The Diary of a Desperate Naija Woman

In the Year Two Thousand and 9

B. Essien-Nelson

authorHOUSE®

AuthorHouse™ UK Ltd.
500 Avebury Boulevard
Central Milton Keynes, MK9 2BE
www.authorhouse.co.uk
Phone: 08001974150

© *2010 B. Essien-Nelson. All rights reserved.*

No part of this book may be reproduced, stored in a retrieval system, or transmitted by any means without the written permission of the author.

First published by AuthorHouse 3/2/2010

ISBN: 978-1-4490-8283-3 (sc)

This book is printed on acid-free paper.

Thank You

I have never really liked the word 'acknowledgements'. It's a good word I am sure but I don't think it captures what I want to do here. I don't want to merely 'acknowledge' people. I want to thank them. OK, maybe it's just me but anyway, that is why I have decided to call this page what it is. A 'Thank You' page because this is where I shall be saying 'thank you' to people. Simple.

Dear Lord, I think it would be rather rude if I did not thank you first cos without you, none of the other people I will be thanking next would even exist in my world. You are beyond wonderful and I could use up every single page in this book to try to thank you and it still would not do. Nevertheless, I will keep on trying. Thank you Father, for loving me so boundlessly. So unconditionally. So completely.

Ayoka. You know who you are. You pushed me to start 'blogging' so this is really all your fault! You believed I could and I believed you. You pushed me off the side of the cliff and wisely, I grabbed on to my God's hand and began a free fall that has led me to this place. It has been so much fun. A fantastic experience. For that, I thank you and even though I have never even met you in living colour, I will never forget you.

To every single person in my life that said in one way or another 'You really should think of publishing these blogs you know'. Well I hope you are all happy now! See what you made me do? Lol! (Are you allowed to use 'Lols' in proper books? Oh, well, who cares? This is not really a 'proper' book per se and so I will 'Lol' if I choose to!). But seriously, you would not be reading this had I not begun to believe you were right. Thank you. From the bottom of my heart. May you never lack encouragers in your life in Jesus Christ's name. Amen!

My Sistas-Divine. Your love and care towards me in the year two thousand and 9 cannot be quantified. You are all from far places on the globe, yet I felt your sincerity keenly. For your love, your support and oh! For all your prayers, I send you my sincere gratitude sealed with a huge 'Mwaah!' I can only thank you but God will reward you. That's for sure.

I must thank my family – my husband and my children – for tolerating me, as I slowly but surely became a blog junkie. Family is ever so important and you are my family. You mean the world to me. You are my four reasons for 'be-ing'. This book is for you really. It might not sell one single copy but it warms my heart to know that you will always have it to remember me by. It's my keepsake to you. Sealed with so much love, you could never imagine.

And finally, I say thank you to everyone at Author House Publishing for making this book more than just a figment of my imagination and for doing it so elegantly. Most of all, I thank you for letting my book be 'me'.

Before You Start Reading

Goodness! You bought my book. Ok, perhaps you are just standing there in the book shop trying to make up your mind if you want to buy it. Or perhaps you got it as a present from someone who thought you might like it. Still, regardless of the reason for which you are holding this book in your hand right now, I say 'thank you'. Yes, I know the 'thank you' page is back there but hey! Its my book and if I choose to thank you now, I can! Lol!

So before you go on, let me explain what this book is about. First of all, if you are seeking some ground-breaking profound-ness, I'm sorry, you might not find it here. You might however experience some suprising 'light bulb' moments just the same way I did as I wrote. Like I have always said, I am not Aristotle nor am I Maya Angelou. And even as much as I admire Chimamanda Adichie, I am not her either. And no matter how much I respect and admire these people, I will never be them. All I am is a Desperate Naija Woman. A simple Nigerian working woman, wife and mother who is deperate to be like Jesus Christ and who, one day discovered the joy of blogging.

On that day, the 14th of January 2008, I began a journey during which I poured out my thoughts, my views and perspectives on life as I saw it. They are very random, very simple, very *'every day'*. Yet, aren't most of the stuff life is made up of very 'every day' – Love, God, Trials, Death, Children, Growing Up, Relationships, Joy, Tears, etc. ? I think so.

So, in summary, 'The Diary of A Desperate Naija Woman' is simply a collection of my random musings. The every day thoughts of a woman who desires many things but when it comes to her 'deepest desire', it would be this - being a **true** woman of God. This is my purpose in life. For me, every other thing flows out from this high calling. As you travel through the pages of this book, you will share in all my 2009 mountain-high and valley-low experiences and while you may not find earth shattering newness of ideas, hopefully you will laugh with me, cry with me, get mad with me, and maybe even ponder a little with me. And before you know it, you and I would have shared a year's worth of experiences. And who knows, as you go on this journey with me, the Desperate Naija Woman (DNW), perhaps a little of my personal brand of 'desperado-ness' would have rubbed off on you.

The Desperate Naija Woman

The Unforgettables

I dedicate this book to the loving memories of my mother, Moni,
My Uncle Abiye
And
My Pastor, Eskor Mfon

Three totally different people. Same unforgettable impact.

JANUARY

Wednesday, 14 January
N10 Million Naira and a Bag of Sweets

I finally create you today and the first thoughts that shoot across my mind all have to do with wondering if anyone will even come to this spot. Will I get any comments or feedback? But this cannot be the point of you, can it? Why am I really doing this? I have to get it right in my mind and make sure I know that this blog is not simply about hearing from people and having a good followership. That would be great but that's not why I am doing this. I am doing this as an outlet for my random thoughts and musings on all things LIFE. So regardless of public feedback - loads or little - I will derive a sense of joy and contentment from just spilling my guts to you. This place will be my release...Hmmmm...Brain, heart, hope you have heard oh? Be wise this year. No pressure! OK?

Talking about random musings, how I wish I could win N10 million naira. That's all I need and I will quit work and free myself from the bondage that comes with needing a nanny/maid/housekeeper. What ever we call them these days. I am slowly losing my mind (and I need my mind very much) with one of my nannies. I think I shall send her back at the weekend. As it happens younger son does not like her. Anyway back to the N10 million naira. It would not be just to save me from work. It would go into setting up my dream vision of a place. JC Braids and Cuts... I know this vision was given me from on high so it shall come to pass even though it is seriously tarry-ing.

I should actually be working (as this is company time) but it feels good to finally make this relationship come to life and I look forward to pouring out my random craziness into your poor but ever receptive and never judgmental 'pages'. Everyday is a treat. It's just that as I dip into the bag of sweets called LIFE, I never know which one I am going to get - sweet bonbons like those yummy trebor sweets we had when I was growing up (wonder why they don't make them anymore?) or horrible liquorice (apologies to those who love the stuff) or minty peppermints. I guess the point is 'Life' is all about different experiences, different flavours, and tastes. You can either relax and savour the different tastes or spend your whole life spitting.... yuck!

No, I'd rather keep the yucky sweet in my mouth and try to figure out why God let me pick it in the first place.........I trust my God, there must be a reason.

Shalom!

Thursday, 15 January
Dear Lord, Am I being Rude?

I should be renamed and dubbed 'Ms. Inconsistency'. You would think that considering the awesome time I had in church on Thursday last week, I would have been there to open the door yesterday. But no, there I was half asleep as my car drove by the church heading home. I was knackered and just at that moment decided to 'burst' the idea.

I remember last week while I was still on vacation I had started worrying about how I was going to maintain my 're-connection' with God which I had taken out time to cultivate in the 2 weeks I was home. And true to type by Tuesday this week, I could feel the fire dwindling already. How does one find this time and keep it consistent. I mean, in between rushing to get everyone ready for work on time enough to leave before 5.55am and JJC nannies who still don't get the schedule and your 7am to 4pm job and getting home through traffic and homework and noisy 5 year olds and older children with projects that require supplies and even older children that require...well stuff and talks and explanations why he cannot go alone to The Palms to 'hang out' and brisk walking for the sake of your heart and your body that needs to be 5kg lighter!!!!!! Dear Lord, this life of a working wife and mom cannot be as you intended. It just cannot be.

As if this was not enough to have on one's mind, my 5 year old reminds me that he does not want to go to church cos we are always shouting 'Hallelujah'. I tried to explain to him that it was our way of thanking God and praising Him for all He does for us. 'Hallelujah' I said meant 'Praise the Lord'. He stood looking at me. I could almost hear the wheels of his brain spinning into overdrive. Then he said to me 'Mommy, but why do you have to shout at God? He is not deaf. And you always say I should stop yelling at people cos it's rude. You are being rude to God and He will not be happy with you'.

I laughed. He looked at me funny, obviously exasperated, and walked away saving me the agony of having to answer...

Morale of this: Be careful what you say to your 5 year old. It could come back to bite you!

Tuesday, 20th January
Let It Flow Lord, Let It Flow

Dear Papa in Heaven

You know I love you. And not just cos you are good or kind or so full of mercy. I love you cos for the life of me, I do not know how you can possibly love me...still. Yet you do.

Please let your love continue to flow into my life Lord. Cos that thought alone is what keeps me going on days like the ones that have just gone by. Yes, days when I just would sell myself for half a penny. In fact, I would 'dash' me out like an unwanted puppy. I mean, how could one who has been given so much be so careless. So forgetful. So mindless. So weak. So undisciplined.

You have given me so much and what have I given you in return? Hot then cold then lukewarm then hot again. I would spew me out of my own mouth. But thankfully, you are not me. You are not man. Your boundless love drowns out all my 'stuff'. Thankfully, you have a graciously bad memory.... thankfully.

So Lord even as I struggle today to be who you have called me to be. Even as I dabble in and dabble out. Even as I go where I know I should not go and do what I know I should not. Just please continue to let your love flow over my life....

It's all I have got. It's all I know. It's all I can count on.

Wednesday, 21ˢᵗ of January
Can I Really?

YES, I can!

Now you listen to me good. Yes, you! Devil you sitting on the corner of my mind. Thinking you can be the boss of me. Ever taunting. Ever Teasing. Ever wicked.

YES I can kick you out of my mind. This is your quit notice. You don't own me any longer. In fact, you never really did. It's me that had been giving you 'chance' all this while. No more chancing. I am not taking crap from you any more. I am better than that!

YES I can live a godly life cos God gives me the power to crush your ugly head. It's my fault for not keying into **HIS**ability in me to knock your lights out. But now I am gonna and you are a goner!

YES, I can watch what I say so that it agrees with what my Father in Heaven thinks of me and not with your mean cruel lies. You are and always will be a liar. The father of liars.

YES I can control myself by the grace of God. You will no longer be in the driver's seat of my life taking me places I do not want to go. Jesus Christ is the Lord of my life and He is in charge. You are in trouble!

YES I can and YES I will do all of the above and much more through my Personal Person and Personal Saviour Jesus Christ. From the very beginning, you had lost this battle. Yes. It was a fixed fight from the start. I was just foolish but not anymore. 2009 is the year of the wise and boy am I getting my wisdom on!

And boy are you in trouble, you devil you. You enemy of my soul. You need to go look for some place else to live. You DON'T live here anymore!

You see, in 2009 I CAN and I WILL.

Thursday, 21st of January
Rock on O Jare!

This is sort of an ode to a supremely strong woman of God that I know and she rocks!

She rocks for me not cos she is fine or cos she is smart. And believe me, she is both of those things. She rocks for me cos she has been rocked on all sides and still stands. She has been through some stuff that would have levelled most people. Including me. And she still stands tall. To see her, you would probably never know it. And that's what I love so much about this our God. Here is someone crying on to Him. Waiting for Him to move. What does He do? He sends her people to minister to in all sorts of ways. He uses her to bless people even in the midst of her own 'dry lands'. I could tell you about me and her. About how God used her in my life but that would be a whole other blog.

Suffice to say that I admire her cos she has taught me what it means to truly stand on God. I am not saying she has not had a dry spells or times when she just wants to weep or yell at God. Or both. Oh yes, I am sure she has been to these places and even more. BUT yet she stands. Like a rock.

But in all of this my hailing of this 'wo-rock' (OK, so it's not a word and it does not sound cute but you grab what I mean. Lol!). The person I really hail is my God. He is the true Rock that has and still supports her and all of us who need help in time of need.

Now when I sing that Donnie McClurkin's song, it will have an even deeper meaning for me...

'Every Rock Me Rock Upon Jesus, Jesus Name so Sweet'.

Rock on Oge! Keep Rockin' on Jesus.

Friday, 23rd of January
Whatsoever

The first Christian song I remember learning as a child was real simple but now that I am older, I see that it was quite profound in its instruction. I do not remember it all but here is the bit I do:

Do no sinful action.

Speak no angry word.

You belong to Jesus, children of the Lord

Christ is Kind and Gentle

Christ is Pure and True

And His little children must be holy too.

Could it get any easier? That is what our walk is all about. Being like Christ.

Anyway, that is not really what I wanted to gist about today. But it is about another song I was listening to this morning on the way to work. My 5 year old is really into it and does not even allow me to talk on the phone when it is playing. That is how intense he is when Ceecee Winan is singing. Lol!

When we pray, we probably say the name of Jesus more than a hundred times (Ok, if you pray for more than 20 minutes, you could!) And as I listened as Ceecee sang and for the first time concentrated (since my commander in chief had ordered complete silence!) on what she was saying it occurred to me how profound this simple song was too.

The name of Jesus is so potent that it literally 'contains' all that we pray for. I mean, IN his name lies the answers to all our prayers. It's not just that when we ask God for something, we have to end by saying 'In Jesus Name'. For me, it means that the name 'Jesus Christ' is the 'Source', if you like, of all things. She sings

If I need Peace. Peace! It's in your name Lord!'

If I need Joy. Joy! It' is in your name Lord.

Whatsoever I want, it's in your name!'

I don't know about you but for me this realisation was huge! You and I have been given permission to call on a name that is so powerful that it brings to life those things yet unseen. You and I have someone living on the inside of us that has, IN His name, all the things we need to live godly abundant lives. And He lives in you. He lives in me. Awesome stuff.

I am still thinking about it as I blog now and I am wondering in my heart if I am worthy of such a gift. If I am living in a way that deserves such a right. I know I am not. But I know I want to be. And I know I am going to keep on trying but I think... No, I KNOW that I need to rely on HIM more cos Ceecee has shared an open secret with me

The *Grace* I need. The *Strength* I need. The *Discipline* I need. The *Will* I need. To walk worthy of God's awesome love is IN the name of Jesus. And I can call on that name. Praise God! I just need to draw close to HIM day by day so that the power in this awesome name is available to me. Join me?

Wednesday, 26th of January
Plug In The Telly!

God is really something. The moment he sees that you are getting serious about him, He gets serious too. He has been using all means to help me understand cos He knows I really want to live for Him. I have even blogged about my 40 year struggle and I remember someone sent me a mail asking if I was not trying in MY own strength rather than His. I remember nodding in agreement with her as I read but asking myself how do I NOT do it in my own strength. How do I get God's strength to walk in HIS ways?

It's funny how you know something in the day-to-day life but just cannot see how it applies in the spiritual. Let me explain. Would you ever sit in front of your television watching the empty screen waiting for it come on WITHOUT plugging it in to the socket? I mean, who would do that? Yes, the telly has the 'potential' to work. Indeed, it has been programmed to work and everything in it has been engineered to function BUT it needs a power source. Without that power source ALL its potential will remain untapped.

Now as a spirit filled Christian, I am like that telly. Yes I have given my life to Christ and Yes, His spirit is in me (Thank God, now I feel it better) giving me the potential to do great things but being filled with God's spirit is not enough. It's great but it's not enough to live a victorious, fruitful life in this world we live in. To live the kind of life I want and have been whining about, I need to be plugged in to the Source of Power. And how do I do that? How do I transform my 'being filled with the Spirit' to 'walking in the POWER of the Spirit? How do I get some sound and picture images going on the screen of my Christian life?

My newfound answer? Praying in the Spirit.

Praying in the Spirit until I pass from the outer courts to the inner court and finally into the Holy of Holies where I can bask in the presence of God. That's where the real deal POWER is. I need to get into this place and spend some good time with God so that He can zap my potential energy and turn it into Power <u>TO LIVE</u> and <u>TO DO</u> as He had ordained from the beginning!

You know why I am sure this is true for me. For the first time, in a long time, I went for my Church's Prayer Meeting on Saturday and as we prayed in the Spirit I could feel my issues fall away as I approached God's presence. I did not make it all the way but by the end of the meeting and after listening to our Prayer Leader's exhortation, I had answers to many of my questions about why I was the way I was.

Then God made sure I got the message during the Iron Sharpens Iron Meeting 3 friends and I had on Sunday. We actually spent some good time praying in the Spirit and we KNEW we had approached God's presence. If I was a rechargeable lantern, I got a recharge on Sunday that's for sure! All my stresses and anxieties just melted away and when I got home, as usual, there were things to yell about, but I just couldn't. I was still floating on the wings of my encounter. God was ALIVE in me and HIS POWER was and still is coursing through my being.

But I know that just as the telly will not work if it's not plugged in. And just as the lantern will eventually die if it does not get recharged. So will this love for all people, peace, calm and sense of equilibrium I feel begin to dissipate if I do not find time to go before God again and spend time in His presence. And cos I know my history and I know the devil always likes to be in my business, he will do his best to prevent me from finding time.

But he is in for a big surprise cos I know you all will be praying for me as I go into a time of fasting and prayer for this season I am about to enter, won't you?

Please do, cos my 'telly must stay plugged in!

Shalom!

Wednesday, 28th of January
My Word! How Many Miles!

Dear Lord & Heavenly Father.

You are just too much! You take my breath away all the time and just now as I count the hours to my husband's return from a trip abroad, it just struck me how many miles you must travel!

Yes, all the miles you travel by the side of your children as they go up and down about their daily lives. I know you go everywhere with me and I mean everywhere. On the road, in the air and recently, on water!

You are a super duper Voyager! I mean you must be cos my bible says you never leave me so that must mean you go everywhere with me. And boy! That is a lot of miles Lord. Thank you!

Thank you for protecting me as I travelled from point A to B

Thank you for watching over my children cos you know how many times they go and on that dreaded Lekki -Expressway. And you have always kept them. Thank you! And thank you in advance for all the times in the future you will remain faithful.

And my deepest thanks go to you for all the miles you travel with my husband. And Lord, compared to him, the children and I are standing still! This year alone, I cannot count the miles you both have covered together and we are just in January 2009. In the air, on the road, in boats! O Lord, I could thank you for all eternity for this single blessing and it would still never be enough.

Nevertheless Lord, I will keep on trying. Thank you for being my family's Travel Companion all these years. I thank you from the bottom of my heart. I could never take it for granted cos there are some who simply step out of their homes and that is it.

And I use my family as a point of contact to all my relatives and friends. May we all have reasons to thank God as He travels with us everywhere we go.

Since we cannot give him any bonus miles or special discounts, I guess all we can do is continue to thank and praise Him for all He does for us. He is simply the best!

Shalom!

FEBRUARY

Wednesday, 11th of February
What Time Is It?

A Set Time. Yes, that's what time it is.

No matter what I have seen so far in this year 2009. I will not be moved. I still believe the 'Set Time' has come for God to favour me. And you. If only we will remain true to Him. As we say, there will be no shaking for the child of God.

You see I even think God loves to do '*nyanga*' small in times like this. To show us who's 'The Boss'. If He moves for us when things are easy. People will say it was 'luck'. Or 'being at the right place at the right time'. Or some other funny 'man must be in control' reason. But when God moves for us and causes us to prosper in the midst of plenty economic, political and spiritual *katakata* like 2009 is promising to be, then He gets even more glory. And deservedly so too.

So for those who choose to align (or re-align) their lives to the will of God, He will ensure that, like Jacob in the midst of a famine, we will reap what we sow in the very 'same year'. Imagine that. Here we are saying there is a drought, which means there was no water. Abi? Then this man comes, plants seeds and reaps in the same year a hundred fold! How is that possible? Where did he get his own water? How come the drought-ridden soil yielded harvest for him alone? Na God oh! Our very big God who is always by our side.

He is the only one able to keep us in the eye of the storm. Yes, storms will come. Yes, fires will rage and yes, yes, yes, the enemy will come a-tempting. BUT I know that my Redeemer lives and he is able to command the storms. He is able to ensure that not even one single hair on my head is singed. And triple yes; He is able to provide me with the grace to resist the devil and the wisdom to know when to flee!!! Believe me, there are temptations you resist and there are the ones you roll up your sokoto and flee! God will give us wisdom in this season to know the difference. In Jesus Name! Amen.

No matter what we do this year, we must not allow what we see make us conform to the ways and thinking of this world. Seek God earnestly. In His word and face to face. Let His voice be the only voice you listen for and heed. He knows all things and is wiser than any banker, stockbroker, realtor, guru, *woli*, seer, *baba alawo* ...etcetera etcetera! All these sources have limited knowledge and no matter how hard they try, cannot predict the future as accurately as the Inexhaustible Source of All Knowledge in this age and all ages to come! Why would we short change ourselves by settling for mere imitations when we can tap into the Original Baba-God, Creator of All things?

I am sure we no better *ke?*

P. S. Sorry for the long radio silence. Much to say. Not enough time to blog. The Lord will help me. I do so miss it. I tell you, there is no mental vacation like blogging!

Thursday, 12th of February
Girls Behaving Badly

I was OK until about 20 minutes ago when I logged on to my Face book!

I wish I had not. I would have been able to go home today in peace. But as I watched the clip of the shameful incident that happened at one of our most prestigious secondary schools for girls in Lagos, my jaw dropped in shock as my eyes were assailed by the image of girl on girl 'brutality'. I know that is a hard word but you need to watch the clip to understand. I do not know what the poor victim did to the ones beating her up and I really do not care. All I know is that WHATEVER it was; no one has the right to beat another person up like that.

As I watched I kept wondering to myself 'but where are the teachers? Was no one on duty? I guess not and therein lies my point. In the end, sending our children to posh schools is great and we thank God for being able to do so BUT much still lies in the hands of parents. Where would these girls have picked up such *'agbero'* tendencies to deck another person like that? Such displays of 'craze' remind me of bus conductors 'displaying' as they prepare to fight!

Parents! Mothers! Fathers! Please let's participate in the upbringing of our children. From this scene I am just reminded that there is so much teachers and posh schools can do. Assuming they are even 'present' for the children you place in their care. And even the most committed teacher cannot take the place of a concerned parent that tries to be there for their child. I do not really have any answers cos for all I know, their parents are nothing like this and have done nothing to result in their children, their daughters behaving so badly.

What I do know is this. God helping me, I must make sure I continue to do all I can so that my children grow up to abhor the kind of behaviour I watched on that clip.

I am still in shock!

Monday, 16th of February
My God Is A Consuming Fire. What Am I?

The question does sound odd but nonetheless, it is a valid one. The bible does tell us that God is a consuming fire. I do not know about you but I always pray to him and sing along with Ceecee Winan, that I want to 'be like Him, walk like Him, love like Him'... so why not 'burn like Him?'

No, am not going too far cos I know that my bible also tells me that as his minister, He makes me a flaming fire. Like Father. Like daughter. You do not believe me? OK. Check it out in Psalm 104:4. You see, once we become born again, we take on, via the redeeming blood of Jesus Christ, all aspects of the nature of God. At least, we should. At least, that is what I am trying to do....

Anyway, the real crux of the matter for me is this. What does a flaming fire do? How does it behave? As a Christian, what does it mean to be 'fire'? How should that affect the way I run this race? Live my life? If you are like me, then all you need are some questions to ponder on..... if you mull over them for some time, you will begin to see clearly where you stand today in your walk with God. And if we are wise, then we will check ourselves and begin to work on the areas that need fixin'. So let's go!

Let talk about fire babe
Let's talk about you and me
Let's talk about all the ways that we should be like fire babe.
Let's talk about that.
Let's talk abooooouuuut that! Let's talk about that!

(Sorry. I could not resist that. If you are lost, then you have never heard of Salt and Pepa!)

Anyway, back to serious matter. What are the traits of Fire?

Fire is ...**Focussed**. All it wants to do is BURN. Are you focussed?

Am I focussed on doing God's will? Am I focussed on winning souls and wanting to tell people about the love of God? Am I focussed on resisting sin? No matter what comes my way, do I stand on the word of God? Do I put my faith in the Solid Rock or do I let myself be carried away by every storm. Every trial. Every fad. Every doctrine.

Fire has.... **Integrity.** You can COUNT ON fire to burn. No matter where. No matter who. Fire will burn. It can be trusted to do what it does. How far can I be trusted as a Christian? Can God trust me with my tithes, vows, and pledges? Do I have integrity? Is my word my bond? Do I say 'yeah' when I mean 'nay'?

Fire is...**Dependable.** Can my family depend on me? Can the Pastor or the other prayer team members depend on me to be where I said I would be. Do what I said I would do? You can be sure that if you set something on fire, you can depend on it to burn. Can God depend on me like he depended on Abraham?

Fire is.... **Pure.** There is no additive. No contamination. No dilution. Are you? Is your eye single? Am I pure in thought, word and deed? Am I consistent and uncompromising? Fire does not cut corners. It goes straight for the jugular. It does not bend it rules for anyone. It is consistent. Are you? Am I? Am I a Christian when it is all good and everyone else is the same? Or do I change my 'skin' to suit whatever environment I am in? Is there still some 'world' in me that I am not even trying to bring under the cleansing blood of the Lamb? Is my garment of righteousness truly spotless?

Fire is.....**Hot.** Have you ever heard of cold fire or lukewarm fire? I haven't. Fire is HOT. Period. You know what the book of Revelation says about being lukewarm. God will spew us out of his mouth. I know that I do not want to be spewed out of the mouth of the Almighty God!

So Lord helping me, I will burn! I will, by the power of the God who calls me by name, be a pure white-hot flaming fire. I want to be all the things that fire is as I run this race. No one knows tomorrow. I do not know how much time I have. As God has been gracious and begun to help me to stoke the dying embers, I will continue to release myself so that he can breathe on me...that the small hesitant fires can grow day by day until it becomes what I am meant to be...a Flaming Fire to the glory of God!

Wednesday, 18th of February
Tomorrow

If Tomorrow never comes, will you be set?
Or will your fate be a lost bet?
If tomorrow does not come for you, will you be at peace in Him
Or floating around in hell , screaming?

Dear One, why are you so sure
That tomorrow will let you in its door?

Why can you not see the need to bond your heart
To the One who, in the end, will set apart
The goat from the sheep
The fake from His peeps

The Good Book says, 'Now is the Time!'
To acquaint yourselves with God and your life re-align
Do not put it off any longer, my friend
This journey you are on might, this minute, end

And then all the things you are chasing up and down
Will suddenly hold no attraction
For the dead have no need of all these vanities
You do not dress, or drink or use the ATM machine. Believe!

So come, my brother, my sister
Your spiritual status, please reconsider
For really, really, tomorrow is not a guarantee
You may just sleep today, and the dawn of tomorrow, not see!

This poem was inspired by my cousin. He went to bed on Friday night and never woke up again. He died in His sleep. He was 28 years old. He would have picked up his first job offer this past Monday. It is well!

Thursday, 19th of February
What's financially?

Apparently, I was the last person in my office to hear about the 13 year old boy who has just become the youngest dad in the UK. His accomplice and new mom, 15 years. When he was asked how he would manage financially his response was to ask the mother of his child (obviously much wiser than him) 'What's financially?' And yet he was 'smart enough' to know how to do IT? It boggles the mind doesn't it?

Hmmmm, it really is a sign of the times we are living in. My son is going to be 15 this year and thanks to all that goes in on telly these days and the inevitable biology class lessons on reproduction and top that up with my no holds barred talks (well more like 'if you try me, you will realise that *kaki no be leather* talks!), I am pretty confident that he knows where babies come from now. You should see my daughter's face when I am having these 'let's talk about sex' workshops at home. I am not sure if she wants to cry or throw up. It is so funny!

But this story about the boy and girl in the UK is not. Between them, they are 26 years old! But they have made their beds so now they will lie in it and of course change baby diapers on it. They should know *sha* that their lives will never be the same again. Even if their parents take over the *katakata*. Really the truth is that whichever set of parents decide to take this on have just gotten themselves one more child!

Anyway, that's done. May God help them all. My focus now is on our children. My son, your daughter. My daughter, your son. How are we going to ensure that we do not become grandparents ahead of God's appointed time?

Even as I write (or type), God just reminded me of something else I wrote about this morning. It was captioned 'Whose children are they anyway?'. It is true, in this world we are living in we can shield our children as much as we like. We can ensure they get good teaching in the Word, we can preach to them, scream at them, threaten then, encourage them, bribe them, and even entice them BUT if God is not in charge of them, we truly labour in vain oh!

So even as we continue to do all of the above (not the negative ones oh. please bribing children is just a set up for your future failure. My 5 year old has shown me the errors of my way. Funny enough, it worked for his older brother and sister but I guess the children we are *'borning'* now are drinking a different kind of water. They must be if they are having sex at 13 years old!)... as I was saying *sha*, as we continue to do the right things by our children, let us make sure that we are PRAYING for them. And praying HARD!

Stormie Omartian's 'Power of Praying Parent' is one of the best tools I know for praying effectively and comprehensively for our children. Please go buy it. If you have it hidden somewhere, look for it and dust it off and let's begin to pray for our children. Errr, yes even you, my sisters who are not yet married. Now is the best time to start praying for your children who are still waiting on the other side for you and their papa to find yourselves. As a friend of mine says, Prayer does not have overdose!

Don't know about you, but I would prefer to become a granny when the parents of my grandchild are actually husband and wife. And are old enough to be so called!

It is well oh!

Thursday, 19th of February
14,881 Days!

You have got to love technology *sha*! Here I was trying to spice up the look of my blog and I stumble on some techno gadget that tells me something incredibly awe-inspiring. What?

It actually calculates how many days I have spent in the land of the living! Believe it or not, it has been 14, 881 days since I took my first breath. Now that is something to give crazy thanks about!

To be honest though when I saw the number at first, my first reaction was actually ' Ah ah, is that all?' I took out a scrap of paper and did the maths - 365 X 40. I got 14, 600 days. So give and take the leap years I did not add in, I decided that the machine was right after all. Only fourteen thousand + days. It seemed small. I know I felt older. Like at least 60,000 days! Lol!

But quickly quickly, the Spirit of God that resides within me jacked me up and reminded me to be grateful. It was all in my head. 40 years, 14,881 days was A LONG time and a huge testimony! But isn't that like us sometimes, to downplay or allow *'see finish'* to affect the way we look at the mercies and blessings of God?

So today, as I celebrate my 14,881st day on earth I want to ask you to join me in giving our God, the Giver and Sustainer of Life a day filled with praise and thanks. Let's do it this way:

1. Each time you cell phone rings, say 'Thank you Lord. For you have been so merciful to me!

2. Each time you get a text message today; as you open it, say ' I praise you O Most Loving Father for my life and for keeping me all these days. (You can paraphrase and thank him as the Spirit leads you as the day goes on!)

If you are like me and your cell phone never stops ringing or buzzing, then by the end of the day, we should have lived a thanks and praise filled day to the glory of our God and He richly deserves it and more!

Shalom!

Friday, 20th of February
'The Axe Head' of Our Lives (based on the story in II Kings 6: 1- 7)

How on earth could an axe head made of iron float on water? You and I know that iron is not meant to float so what does this tell us?

It tells me that God is not bound by any physical laws of nature. In fact, He put these laws in place and He can re-arrange them if He wants to. Just for me! Just for you. Hallelujah!

It tells me that my God is able to do anything for me including restoring stuff I had lost. Stuff that had sunk to the bottom of the sea of life, supposedly gone forever.

It tells me that just as the men with Elisha did not have to go get a deep diver or some big mechanical object to fish out the axe head, the same way I don't have to rely on some specialist 3rd party or gadget to experience restoration in my life. I got the Great Restorer on my side. I can call him direct. His line is never engaged. Never busy. Never crosses.

It tells me that I cannot be working for God and lose stuff and He will turn a blind eye. No, He will fix the situation. He is a rewarder of those who seek him and those who labour lovingly in His vineyard. These men were working to build a place for Elisha, a man of God to dwell. When trouble struck. God moved.

It tells me that just as God moved and the axed head reappeared and Elisha then told the man to pick it up out the water, the same way I must always be ready to do my own part when God moves. I must reach out and take what He is giving me. My faith must move me into action. Walking with God is about partnership but trust me He is always doing the lion share of the work. After all, He is the Lion of the Tribe of Judah!

It tells me that if I have lost my health or wealth due to sin in my life. Due to bad habits I had. When I repent and call on God. He will restore my insides back to the way they were when I was a baby. He is able to turn back the hand of time and reverse the irreversible.

It tells me that it is never too late with God as long as one is alive and able to call on Him. I am so happy I called on Him. I know He is restoring all that I had lost and is even giving me some brand new stuff to the glory of His name! Amen.

Take time to read this story. I wonder what it will tell you. Shalom!

Monday, 23rd February
'Hannah's Vow': A Key to Fruitfulness

Below is a mail from my favourite Uncle in the whole world (sorry all other Uncles but truth must be told). I take after him in so many ways but the 2 major ways are 1. We both share a love for other languages. We both speak French. Just that he speaks about 3 others as well. And 2, we both love to write. He has two books that have just been published and I would like to share the information on how to get one of them with you. Go on, go get a copy! All details are as stated below.

****

Dearly Beloved,

Calvary greetings to you all once again. Glory be to God, the Giver of all things pertaining to life and Godliness. He has manifested His amazing grace in a new dimension. I am delighted and humbled to inform you that my new book, Hannah's Vow: A Key To Fruitfulness, has just been published and is now available for order online at:

http://www.amazon.com/

www.CreateSpace.com/3367438

When you order direct from the publisher at: www.CreateSpace.com/3367438, there is a promotional discount of $1.50.

Please remember to enter the discount code:

ZNJUM84M

In buying this book, you are helping to facilitate Kingdom work. All the proceeds are dedicated to the promotion of the Gospel and to charitable causes. The first beneficiary will be the ongoing building project here at The Redeemed Christian Church of God, Living Waters, Greensboro.

You may read excerpts from the book online at www.BibleArena.com/hannah.html.

Kindly forward to friends, family, and co-workers. May our Heavenly Father bless you richly even as you purchase and help to promote this publication.
Remain blessed.

Joseph Adefolalu
February 02, 2009

Monday, 23rd February
WWJD – What Would Jesus Do?

I know we have probably all heard of this acronym. I know I have and I know I have purposed at least a 1000 times to live by it. You know, in all I do, say or think, I would first of all consider what Jesus Christ would do, say or think in the same situation and model my actions or speech or thoughts on Him.

Sounds easy enough *abi*? Not!

But why I ask is it so hard? And why oh why do I feel such a sense of urgency about getting my 'Christ like' act together? As I believe that God has blessed me with long life. And I strongly hold on to His promise that I shall live to see my children to the 3rd and 4th generation, so it cannot be because I think the wind is going to blow out my candle light anytime soon. Heaven Forbid! Yes, God forbid.

But what if God has not forbidden it? What If my tomorrow does not come? What If, as I am typing this right now, my lights are snuffed out by a God who simply wants me home? My children? He will sort them out. My husband? He will sort him and might even allow him find another (ouch! that was so hard to type but alas it is true). My family, oh for sure, they will mourn and weep but my God will sort them out too. My job? Please! In a minute, they will find a replacement. My church. They will miss me but even for them, time will heal all wounds. Indeed for all that love me and are close to me, time will heal all wounds.

But what will Time be doing with me? My soul? My Spirit? I know where my body will be. 6 feet under! But where will I be? Heaven or Hell? Or waiting to enter one or the other depending on how things work out (am not really sure . I just want to be on the right side of the fence when that time comes.)

Anyway that brings me back to my WWJD thing. Only by living a WWJD life do I stand a chance of assuring myself of a seat on the 'sheep side' of the line at the pearly gates. We all know this so what do we need to begin to live it. What do we need to do to, in our own little spheres of influence begin to be 'The Change' our world needs? By world here, I am even only talking about the world of our homes, the world of our work places, the world of our churches. We have so many many many churches yet so few true Christians. Christians living like Christ for real.

I want to be one of those. a WWJD Christian. I NEED to be one. I meet with 3 friends to sharpen our 'irons' so to speak. We agreed we would live like we knew this was out last day here. And we agreed that on this our 'pretend' last day, we would live it the WWJD way.

How? There is no other way really than by tapping into the power and grace of God by spending some quality time in His Presence. So let's all begin to approach 'The Zone' via praise and worship and pray the Lord to 'fill our cups'.

We need the power!

P. S. forgive me if this was a tad too morbid for you. But am just being real and I REALLY feel that this is no longer the time to be messing with God.

Tuesday, 24th of February
Of Women and Mirrors

OK I admit it. I tend to sneak looks at myself in anything that reflects. But I am still better than my hubby and my teen son. At least I am female. Not sure what their excuse is. Lol! I want to believe however that they look cos they know they look good and are just reconfirming. In my case, I am looking cos I am sure something is out of place and I need to be fixing it quick quick before someone spots it.

Honestly and I speak for myself when I say that my perusing my image wherever possible whenever possible is not cos I believe I am ' all that'. Actually it is quite the contrary. When I look, my first thought is ' Oh Lord, was that my belly fold showing through my blouse?' Or goodness, this bra is not doing it for me today. There is no lift!'. Or if it is a really bad day ' No! That is not VPL I see!' Yes, some days are THAT bad!

Where am I going with this? Well, it may just be me again but this is exactly what looking into the Word of God does for me as well. Looking into it, I see my shortcomings and my imperfections in comparison to a Holy God. The Bible is my spiritual mirror and I wish I can say I look into is as often as I look at any reflecting surface but that would be untrue. But I am doing better than a while ago and give God the glory for that.

And you know what?, No matter how long I stare at the mirror in my room or the mirrors in the elevators at work or the windows of that car parked outside Shoprite, all the imperfections I see never go away. Nothing shifts. Nope. Nothing changes in spite of my tugging and pulling. No matter how much I hold my breath that rolls is still there! Sheesh! It is such an unloving, unforgiving object, the mirror!

HOWEVER, the Mirror of the Word of God is much more compassionate. Its very forgiving and works miracles on the soul, spirit and yes, even the body. The more time I spend looking into it, the more God works on me and refines me and re-moulds me until little by little I begin to look like Him. Like His Son, My Saviour, Jesus Christ.

Now isn't that awesome.... A life-changing mirror. To be the best version of you. To be the best version of me. We need to spend some quality time looking at ourselves in the Mirror of God's Word. Now that's a hot beauty tip if ever there was one!

Shalom!

Wednesday, 25th of February
Alex Linley's Top Ten Strength Spotting Tips

A friend sent this to me and it really struck a cord.

As a child I used to always organise the children who lived in our flat block and around the neighbourhood and make us (well them as I was the 'choreographer'!) practise for hours. For what? A grand TV performance! We would rehearse songs with all sorts of choreography and my bait was that my dad was going to take us to NTA to go and perform. Of course they believed me cos I used to appear on a TV programme called ' Animal Game'. Do not laugh oh. It was a hot kiddie's programme at the time.

Anyway, my point is that, even at this age (I was about 8 or 9 years old) I loved rallying my friends and making them believe in themselves. I made them feel like the next stars of TV and as far as I was concerned, we were just too hot! We could sing, we could dance and we could act! In some way, I see my love for making people feel appreciated, wanting those around me to be the best and feel good about themselves stemming from these my early 'star building' days. I identify with most of the other stuff Mr. Linley says as well. Read for yourself:

Alex Linley says that if you want to identify strengths, whether in yourself or in other people, these are his top ten ways of doing so:

1. Childhood memories: What do you remember doing as a child that you still do now – but most likely much better? Strengths often have deep roots from our early lives.

2. Energy: What activities give you an energetic buzz when you are doing them? These activities are very likely calling on your strengths.

3. Authenticity: When do you feel most like the "real you"? The chances are that you'll be using your strengths in some way.

4. Ease: See what activities come naturally to you, and at which you excel – sometimes, it seems, without even trying. These will likely be your strengths.

5. Attention: See where you naturally pay attention. You're more likely to focus on things that are playing to your strengths.

6. Rapid learning: What are the things that you have picked up quickly, learning them almost effortlessly? Rapid learning often indicates an underlying strength.

7. Motivation: What motivates you? When you find activities that you do simply for the love of doing them, they are likely to be working from your strengths.

8. Voice: Monitor your tone of voice. When you notice a shift in passion, energy and engagement, you're probably talking about a strength.

9. Words and phrases: Listen to the words you use. When you're saying "I love to…" or "It's just great when…" the chances are that it's a strength to which you're referring.10. "To do" lists: Notice the things that never make it on to your "to do" list. These things that always seem to get done often reveal an underlying strength that means we never need to be asked twice.

So what do you think? Ring true for you too?

Hmmm I wonder how come those my olden day street mates never asked me 'when?' When is your dad taking us to this show? I guess we were all sweet and gullible like that!

For more information on strength spotting, see:
Average to A+: Realising Strengths in Yourself and Others, by Alex Linley, published by CAPP Press, 2008

Thursday, 26th of February
The Desperado in Me

A friend stood behind me once as I was typing up one of my blogs. 'Desperate!' Ah ah what do you mean by 'Desperate?' she shrieked. She could not understand why I would go out in public with a 'desperate' label stuck to my forehead (well that's a bit extreme but a blog is open to a whole lot of people!). I understood where she was coming from. We all know what that term connotes in the days we are living. Especially when it is used to describe a woman.

Anyway, I took out time to explain to her and I feel it is time, after 18 blogs or so, I should do same here as well. Again. But this time, in the form of a poem (and pls remember, I am not Wole Soyinka nor am I Maya Angelou!). As we say, *'Idea is need!'*****

I am indeed a desperate woman.
But desperate for what, did I hear you say?
I am desperate to be like Jesus Christ,
For in Him I am always blest and will be at my best
I am desperate to be holy like God.
For in that, my eternal life will be assured
I am desperate to know not only God's acts but also His ways
For that means that His voice I know and heed always

I am desperate to experience more of God's love each day
For when I do then I can share same with all He sends my way
Indeed I am a desperate woman. But don't feel bad for me.
I am so full of glee.
I am desperate for a God who has given up so much for me.
There really is no mystery at all you see
I am a Desperate Woman, that's just ME.

Praise the Lord!!!!!

****As long as the idea is conveyed OR You understand the main idea!

MARCH

Friday, 06th of March
How Do I Love Thee? Let Me Count the Ways

This blog was actually inspired by the write '5 things I appreciate about my Husband' request I responded to on 'The Praying Wife' website (http://www.prayingwife.net/) AND a letter a sista-friend of mine wrote to her own hubby as a Val's present.

I was only allowed five things to appreciate and had to put them down sweet and sharp like bullet points so when I was done my brain was still on overdrive. It continued to work with my spirit to throw up my 5 things and why I appreciated them in him and on and on and on. I smiled as I thought about them and the more I thought, the more I smiled. And then I had a great idea!

Why not do my own 'expanded' version of my list here? Its not in any particular order and is more or less the same as what I had on PW. Just more detailed in some cases. What makes this such a GREAT idea? Mailing it to him! Yes, I would mail this blog to him as my 'no-special-reason-but-just-becos-present'. I smiled some more. Yes, me thinks this would be a good surprise for him. My mushiness is usually expressed only in cards on special occasions so apart from our 'love Us' at the end of sms messages, this would be one of the few times I would be sending him a proper 'manifesto of love'. In fact, if I remember correctly, the last one was a home made scroll of love I did for one Val's day like this. Or was it a birthday? (Anyway (said in the *gbogbo bigz* girl way) I think you get my point. Now is as good a time for this as any.

So Love, how do I love and appreciate thee? Let me count the ways...

I love and appreciate you cos:

1. You know all my faults yet you continue to love me more each day. Yes, I can feel it. In fact, I sense that you love me now more than when we got married. Yes, you love me, warts and all yet you encourage me to be the BEST me I can be for ME. You always knew I could do more than I was doing all those years I worked as a PA (all due respect to PAs

round the world. PAs rule! I loved doing it and I did it well). But you just KNEW I could more with my talents. And I am.

2. You are doing your best to love and serve God. I know it's a struggle not cos you are bad but just cos life and the world and all have such an attraction for most of us. And sometimes, this 'enjoyment' can be a divide between us and God. But you have purposed to keep at it. And I am praying for you. As far as I am concerned you are a mighty man of God.

3. You are so much more tender and loving with the children than I am (really maybe its the Ekiti girl in me, or maybe cos I did not really grow up with people hugging me and all that so it is something I am still learning to do even after 3 children). Its not that my parents were hard but I guess for them to feed me, clothe me and send me to school - that WAS Loving me. Plus *sha*, you got the *oyinbo* blood in you so that makes it easier abi? Lol!

4. You are a truly responsible man in all the ways that matter most especially in your role as a father. I see your pain at not being around a lot but I know why you do what you do. I am proud of you and so are the children. Is that not why our 5 year old 'mini-you' insists on wearing a blazer to school everyday. To look like his Papa?

5. You are able to shop for all of us and everything fits! I do not know how you do it. Yes, you are a better shopper than I could ever be. Me? I enter a shop, I see it, I like it, the price is right, I buy it. You, if you do not go round 3 different shops first, Hmmmm, let's just say, I love watching the children while you shop for us and trying on all the suggestions you pass to me in the dressing rooms! Lol.

6. You genuinely care about my father and his family. This matters a lot to me. Family can be...well you know sometimes. Yet you always seem to find a way to help me help them. Sometimes behind my back I suspect.

7. You have always been and still are a family man. Now that I have come into my own... This does not bug me anymore. You can fawn

over your mom, sisters and brothers as much as you like now. I get it now. It does not take anything away from me. Sheeesh. How ignorant one can be at 25 years old! As the song goes, 'If I knew back then what I know. If I understood the what when why and how....'. But thankfully I know NOW. Better late then never!

8. Yes, and that is another thing I appreciate about you. You stuck around long enough for both of us to grow up and mature. And like fine wine, we taste much better than we did 15 years ago!

9. Your sense of style and your charisma. I always told you I loved to listen to you speak at engagements. It is still one of my favourite past times. Listening to your business calls, wheeling and dealing. So confident. So 'Just do it'. A true orator.

10. Your sense of humour. It does not match mine or our first son's. But I still love it cos when it is tickled, you let out this high shrill laugh that me and the children say sounds like a girl laughing and choking at the same time. Even now I can hear it and yes, I am smiling.

Yes, mighty good man, these are the ways that I love and appreciate you. And my highest praise and the most sincere thanks go the One who made you. The One who brought you into my life. The one who ordained that 'it will be and nothing shall put it asunder' - Our Most High God and Loving Heavenly Father. But for Him, I would not be here appreciating you at all and by His grace, perhaps I can do this again in another 8 or 10 years! Just kidding!

So take it from me, I love you babes and do not get me wrong. There are still a number of things that you do that rub me off the wrong way BUT they pale into insignificance when I remember the above. Errrr, and no, I am not doing a list about those!

Friday, 06th of March
An Ode to My Son

To be honest, I am not really sure what an ode is. Sorry, Mrs. ...sheesh I cannot even remember the name of my fifth form literature teacher! Sad.

But still I am full of joy that you, my son just turned 15! Wow! I still remember VERY vividly being in labour for your birth. Taking you home for the first time. Staring at you in awe as my sweet sweet mom in love (as taught by Ms. Bardot) gave you your baths. Boy could you scream! I think you hated water. Actually come to think of it, I think you still do judging by the briskness of your showers sometimes! I can see in my minds eye the window I used to stand by and peek at you on your first days in school. And yes, you cried for 3 weeks straight! I remember the first time I saw you on TV talking about oranges and watermelons! Shriek! You remember, don't you? Still I was proud of you as I hoped no one heard what you said. LOL!

Like I said, I do not know what an ode is but I do know that I love you from the bottom of my heart. Yes, it is a fact that I do not know what an ode is but I am 100% confident that the day you were born launched me on to another level of existence. Of self awareness. The awareness that there is love and there is LOVE. My love for you is such that I get scared.

Scared that you will not be as safe as I want.
Scared that you will not be as happy as I would want
Scared that you will not be as healthy as I would love
Scared that people will not be nice to you as I want
Scared that some girl will come and break your heart
Scared that some man will come and hurt your ego/feelings.
Scared that I will not be a good mother to you
Scared that you would 'hate' me cos I am always on your case.

Yes oh, there is a lot of 'fear' in my life as a mom. And you know the only thing that has not allowed all these fears to reduce me to a blubbering mess is the TRUTH I hide in my heart that you are really not mine. You belong to God. He just gave you to your dad and I as a sort of 'ward'. Someone to take care of here on earth. At the end of the day, God is your true parent. AND He will make sure that all the fears that I listed above will not come your way. But even if they do, He will make sure that you grow up to be someone who can deal with whatever life throws at you.

And you know, my son, I see that you are. You are growing up into a fine young man. Yes, I know I yell and shout. And yes, I know my mouth needs spiritual surgery and God is helping me on that score. But one thing you should know is that when I talk mean. I am crying inside cos it hurts me too but I bear the pain in the hope that what I am saying will shock you into positive action. But no more. No more shock tactics. I have now handed you over to God full time. I will do only as He leads to me do , tell or enforce. The rest I will raise to God in prayer. For you, for your sister. For your baby brother.

As you turn 15 , I celebrate you. Your humour. Your charisma. Your talents. Your 'entrepreneurial' skills (a.k.a. money mindedness) and your intelligence. Most of all I celebrate your heart cos it is good. And still I see it, underneath all the 'big boy' moves. You are still you. Caring and sensitive. A good person.

As you turn 15, all I can ask is you be true to your heart. Let Jesus Christ be your number one mentor and role model and even as you shine in all you do, make shining for God be on the top of your list. Every one loves a winner and with God on your side, that is all you can be. An all round winner!

Happy Birthday son!

Your mother who loves you more than you can ever understand.

Monday, 09th of March
Standing On What, Pray Tell?

If you are like me, you probably say 'It is well!' about a thousand times a day. Actually my MGM and I probably account for 2% of the total times that phrase is said in one day in Lagos State! OK perhaps that is a tad too much but I am sure you catch my drift. We say it ALOT. Like 'It is well' I tend to say a whole bunch of other things as well . A whole lot of Christianese as it is called by some. And not that it is bad per se but I am convinced I need to check myself a bit.

First of all, "What is well? and "Why is it well? Instead of just throwing up an 'It is well' anytime there is a pause in a conversation, I want to begin to say WHY it is well as well. I want to begin to link this my confidence to some particular scripture. For example, if I am trying to encourage someone that is still seeking a spouse. I will say to her 'It is well cos the bible says that He shall set the solitary in homes' . Or I am trying to encourage my MGM when he is setting off on another trip, I will say to him 'It is well love, Cos the Lord has gone ahead of you. He will make the crooked road straight for you'. I am sure you are getting my jist better now.

And trust me I know there are sometimes that a simple "it is well' is all you can say but I promise myself, I shall finish off that phrase in my heart with the bible scripture that the Holy Spirit lays in it at the time. I need to be able to show the enemy that I KNOW what I am talking about. But if I have not hidden anything in the heart what is the Holy Spirit going to remind me of????

That brings me to the title of this blog and another favourite of mine. "I am standing on God's promise. I know He will do it' Which one of God's promises am I really standing on? Have I really taken out time to search this His Word to find the applicable word? If the person I am confessing so boldly to happens to say to me. 'That's really good. Tell me, which scripture are you standing on?' Would I be able to respond? Knowing me, caught off guard like that. Methinks not. My flustering will not be cos I do not know but obviously becos I had not taken the time out to 'hide' this word in my heart to the point of it being 'close to my mouth' when this nosey person asked me. Lol!

But seriously, we have to get to that point where we are brimming over with the Word. Look at Jesus Christ for instance. Can you imagine him facing the devil's temptations and with each one satan threw at him, Jesus said ' Errr wait, OK, No, you cannot make me turn these rocks to bread because.... where is that my bible now? Eh hen, I will show you why now now, emmm, eh hen, man shall not live by bread alone but by...oh what is it now?????...

Ludicrous abi? Thank God Jesus Christ himself had hidden the word in his heart and was ready to fire the devil *fiam fiam fiam*! No shaking. No hesitation. Now if the big JC himself, who is the Word did this, what is our excuse? I mean, He could have just turned to the devil and said ' *You no fear at all oh*. Me, bow to you? Lightening strike him now!!!' Boom, Thunderclap, Blast!!!! LOL! But as in everything He was careful to give us an example of how battle with the enemy must be done. It is with the weapon of the Word of God.

And please know that this is not just for fighting temptations but it is also the greatest antidote to worry and discouragement and fear. We should be able to store up the applicable Scriptures that we will use to bring every contrary suggestion of the enemy to obedience. Whatever it is we are trusting God for, let us look for that bible promise that proves to us that God will do it. And let us keep it in our hearts and close to our mouths.

As for me *sha*, I know that the next time I say 'It is well' for a particular situation, I will be sure that I know what I am standing on to be so confident! So next time you hear me say it, you are free to ask me "Please, what scripture are you standing on? How do you know it is well?

Shalom!

Tuesday, 10th of March
So I Think I Am Clever?

So I think I am clever?
I sit in a taxi with a stranger at the wheel
And trust that he will
To my destination take me safely

I walk into a restaurant.
Don't know anyone but
Trust that the food will not kill me

I board a great big plane.
Cannot even see the Pilot. Just a voice
Yet to 'The Voice' and his co-pilot I trust my life forty thousand feet in the sky!

A cheque is given me with a mere man's signature on it
And off I go to the bank smiling happily trustingly
For sure, in my hands will some good money be shortly

Ha! How clever am I really?
To feel justified to second guess a Mighty God
To distrust the One who created ALL things.
To lack confidence in the One who can hold all the
Waters of the worlds in the cup of His Hands.
Yet in a mere man I trust completely

I see it quite clearly now, I really cannot be that clever, can I?
If, in the One who
Gave breath to the taxi driver
Taught the Chef to cook
Keeps the plane in the skies
Gave the mere man the power to make money
I apparently have no confidence at all

Let' see how foolish I am:

It is HIM I begin to ask to show me proof
Who taught you how to drive? Where is your licence?
Where did you learn to cook? Show me your accreditation.
How many miles have you flown? What Flying school did you go?
Let me see your credit history and your bank statements? Who is your Banker?
I think I am clever to ask the I AM that I AM all these questions? How shameful!

But Yet, He smiles down on me, always the doting Father
Knowing my frailty, He gives me time to ponder
On all that He has done in my life and for others
He smiles, always long suffering, in the belief that one day *sha*
This My child will eventually get Me. *Na wah*!
And cease to be so foolish. So Faith-less.
In short
So incredibly un-clever.

Wednesday, 11ᵗʰ of March
Happy Birthday, My Personal 'Love of God!'

Anyway you slice or dice it. Love of God. God's Love. Your name is special. My dear daughter, my personal Love of God. My symbol of love from God. You are 12 today and I am once more reminded of the boundless love God has for me. For your dad. For you. For us. Isn't it just awesome? Bless His Holy Name!

Imagine that. You are 12 already! So this time 12 years ago I was waddling around getting ready to go to the hospital. Actually I remember it quite clearly. I was at the PC trying to put some finishing touches to something your dad has asked me to type up for him. For the life of me I cannot remember what that could have been. But the point is I was quite comfortable. Quite relaxed. Knowing that you would be born that day. My plan was for you to come a week earlier on the 4th just like your brother. But obviously you had your plans. Independent woman that you already where from the womb. You wanted your own day. Who can blame you?

God on my side, you were born at 4.30pm. Your labour was hard but quick. You came out screaming like a banshee but boy where you a sight to behold. Your dad could not stop gushing. Your hair, your fingernails. Your face. Everything was perfect. And of course everything looked like him! Lol! I wish you could have seen his face when days later ALL the hair fell off! Yes oh, you were one of those *oyinbo* looking babies who had no hair on your head. To this day, I have a friend who cannot believe your hair is not attachment. That is how God does His things *o jare*. That is why it is wise not to despise little beginnings. Now your hair is so long and lovely and luckily for your papa, your nails are still nicely-shaped. Positively not from my side of the family. We have nails like the cocoa farmers. Good stock though.

My dear lovely girl-child. Happy Birthday! I bless God for your life. He has indeed made you for signs and wonders. And we have begun to see this in your intelligence and quest for excellence always (although it sets my teeth on edge sometimes, this your desire for EVERYTHING to be just so!). As someone told me, it is who you are and as you grow up, it will serve you well when tempered with maturity and experience. Keep on doing the best you know how love. God is watching and He will reward all your efforts. You will be on top always and never beneath in Jesus name. Amen!

I bless God for your caring nature. But for you I am not sure your brother would ever get his homework done. Ever. It is you he cries for when he is being disciplined. You are his little saviour, his mini-mommy of sorts and I appreciate you for that. And though you sometimes drive me to distraction with you 'Jeremiah's anointing'. I know that this just shows another side of your sensitive nature and as God answers prayers I notice with great joy that you do not cry at the drop of a hat anymore. Bless God. May your heart always beat with the love of God. Know that though your dad, your brothers and I love you loads. No one loves you more than God.(Yes, AK loves you too. You know guys, he thinks its cool to act otherwise. Pray for him to see the light. Lol!)

You, my love, my one and only princess are a rising star and I am waiting bated breath to see what God has in store of your life. I know it will be good. Cos you are His love child. Your name reminds his children of one of his most important traits. Love. And Lord knows I love you girl. The way you sometimes go off in those your freaky bouts of laughing for no reason. The way you are such a snoop. Yes, you are ! The way you always look like you are going to faint if you think something is wrong with me health wise. The way you play the piano (this amazes me and I admit this must be from your Papa's side. We do not pay piano in Ekiti. Drums? Yes. Piano? I don't think so. Your addiction to Oreos and chocolate chip cookies. These are just some of the things that make you YOU for now. I know as you grow older, some will change. You will change and for good too by God's grace. But I am confident that one thing will never change and that is how much you are loved. By Me. By God. Know this always. Deep in your heart. OK?

Happy Birthday Avosinha!

Thursday, 12th of March
Hey Mr. Temper, Please Stay Lost!

A while ago, I lost a pair of my favourite ear rings. If there was any such thing as 'jewellery uniform; this would be it for me. They came with this gorgeous necklace and I wear them all the time. To work. To church. To weddings. Everywhere. They were a birthday present from me to myself in 2007. Anyway, now one of the earrings is lost. It has stayed lost. It has not come back.

Way before then, I also lost my I-phone. Yep! That big old thing is hiding somewhere in my house (as I refuse to believe it has been stolen!). It too has not come back to me. It has stayed lost.

Now watch this! Watch this! (God Bless you Pastor Eddie Long!). I have lost my temper many many many times. In fact I lost it big time a couple of nights ago when my son decided that blowing soap bubbles into my dinner was just so much fun. 1st warning. No change. 2nd Warning. Some more giggles. The 3rd time those coloured soap bubbles popped all over my rice and fried egg (errr I know not a well known combination but yummy all the same. Big up to all the FIRs in Uyo for making this one of my preferred rice accompaniments) I lost it completely. You know what happened next right? Yep! The rod and the child had a nice 'getting to know you' party. Moms, take it from me the wrongest time to discipline your children is when you are boiling mad. I know this but I just could not help myself.

So you see I have been losing my temper for quite some time now. What I cannot understand is why it does not just STAY LOST! I would seriously not mind at all. You hear me Mr. Temper, Since I lost you the other day, you have not come back. I have repented and asked God for a double portion of self control and I promise you I will not mind at all. JUST stay wherever you are hiding. Please!

As my experience has proven that Mr. Temper is also deaf. I am sure he will try to make his way back. In fact I am sure he is already looking for the next opportunity to slip right back into my life. So I am going deeper into the bunker of the Word of God so that I can continue to renew my mind.

Methinks if I do this, even if the Temper-man comes back, I will not be home for him. He will have to go look for another 'appurtenance situate'

So it is and so shall it be in Jesus Christ's name. Amen!

P. S.
FIRs means Food IS Ready . Little food joints around the Universities in Uyo and Calabar. Not sure if they existed anywhere else under this name!

Yes, I have made Temper masculine just cos..... well cos I wanted to. Ha!

Friday, 13th of March
A Rare Breed of In-Laws

An old friend and sista recently dubbed me 'Queen B'. It made me smile. Over the years I have been a number of 'Bs'. In University and when I just started dating my MGM, his brothers and friends used to call me 'Miss B'. After we got married I was elevated to 'Lady B'. The moment I started having children, the chic and elegant sounding titles just disappeared and I just became 'Mama - my first son's name'. I actually thought that was the end of my 'B-ness' until now. But no, I am back with a vengeance. Queen B!

That's really not what this blog is about though. It's about the guy who started the whole title thing in the first place. My brother-in-law (or in-love as as Ms. Bardot puts it). My MGM's immediate younger brother. Mr. P! He was something else. In the early days of our marriage, he, it was that was my main buddy. I still recall how he and his then girl friend would go to the market, cook and then clean up the whole kitchen. There was nothing that he did not take on. To be honest I was quite shy asking him for all the help but he would just go on and do the needful himself. Oh where was I do I hear you ask? Sick as dog. For a good reason though. Upon all our bravura after the wedding, telling our parents they would have to wait 2 years before any grand children appeared on the scenes. I fell pregnant (funny term that, where did I fall pregnant from? The sky? LOL). Yes oh, 3 months after the I Dos, we were preggers. I can still hear my mother in love laughing at us! And so in those days, before this same MIL arrived on the scene to take care of me, it was my BIL that acted like my 'mom'. And I will never forget that.

You see my MIL had trained her 3 boys such that they could do anything that any well brought up girl could do. In fact, I sometimes wonder if they do not do it better than my SIL actually. In fact, if this my BIL cooks for you.... hmmmm. Let's just say he is talented like that. In fact, all of my MIL's children are good in the kitchen and they all also have various other skills and talents. I thank God so much for them all. However, I will always single out this my one BIL because he was good to me when I needed it most.

You might say he did it out of respect for his older brother but please he could have done just 50% of what he did and no one would have begrudged him. But he went the extra mile. I prefer to think he did it out of genuine desire to help a young SIL out. He was just a good in law and I doubt I ever told him properly how much I appreciated his help and care. I did then and I do now, so many years after. Now he has his own family and I want to believe he is still the same hands on kinda guy. Thank you Mr. P and I pray that God will reward you in this season just for all you did for me way back then.

You see, somehow God always works things out for us. He balances things out. There I was a young woman in a new marriage. No mom to turn to. No older siblings to call on. So God gave me a loving and caring family in love. In that family my MIL and BIL stood out as the champions of my cause. They are truly a rare breed of in laws. And today, I salute them both!

Mr. P! Nana! Thank you both for your labour of love towards me. I pray for God to do something special for you in this season and let you know somehow that it is because of how you showed me care and love those many many years ago. So shall it be in Jesus Christ's name. Amen!

I do hope that I can be your kind of MIL when I grow up and that my children will emulate you Mr. P. That would be real neat.

Friday, 20th of March
My Sistas-Divine in Dispora, I Hail You!

To mark my first day back to my dear blog (not sure why but the network refused to allow me in!) I feel like focusing on the good side of Facebook. I am loving the way it is expanding my coasts and broadening my horizons. And it's funny cos that is one of the things God told me he would be doing in my life this year. But you know me now. Typical human being I was thinking about some grand plan to make me the next female president or something! LOL. Well not really that but you know what I mean. But in His infinite wisdom He has been using FB to bring me in touch with some phenomenal women.

Yes, awesome women who by their day to day lives, have inspired me to be a better me. Women of prayer, strong women of faith. Daughters of Zion who are ever ready to encourage and build up. Yes, God is taking me to higher heights and I am doing it on the wings of new found friendships with these women and it is all thanks to Facebook. Praise God!

Last night I was online chatting with one of these divine divas who lives way away in the US and runs a crèche. I am not sure about you but just the thought of what that means makes me cringe with fear (All due respect to babies and all. I know y'all are cute but no way will I take a job to look after more that the ones God has blessed me with!). I have one 5 year old and he makes enough noise to make it seem like I have 3! But this diva does it and loves it. Today, I am hailing her, this woman of faith. Only God can reward her for what she does. Me, I can only thank you and claim you.

Then there is another new found friend who I am quite sure wears a Superwoman suit underneath her clothes. She really cannot be just human. She has blogs. She officiates on more than 3 websites. She is a wife, mom, sister, and daughter. In short. She is superwoman! Even though she lives in Naija, this piece will not be complete without mentioning her. She inspires me. I hail her and I know God is taking her somewhere. I wait with bated breath.

Then there is this my '*Ore*' (friend) par excellence. She, I did not actually meet via FB. Have known her for quite a while and from the first time I met her. I stood in awe of her. She lives in the UK and is what I call the 'perfect hostess'. On two or more occasions, my family has stayed with her family at some point and she is always wonderful. She cooks up a storm and once my 5 year old would not eat jollof rice unless you told him it was 'like Aunty Ys' jollof rice'. What amazes me is that she has no nanny, no cook, and no driver. She is all of the above ALL THE TIME and she works!!!!!! I mean, I have all of the above (well barring the cook) and I know how tired I feel just managing the things these staff cannot do for you and my job. I am convinced that for any woman out there to cope the way you all do, it is the grace of God.

So this little piece is just to let you know that I have a healthy amount of respect for you all, my sista-friends in diaspora and out of diaspora (abi is that not the opposite of 'in diaspora'? Lol!). You are indeed blessed and highly favoured of the Lord. I thank God for bringing you into my life at this point in time. That I am on this site doing what I am doing is thanks to one other lovely lady who, till this day, I have never met. Never seen. But it was she who encouraged me to start blogging. And now, what looked so daunting is almost second nature. Women can truly be joint partners with God in lifting up their sister folk. If only we will all catch the revelation.

Anyway, to you my divalicious chics of God, as you continue to go about your daily lives, being the women God has called you to be, I pray for you. May you always delight yourselves in the Lord. May you also find joy in pleasing Him. May your husbands and children hail you at the gates. May your family members call you blessed. May you be surrounded by solid friends. True blue ones. And may you be a true WOMAN AFTER GOD'S OWN HEART in Jesus Christ's name. Amen!

I am proud to know you and I am sure God is proud of you waaaaaaay more than me!

Shalom!

Monday, 23 March
No Comments? *Kini Big Deal?*

I have been doing a lot of self-examination recently on the reasons behind my actions. Especially the good deeds. At least, in my mind, they are good deeds. Why do I do them? Is it to make me feel good inside? To make the other person think I am a good person? Or is it just my normal response to certain situations. Or is it about wanting to please my Maker and be like Him? For instance, why do I blog? If it is indeed cos I love to write then why does it matter so when I get to my blog and still see '0' comments? Why do I revel so in seeing other people's comment on my FB page? Why does it matter so much when I tell myself I am really only doing it for me. As an outlet for my thoughts. My musings? As one more way to reach out to people with the good news of the Gospel of Jesus Christ. Ok, well there are many ways to bell a cat. As long as I do not add or subtract from what the good book preaches, I am still safe *ke? abi?* There is no doubt oh, this blog belongs to an *omo Jesu* through and through. No controversy at all at all oh!

Anyway back to my self-examination. You know what? After a lot of to-ing and fro-ing in my mind. I have arrived at a conclusion and it has just got to be said. I just have to confess it. I LOVE feedback! There! It's out there and I am free! I love to hear from people. I love to see that people actually read and feel led to write something in return. I have this huge oafish smile on my face every time I log into my FB and see that I have a mail or some comments have been logged in response to my status or some comment I had made earlier. It just gives me a warm fuzzy feeling inside. It's like winning a mini-lottery. It's a big deal! It's a big deal! So, my secret is out. Phew!

I think in the end, it is again part of that innate desire in all humans for acknowledgement. For validation. I have decided to agree (with myself of course.) that this is really not a bad thing UNTIL I fall into the trap of wanting it so bad as to veer off my 'chosen path'. You see in as much as I love to hear from people and would love them to read my blogs and write back. I have come to a place in my life where feedback or the lack of it can no longer define me as a person. It would make me happy to see feedback every single day but by God's grace I will continue to be happy and filled with joy whether or *'whethernt. Kosi big deal. Kosi big deal!*

As for all the other random acts of kindness or goodness that I may be blessed enough to impart on those who come along my way, I just say' to God be the glory oh!' *Who dash Jero* life to be helping people. *No be God?* Let people now know. It is not me oh! And let me myself now know, woman, it is not you! So get over yourself and give all the glory to God for anything He enables you to do for your neighbour. *Kini big deal?* Well, *shebi shebi* Jesus Christ did say, if you love me, 'feed my sheep.'

I am just trying to obey the last command!

Shalom!

Wednesday, 26th of March
A Simple Woman

I thank God for my job. It is a really good one and I love it. Mostly because of the people I get to work with and mostly cos the pay is good too (Yes, truth must be told and yes, it's my blog so I can use mostly twice in one sentence. Lol!). And it is this work that has been taking the lion share of my time lately so that I have not been able to pay a daily visit to my blog. It is well *sha* because the Lord will keep on making ways and time for where there seems to be none.

Anyway, I have been meaning to do this particular blog for about 3 weeks now. And you know if I had, it would have come out in good time for Mother's Day. But O well, better late than never. You see, I have been thinking about my mom a lot lately. There is no deep deep reason for this. I think it just has to do with my age, watching my children grow up and hearing me say things to them I remember my mom saying to me. Also, for different reasons, I have been talking about or saying things that bring up memories of her a lot. In short, *mi Madre* has been on my mind a lot. So I am going to blog about her.

And the first thing I always remember about her is her dressing and it brings a warm smile to my face. You see, my mom wore only two things. She was either in a pair of trousers and a simple top or she would be wearing some simple yet stylish long abada skirt and blouse. I remember the trip we made to Lome once to see my Uncle. During this trip my mother sat down with one of those talented tailors that come out of these francophone countries and together they came up with the most beautiful abada tops I had ever seen. Nothing too loud but every time she wore them when we got back to Calabar, some friend would ask to copy it. She had talent like that. In her own simple way.

Mom was a simple woman. She had no airs about her. She and my dad had lived in the States for many years but as far as I remember, she always spoke to me in a funny mix of Yoruba and English that had a sing song ring to it. I can hear her even now ' *Bola she oni wa clean up table yi ni. You know time ti lo?*' And you can trust me, I would always respond in pure English. It used to annoy me sometimes. People should really choose which language they wanted to speak in. Bu now I miss it. You see how life can be? Funny enough, I did hear her once in a while speaking 'phonetics' and as I think about it now, I actually preferred our own personal lingo. Cos that is part of what made you YOU. My Mom.

My mom had this knack for trying something for the very first time and getting it perfectly. Like when she started baking bread. It was just delicious and I still cannot understand why she would bake all this gorgeous bread and then keep on warning me about putting on weight when I showed my appreciation for her skills by eating bread with every meal! LOL. Oh Mom, I do miss you in my life today. Then she went into making meat pies as well. Is it a wonder that I weighed in at over 80Kg in those days? Thank God I had a mirror that constantly told me I was slimmer. LOL!

At some point close to the end, she began a love affair with adire. She would travel from Calabar to Abeokuta and come back with adire fabric and shirts in uncommon designs. I was her mini sales rep as I would take them to the Uni then to sell them to friends. I even remember one of the birthday presents I gave to my MGM (who was still then just my 'bobo') was one of the adire shirts I was meant to have been selling. I am not sure I ever made any returns on those sales! Till today, I am still not your best choice when it comes to sales and marketing!

Anyway, Mom, I never really got to know you. Cos that kind of knowing can only come as one matures and the relationship moves from just being mommy-child to that one where you are now mommy/friend to daughter/friend. You died before I could get to know you as friend. We used to talk but mostly about the sad stuff going on in your life. I remember still how committed you were to us children and how that had driven you to make the choices you had made. I look now in my life and know that I too, am committed to my children like that but I also have the added advantage of knowing Christ as my helper.

You were a Moslem and I know that you converted to Christianity at some point though I do not know exactly when. A friend of mine was encouraging me recently not to fret over where you are and the reasons she gave me made sense so I have laid that worry to rest. God who saw your heart and saw your desire to get to know Him would have done good by you. Your favourite past time was reading your bible and even the day you died, you had your bible face down on your chest opened to Psalm 27. Though I cannot understand the timing of your death I know that I have a God that knows best. And even as I type this now, I remember some stuff that I got up to after you died that no mother would have missed. Poor dad, in his ignorance, he was at peace! Perhaps God had to spare you all that!

Time does go by and here I am your daughter, a mother to some seriously blessed children. You would have so loved your grandchildren although I think they would have exhausted you no end. I am sure my MGM would have also won your heart cos he is charming like that. But more importantly he is a good and respectful person and since I am your daughter and he loves me, he would have loved you too cos you were an easy to love person like that too. Mom, I miss you. So does your baby daughter who sometimes calls me sista-mom. She misses more the idea of you cos she was just 4 years old and really cannot remember much. But lately I have even begun to look like you so she is getting the picture better. But I could never be you really mom. You were just special like that. You need to help us with your son. Only you and God know what he thinks and feels. I know he loves us though. Of course he does, we are his sisters! But talk to Jesus about him. He needs help from above. God told me some days ago to pray specially about his health, finance and salvation. But am sure you know about that *abi*? I cannot help but thinking had you been here that boy would have taken a different turn all those 19 years ago? Who knows!

Your sisters and your mom still live life in mourning really. It is almost as if you died just yesterday to them. They cannot get over it. You were their personal star. The light of the family. The one they all looked up to. They smile when they see us. But even I can see that mixed in with those smiles is a sadness that no one can take from them. I doubt they even want that sadness to go away. They seem to cherish it. As if it keeps you close by. Alive.

I am desperate to be like you mom in the good things you did and in the good woman that you were. But I am sure now even you know that if I really should be desperate for something, it should be to be like Jesus Christ. So I am working on that now with all my heart.

Still, this is for you mom, the outpouring of a desperate Naija woman missing her mom. A simple woman. A good woman. A woman I hope to see later.

Ciao Mama! Je t'aime tant!

Tuesday, 31ˢᵗ of March
In The Valley

What a ride I had been on all this while. Days, Weeks, Months even. Just basking in the glorious love and mercies of my God-Father who loves me so much. I was the personification of Excitement, Conviction and Spiritual Anticipation. Prayer time restored. Victories through prayers being recorded here and there. Peace on the throne in areas of my life that mattered. In short, I was once more getting reconnected with my Maker.

Hmmmm, it is funny how you never see it coming. The curve ball heading your way. At least I did not see it coming. I guess I was all wrapped up in the 'high' of the mountain top experiences I had been having. Or maybe I was only on the look out for the 'usual suspects'. You know, those 'besetting sins' that so easily come upon me. I was so intent on watching out for those ones that I didn't know trouble was brewing until the hot mug of *katakata* landed square in my laps!

Whatever, the point I am trying to make is that I am not in a good place right now. And it is not about Who? Or What? Neither is about Why? Or When? Or How? The important thing for me now, as I try to work my way out of here, is making sure that I hang on to the 'In spite Of' The 'Though' and The 'Yet'.

Yes, INSPITE OF how I feel right now, God still loves me. That can never change. I am indeed a beneficiary of all the things that Jesus Christ died on the cross to give me and the key ones for me now are Joy and Peace of Mind.

Yes, THOUGH I am in a dark place and I am wondering what the point of it all is again, THOUGH I have fallen again into the sin that so easily besets me, I shall rise again in the name of Jesus Christ. Amen! I am more than an overcomer regardless of how miserably defeated I feel at the moment.

The enemy has come again brandishing his sickle at my Achilles tendon. Yes, right now, I am out for the count. I am sitting in my corner all bloodied and battered emotionally YET I will rise again for in the name of the Lord, I will overcome him and all his cohorts. Now I may be mourning but I know I shall dance come morning! I shall sing to the glory of my God. Yes, I will!

I just have to stay in the Word whether I feel like it or not. Just like loving someone, this is not about how you 'feel'. Once you have made up your mind about loving someone, the truth is that sometimes, it does not come naturally. Sometimes, that person does things that are not at all lovable. So then you make a conscious choice to keep on loving him or her. And if it is real love, it will weather that incident or storm or whatever and the love will survive.

It is the same, I think, that we have to do when the enemy comes A-Lurking. A-Roaring. A-Destroying. I must choose to remember that, EVEN in that dark place, God is there with me. Nothing can separate me from the Love of my Father. The taunts and jabs of the enemy must not sway me from my path. It must not move me from my stance on the Rock that is higher than I.

That is why, at this time, I chose to set my face like a flint. I chose to hold on cos THIS TOO SHALL PASS. In Jesus Christ's name! Amen!

P.S S.
And Amen! It has passed. I actually wrote this on Sunday evening and shame on the devil. What he meant for evil and destruction has actually worked out for good and REVIVAL! But it was a hard place to be especially after being on the mountaintop for so long!

So I guess the learning is while you are enjoying your mountain top experiences, keep an eye out on your hedge. The enemy sure is!

Shalom!

Tuesday, 31st of March
The DNW's Seven Steps To Spiritual Rejuvenation

I met a man 2 Saturdays ago. His name is John Piper. My Pastor introduced him to me during our Saturday Morning Prayer meeting and I am so glad he did. OK, I did not actually meet him in person but by the time my Pastor was done making us pray for our souls using John's prayer points. I felt I knew him personally. At least I knew that he desired something that I have been seeking for a long time now. He wanted a Revival. In his soul, his mind, his spirit. He wanted to be so aligned with God that no one would doubt that he was a Christian. A true follower. Not just a believer.

I want that so much and in the hope that you do too, I am sharing these DNW's 7 steps towards 'A Spiritual Awakening'. I have adapted John Pipers scripture based prayers somewhat to come up with these prayer points which I am now sharing as we cross over into this 2nd quarter of 2009.

Dear Lord, Make Me WANT To Know You and Read Your Word (Psalm 119:36)

To even begin to walk this path, I have got to WANT it badly. I have got to desire to know God. I have got to be inclined want to spend time in His word. Where does this 'want' come from? It comes from God. So I will pray asking Him to:

Incline my heart to your testimonies...

Dear Lord, Open my eyes, Open my ears (Psalm 119:18)

OK, so now I want to know God and I want to read his Word. But how do I really 'see' all that His word has for me. Who can open my eyes so that I see exactly what God wants me to see and not just my own ideas? Who will prepare my heart so that I can understand? God will. So Psalm 119:18 teaches us to pray:

Open my eyes, that I may see wondrous things from your law.

Dear Lord, Enlighten my heart with these 'wonders' (Ephesians 1:18)

So I am getting to know God better and my eyes and heart are seeing all sorts of wonders from His Word. Yet I do not want to just read it like a novel and be entertained (and indeed there are some very entertaining stories in the bible!). I want to be able to appreciate the glory in them and who will enlighten my heart so that it can do that? God will. So Ephesians 1:18 teaches us to pray:

That the eyes of my heart may be enlightened in order that I may know the hope to which he has called me, the riches of his glorious inheritance in the saints (You need to see how this is captured in 'The Message')

Dear Lord, Unify my Heart (Psalm 86:11)

What would be sad is if some parts of my soul and spirit are receiving light from the word while some others remain in darkness. I need for my whole heart to be united for God. I want ALL of me to aligned to Him. All areas of my life. Where does this unity and wholeness come from? From God. So he has asked us to pray:

Teach me your way, O LORD;I will walk in your truth; Unite my heart to fear your name; Dear Lord, Satisfy my Heart (Psalm 90:14)

What I really want from all of this time being spent in God's word and the work of His Spirit in answer to my prayers is that my heart will be satisfied with God and not with the world. Where will this satisfaction come from? It comes from God so Psalm 90:14 helps us to pray:

Satisfy me in the morning with your unfailing love that I may sing for joy and be glad all my days.

Dear Lord, Strengthen my Heart (Ephesians 3:16)

It would be a shame if I were just happy in my own private world with God. I want my happiness to radiate outwards to all around me. So it has to be really FULL, I want to be strong in JOY. This will help me be durable in the face of threats or storms. How do I get this strength and durability? I get it from God. I get it as I pray:

…that out of his glorious riches he may strengthen me with power through his Spirit in my inner being,

Dear Lord, Let My Life be fruitful (Colossians 1:10)

Finally, I want to be strong in Christ so that I can produce good deeds for others so that the glory of God can be seen in my life. Who produces these goods in and through me? God does, so please join me as I pray:

… That I may walk worthy of the Lord, fully pleasing Him, being fruitful in every good work and increasing in the knowledge of God;

May I remind us all as I end this that Jesus Christ died on the cross to accomplish 2 main things: He died to give us stuff and He died to remove stuff from our lives. All of the things we have prayed for above are part of the things that God has 'freely given us' through the bloody cross at Calvary. As we approach Easter, I think it is a wonderful time to begin to take possession of all these free gifts paid for in a currency beyond treasure and measure. It would be such a shame not to do so. It would be just as if Jesus Christ died for nothing!

Shalom!

APRIL

Wednesday, 01 April
It's A New Month. I Declare!

Yes! It's a new day. It's a new dawn. It's a new month!
And I declare that
In the name of Jesus Christ
And
By the power of the blood he shed on the cross for me. For you.
And
By the authority of the scriptures
As I move into this new month. As you move into this new month
A mighty blessing will come upon our lives
Our now
Our future
And all that has to do with our lives
Our health
Our homes
Our finances
Our friends and
Our churches
As we step into this new month of April, the 4th month of 2009
I proclaim that this is our time of favour, blessings, new spiritual power, increase, expansion, fresh anointing and great personal breakthroughs for the glory of God.

In Jesus Christ's name!

Amen!!!!!!!!!!!!!!!!!!!!!!!!!!!!!!!

Now say a better AMEN!!!!!!!!!!!!!!!!!!!!!!!

Thursday, 02 April
Funny Things Are Happening.

A funny thing happened to me today. Actually a lot of funny things have been happening to me lately. And God is having a good laugh I am sure. Thankfully I am smiling too. Yes, I cannot lie. I am not laughing with him. But I am smiling whimsically cos God really does KNOW what we need at different points in our lives. And even though they are 100% the opposite of what you think you need at the time. He is always right.

About these funny things now. I shall not bore you with details but all I can say is that 'IT IS ALL GOOD!'. In the midst of my issues and my struggles with my every day life. God is showing me that it is NOW, in this season, that He is now ready to use me. And the different ways He is showing me this are indeed funny. My MGM said to me, 'maybe you have a calling...'. Maybe. Just maybe.

Yes, just maybe in this my every day life, there is something good that I can do for God. Something small that is BIG in his own eyes. It is clear that He is sending stuff my way that make me look into the skies with a questioning look on my face. ' Err, excuse me Lord, what's up?

I am sure He is just looking at me smiling.

Me, too, I am smiling and I am thinking 'Lord, you know what? Carry go! I am free falling with you. Where ever you lead, I will follow'.

Funny how free you feel when you just let go and let God...

Friday, 03 April
And The Saga Continues.

God is really up to something. I know I said this yesterday but I just have to say it again. God is working out something in my life. And THIS TIME I will stand. I will stand against the enemy of my destiny. I will not let him trip me up. I am so excited because I really love surprises and have decided to just go along with whatever God is up to. He loves me so it will be good.

So as you go off into the weekend, you too lean into God. He has a special plan for you too. I do not know exactly what I did that has made God open up his store house on to me. But I am glad and please I hope you know I am not talking about store house of money or anything like that. I am talking about stuff better than money. I am talking about hot connections. I am talking about doing God's business. The business of Love. The business of helping people. Of talking to people and helping them to tap into God so that their paths might be aligned to His. I mean if God had any particular favourite dish, it would be the dish filled with souls won over from the clutches of darkness. And for some reason, all sorts of opportunities are opening up to me to do tiny tiny things to provide this meal for my God. Praise His name!

Anyway, as I was saying, go into this weekend knowing that God is the same and He loves us the same.

So if you want this. Go get some! Go knock. Go Ask. Go Seek. You shall find!

Shalom!

Monday, 06 April
The Small 'Big Deals' Of Life

My sista-divine published a blog today and it was funny cos I had been thinking about the same thing a while back but never really got round to putting anything down. It was still there in my little black book of 'possible stuff' to blog about. I took out my book again and saw it 'Gratitude'. I am not sure I remember what was on my mind back then when I decided to write on it but when I shared with her, she said to still do my own piece and I believe she was right cos it came to me differently. Its a long one but try to read on if you can.

It is true that we all know what being grateful or thankful is about and I am sure we all know we could never thank God enough for all He does for us. But my question to myself is this? Am I really aware of ALL the things I should be thankful for? There are so many obvious things to thank God for (and I am not even coming close to doing justice to those ones!) but on top of that is my new awareness that I may have fallen into the trap of not being grateful for the small 'big deals' of my life. Those tiny almost insignificant stuff that should they NOT be there or NOT happen as they do, will cause a huge amount of *katakata* for me. Let me try and explain.

When you woke up this morning and you opened your eyes to look at the time. Did you even think about it? You just opened your eyes like that and you looked at your clock or your phone, saw the numbers, your brain understood the message your eyes relayed to it. If you were like me, you ignored the fact that you were late and plumped you head back on the pillow! But you did all of this without thinking about it. You know what? It is not a given. It's a gift. It's a blessing. One that we take for granted.

Ok, so you finally decide that its time to get out of bed, you throw off the duvet and throw your leg out of bed. Up you get, stretching as you go. Did you give it any thought? No of course not. We do not have too. All is working as it should. We move our limbs, we walk, we run, we sit, and we stand. No effort. No thought required. You know what?

It is not a given. Its God's favour. It's His blessing. And we take it for granted.

You proceed to brush your teeth. Ah ha but first you must pee! Easy *abi*? No thought required. No concentration. Just sit, do the business and get up. Oh what a relief so easily obtained. But my people, this is not a given. There are many who would love to know what it is to simply sit and pee. But they cannot. But you can. God loves you like that. And yet, we take it for granted. OK forgive me, my bad, I am the only one who cannot remember the last time I thanked God for the blessing of being able to pee and poo! *E ma binu*. I know it is a tad TMI. But we need to be real now.

Do you know there are people who are allergic to the sun? Whose skin cannot stand the rays of our God given sun? On a normal day, do you even THINK about your skin or its purpose? Well OK, I know we women think of it in terms of what lotion to smother it in or what shade of foundation will suit it most. But I am talking about it in terms of the actual purpose God created it for. Do you? And when you do, do you remember to thank God for it? Maybe you do but it has never occurred to me.

Watch a child gasping for air in the throes of an asthma attack and you will appreciate the 'small' feat of breathing in and out. Watch a young man trying to relearn how to carry a fork of food to his mouth as he recovers after a road accident. You will appreciate better all the simple movements you make in the course of the day. Tune to that channel that features medical victories or mysteries and you will be so so grateful to God for the tiny 'big' things that you are able to do without thinking. I watched one once about this girl who would for no reason, fall asleep, mid stride or mid sentence. Honest. One minute she was walking with her friends in the mall, talking and laughing and the next, she had fallen dead asleep. They call it the *'petits morts'* – little deaths! That too is some funny illness. May we never see. In Jesus Christ's name. Amen!

So tell me, how can we say, even in our maddest moments, that God is not interested in our lives. Look at all these small BIG things He is keeping an eye on for us. I am sure if you give yourself some time, you can come up with even smaller things that we do or that happen in our lives that we never give any thought to. So you know what? Let's cut a deal. As you are waiting for the HUGE breakthrough. While you wait for God to move your mountain. Open that door. Or close it. As you wait for God to open the eyes of that man. Bless you with that baby. Make straight that crooked road. Send down that job or promotion. As you wait for all of these mighty things, take out some time to thank God NOW. Yes, thank Him now for the little little things He is doing in you every single day. Yes, the small big miracles of life you experience every day you get out of bed.

Do you know what? If any of those small things went wrong, all the other big things you are waiting for will suddenly lose their appeal. They will no longer be such big deals. But we are wise people abi? Yes, and by the special grace of God, we will be thankful for the small big deals we have today! And we will let God know.

Shalom!

Tuesday, 07 April
What Are YOU Going To Do About It?

I think I have heard it said more times than I care to remember. And now it has begun to bug me. Maybe I am just still in a rotten mood trying to get over my friend's death yesterday. Maybe I am just mad that too many of us Christians sit around and let the 'heathen' say all sorts about us and our faith. Maybe I am mad cos what they say is true. Maybe I am mad cos no one seems to be doing anything about it. And if I was any madder, it would be cos I am also part of the problem. OK, before you gather together to commit me, here me out.

We know that there is a church on every street corner. There is a Christian in every office. Go into any main market and you will surely hear some shop owners singing songs of praise early in the morning to usher in the 'god of the shoppers'. I say this cos if it was the true God they were singing to then there should be fewer fight breakouts in the market. There is also a Christian in the House of Assembly and at every level of government. I am sure that you will find one professing Christian in the Police, The Army, The Navy, LASTMA, in our Schools, in our Hospitals, etc. In short, there are Christians everywhere. And please I am talking about 'supposed' born again, Holy Spirit baptised, Tongue-Speaking, Bible scripture quoting Christians. Vision seeing and believing, christianese speaking Christians. So can someone please tell me why are we not having any effect on the environment we live in?

Are we not tired of the people of this world asking us ' wherein now is your God?'. They ask this cos they see nothing in the way we live that resembles the God we claim to be our Father or the Jesus Christ we say is our brother-Saviour. This makes me so mad and so sad. Instead of blaming the 'church' or 'Pentecostalism', how about we look closer to home? Is it not people that make up the church? Take a look in the mirror. Is the person staring back at you doing anything to dispel this notion of fake Christianity? Is your life a shining example of what a true Christian should be? Will someone see you and be attracted to the faith you so loudly profess with your mouth yet equally loudly negate by your behaviours?

I do not know about you but I am sick and tired of hearing how awful we Christians are. I am sick and tired of hearing 'please if that is how it is in the church, let me just stay outside *jejely*'. I will not regal you with tales of what people have been through in the hands of so called Christians. Christian brothers. Christian Agents. Christian businessmen. Christian women. All of us Christian. All of us throwing a mantle of disrepute over a glorious God. What a shame!

But you know what? We can fix it. Yes, one Christian at a time. Let's not wait for some grand move or revolution. Let's take this up as a personal challenge. Happily, God will always be God whether we portray Him well or not. We need this for ourselves. For our children. For our society. For our future here on earth.

Let's be the change we want to see. OK, I have finished venting... you can drop the phone now. I am no longer mad. No need for Aro Hospital again...

Wednesday, 08 April
The Threefold Battle We Face

Do not get me wrong. I am sure I knew this before. But sometimes, you catch fresh revelation about old wisdom when it is presented in a new packaging. What am I talking about? It is the battle every born again Christian begins to face the moment he or she decides for Christ.

I was there busy surfing the web *jejely* trying to find material on personal evangelism when I came across an article on the 'Three Fold Battle' of the Born again Christian. For me, very eye opening to say the least. I shall try to rehash it here for our learning.

Before you and I became born again. Before we decided to say 'goodbye to the world and its pleasures of sins...' we were just there *sha*. If the devil had time for us at all, it was simply because, well he is evil like that and anyone is fair game to him. BUT the moment we decide for Jesus Christ, all that changes. Before JC we are just like all the other fish in the river swimming along with the current, going wherever it takes us. As Believers and Followers of JC, we make a conscious choice to swim AGAINST the current and all that mean current wants to do is drown us!!!!! And here are the 3 things we are swimming against:

The World - You know we are always being told to be IN the world but not OF the world. How we cannot love the world and love God at the same time. Well it is becos the World is the enemy oh! It is out to get us. The World is out to trap you. It uses all its trappings and Egyptian offerings to entice you. Fight it! Flee it!

The Flesh - Pre JC, you and I were just 'Sin' walking around in a body of Flesh. We fulfilled the lusts of the flesh and had no clue nor any desire to crucify it and all its desires and longings. Post JC, we are asked and by the grace of God we begin to walk in the Spirit, which helps us to die to the Flesh. The Flesh is all out to subdue us and make us do all it wants. And I tell you the Flesh wants to do everything that God would rather you not do! Fight it! Crucify it!

The Devil - Remember before we finally gave into JC. It is he, the devil that had our eyes all scaled up so that we could not even recognise our needs. The devil is the god of this world and the enemy of God and therefore of all God's children. That is you and I. He hates us and has only one thing for us - SKUD missiles. Yep! He wants to Steal, Kill and Destroy us. Fight him! Overcome him!

So you see, there are 3 'faces' to the battle we face daily. To be honest, methinks sometimes our issues can come in one ugly mishmash of all the 3 faces. Yikes! Scary stuff. But thank God, we know who we are in Christ Jesus! There is no doubt that being a Christian is wonderful BUT it is a good thing to realise that this DOES NOT mean that life will be all nice and rosy.

Actually quite the contrary. As you can see, that is when you become very visible on the enemy's radar. But the good news is this - Jesus Christ told us not to worry, that we should be of good cheer cos we HAD overcome the world (inclusive of the devil and the flesh methinks). So come what may, I trust that if I just walk with God close enough, I will have all I need to fight the good fight with all my might!

And so will you!

Shalom!

Thursday, 09 April
Can You Sleep When The Wind Blows?

A friend sent this to me today and I absolutely love it. You know when we say that you cannot wait until wahala *strikes before you begin to pray. Prayer should be a part of our every day life. We should be so prayed up that when the enemy comes a lurking, he will not know that 'Hmmmm this one may not be as easy as I thought oh!' Most of time, before we even hear 'pim' we have shouted 'ye pah! (At least if it is 'Jesus' we shout, one could say we praying for help! Lol) Anyway read on, you will understand better once you do*

Years ago, a farmer owned land along the Atlantic seacoast. He constantly advertised for hired hands. Most people were reluctant to work on farms along the Atlantic. They dreaded the awful storms that raged across the Atlantic wreaking havoc on the buildings and crops.

As the farmer interviewed applicants for the job, he received a steady stream of refusals. Finally, a short, thin man, well past middle age, approached the farmer. 'Are you a good farm hand?' the farmer asked him. 'Well, I can sleep when the wind blows,' answered the little man.

Although puzzled by this answer, the farmer, desperate for help, hired him. The little man worked well around the farm, busy from dawn to dusk, and the farmer felt satisfied with the man's work. Then one night the wind howled loudly in from offshore.

Jumping out of bed, the farmer grabbed a lantern and rushed next door to the hired hand's sleeping quarters. He shook the little man and yelled, 'Get up! A storm is coming! Tie things down before they blow away!' The little man rolled over in bed and said firmly, 'No sir. I told you, I can sleep when the wind blows.'

Enraged by the response, the farmer was tempted to fire him on the spot. Instead, he hurried outside to prepare for the storm. To his amazement, he discovered that all of the haystacks had been covered with tarpaulins. The cows were in the barn, the chickens were in the coops, and the doors were barred. The shutters were tightly secured. Everything was tied down.

Nothing could blow away. The farmer then understood what his hired hand meant, so he returned to his bed to also sleep while the wind blew.

So you see, when you're prepared, spiritually, mentally, and physically, we have nothing to fear. Can you sleep when the wind blows through your life? The hired hand in the story was able to sleep because he had secured the farm against the storm.

We secure ourselves against the storms of life by grounding ourselves in the Word of God. We don't need to understand, we just need to hold his hand to have peace in the middle of storms. I like that. Nothing like some good old God-fidence

Saturday, 11 April
No Matter What, It Will Always Be GOOD Friday!

I have missed my blog. My connection has been , shall we say, NEPA like, over the past couple of days. Logging on has been tedious so I decided to spare myself the stress and stay away for a while. But I have missed you dear blog!

Anywho, perhaps it has been for a reason cos I have been in and out of a gloomy place for a bit. Some hours I feel like YES! God is in control. And at others I am like DEAR LORD, how could you let this happen? Is that not how life is really. Mountaintops and valleys. Rain and Shine. Highs and Lows. Yep. I am no different from a million other humans. I spent yesterday mostly visiting with I, the wife of our dear friend who died on Monday morning. Sometimes it is better not to hear some full stories. The short version I had heard was sad enough. To hear her recount what happened that day was heart breaking. As I sat there looking at her, holding her in my arms. I knew as I always have known that there are some hurts that ONLY GOD can heal. This was one of them. It was not the best part of my day.

Compared to the day Jesus Christ was having some 2000 plus years ago. I guess you can say I was having a ball. I cannot say for sure but Jesus Christ must have been on His way to Golgotha with his cross around the same time I was with 'I'. The teeming crowds around him jeering or possibly just staring at him not knowing what to make of this Man. This enigma. This Jesus Christ. I wonder even what was going on in Jesus' mind as he trudged up that hill. I cannot even hazard a guess but there is no doubt that one of them would have been 'Lord, you know. Just give me the strength to go on.

Lord, I echo that prayer for my dear sista-friend now, 'Lord you know why her husband had to die now, leaving her with 3 Young children. I will not question you. BUT please give her the strength she needs to get through these early days and most importantly, the years ahead. In Jesus Christ name. Amen!'

It is still very well! Why? Cos I know that my Redeemer lives. Yes, he may be dead now. But tomorrow.

He will rise again!!!!!!!

Tuesday, 14 April
Christian? Lying? Please NO!

This is a tad painful for me to share. But share I must. I was caught in a lie.
Yes, I told a lie and as I am hopeless at it, I got caught. And do you know what is paining me the most?

It is not that I got caught.
It is not that I told a lie and then told another one to cover it up
It is not the shame I felt as hot as the shame was
It is not the hard words I got hit with as punishment for the shameful behaviour.
No, none of the above, as painful as they were
As hurt as my self esteem and ego felt
It was not these that pained me the most.

What pained me the most was the fact that by resorting to telling this lie
I had placed the person I was lying to in a position higher than my God.
I had effectively bowed to man rather than to God.
Yes I was more afraid of this person than I was afraid of my God.
If I feared God more. If I held Him in higher esteem
Then I would have chosen to remain on His good side and tell the truth.
Even though I would have had to face the music with man.

And yet as mean as the devil is telling this lie did not even preserve me as I had hoped. Since I got caught in the lie, it proceeded to cause one helluva fight and I am still reeling from the effect today.

Why am I boring you with is. Well one, downloading it all here, helps me deal with it. Two, it is in the hope that someone else might see that lying is not just about covering something up. As a Christian telling a lie, no matter how big or how white (a lie my friend, is a lie) is just a NO-No. The very act negates our claims that God is our only Judge.

If God is number 1, then we should always guard jealously our stance with Him. It does not matter what man thinks of us or can do to us. We must speak TRUTH only.

And you know the deepest cut of all? My Christian testimony was rubbished as well. There is nothing more painful to the heart of one desperately seeking Christlikeness that the words 'And you call yourself a a Christian?'. I have not felt so bad about my Christian walk in a long long time and I promise you, I have not been on the straight and narrow oh! But this was a Mike Tyson like KO to my spirit!

Hmmmm, it is well cos God is a God of mercy and a friend sent me a note today and it reminded me to be thankful in ALL things so I have managed to pull myself up. After all, a righteous man may fall seven times, but the clincher is that he gets up. So I am getting up, dusting myself off and hitting the high road of my Christian walk again.

Shalom!

Wednesday, 15 April
IN All, Not FOR All.

Thanks for all things?
My mind reels
How am I to do that Father?
Give you thanks for matters that bother?

Death of loved ones?
Sickness that bodies burn?
Homes that refuse to be built
Even when wives knees in prayer are bent?
Lack even in the face of hard work?
Injustice, Outright lawlessness, a country stuck
Daddy, how do I do that?
Give you thanks for all these hard facts?

Child, did I tell you that?
My love does not want to break your back
Yes, I AM the God of the impossible
But I will not ask you to do the undoable
Please child, do not be gullible
Go, look again in your Bible
Pray without ceasing it says
IN all things, in all situations, no matter the maze or haze
No matter the storms you face
Give Thanks. That's what it says.
Not For. In

Not For the bad stuff. IN them. As you pass Through them.
Keep Your Joy!
For your joy is not tied to any of these things you cry about
I AM your joy. And I am IN you ALL the time. I never leave your side
So joy in ME.
Be thankful IN me.

Regardless..........

And my child, My dear dear child, Fear not
For to do this, I will also help you. Don't doubt
I am your Enabler, Your Power
Just tap into me, now. This hour.

Monday, 20 April
Pressing On, Regardless....

I am convinced now that I have a dual personality. Seriously. But I don't need Dr. Phil and Sigmund Freud. I know what my issues are. I even have a good companion in crime in the bible. His name was Paul. We both do what we do not want to do. And what we want to do and know to do, that we don't do! Not sure how frustrated Paul was with himself but I am reaching melt down stage. I am just sick and tired of being here and there with my walk with God. I know, I know. Perhaps I am trying to do this in my own strength but God knows I have yelled at him enough. Cried enough. Pleaded enough. Demanded enough. I have even tried to bribe and blackmail him enough times to get him to send me HIS OWN help and HIS OWN strength. So what gives? Somehow, I know it cannot be God that is stalling this engine. He owes no one.

Anyway, like one of my latest favourite t-shirts says *'Nothing for you'* devil! Shame on you cos no matter what, no matter how, no matter when, I will rise again. This race is a marathon and I may not know all things but one thing I know for sure, there is only one name I know to run to when I am feeling like a spiritual failure. There is only one person I know that loves me and accepts me unconditionally. There is one rock I know I can lean on in my schizophrenic misery. There is only one pair of arms I know will always catch me when I fall, embrace me even in the depths of my soulish squalor. Yes, indeed, there is only one you, Jesus Christ. You are the only ONE who can understand how I feel and I need you today. Right now. To help me as I press on. Regardless…

I attended an event on Saturday. It was fun. I am so happy cos I saw some older ladies who I believe are crazier than me. I loved that. There are people out there who are still so full of life. I was impressed and deeply challenged. I was the quietest person on the table! And I can be loud sometimes. Anyway, why do I bring this up? Well, cos I sort of stole my blog title from the organizers of the event. They have chosen to set out time each year to remember people who have touched lives in tangible ways our Nation. You know Nigeria now; until something is a 'big deal' no one wants to jump on the bandwagon so though attendance was pretty good, it could have been better. But the organizers are determined to press on regardless. And trust me, very soon, very very soon, these awards will be the talk of the nation. At least from what I saw on Saturday. I have never seen anyone run around so much in a long flowing dress and high heels. This lady was everywhere making sure all was going smooth. I was impressed. Actually come to think of it. I think she must have cloned herself. It is just not possible to be everywhere like that! LOL! But seriously, it was a good show and I give everyone involved in that day a huge doffing of the hat. *Una try well well!*

So like them, me too, I am pressing on regardless of how I feel today about myself. I have so much to be thankful for and I know it. But I know there is more to this my relationship with Christ than I am experiencing. I know there is much more I can do for Him and I know there is much more He wants to do for me, with me and through me. So I am pressing on…Regardless.

Shalom!

Tuesday, 21 April
It's Strange Innit?

I am still pressing on regardless today. My walk with God is one strange one but I like it like that. It is not God that is strange though. It is just the way that I never seem to catch a break. But in the midst of this, all sort of good stuff happen. So even though the devil seems to be on my case, I find that I am still laughing. I can still smile. Real Strange.

For some time now, I have not been able to connect with God. Yet He finds a way to talk to me. Through friends' sms messages. Through friends asking me to read one bible scripture or the other. Through friends sending me one photo or another. Somehow God is still finding ways of connecting with me. In this midst of my spiritual squalor as I call it, is it not strange that a mighty mighty God like mine will find time in His busy day to look for ways of connecting with me?! Yes, it is strange. Real Strange.

Yes, though I sense the devil is taking out special time to distract me, I know that he is being thwarted even now as I type cos somehow in his bid to distract me, he is actually sending me running into the arms of the One person he wants to cut me off from. You, foolish foolish enemy of my soul. The same thing that happened to you with My Saviour is going to happen to you with me. If only you had known what killing Christ would mean for you, you would have left him alone *jejely*. Ditto for now. If only you knew that this your latest assault on me would lead me down the road I am on now. Perhaps you would have left me too alone *jejely*.

Strange, innit? How you can actually rev yourself up by simply typing a few words in a blog. Yes, real strange...

Shalom!

Wednesday, 22 April
Wordless Prayers

I am so glad that God hears our hearts. Yes, He does not need words all the time. Especially when we are in pain. He hears our sighs and groans. He feels them so much. I am so grateful to have a God like that. Cos sometimes, it is just nigh on impossible to articulate what one wants or is going through. You search for the right words and all you come up with are tears. Hot tears that course down your face, down your cheeks over your lips and down your chin. Yes, but God can read and hear our tears. The same way he hears the cries of innocent blood shed by the wicked. So he hears the cries of our tears.

I was in tears this morning. The hot kind I spoke above just now. Because I knew that God had once again heard my wordless prayers. I have not been able to connect with God on my own for sometime now. But I have been sending up wordless prayers to God constantly cos that is all I could bring myself to do. God's middle name should be Merciful. In His mercy, he heard me and sent a human angel to me this morning to let me know. To comfort me. To encourage me. To touch my heart. Yes, I was touched by an angel this morning.

The Bible says that though mourning may last for the night, joy shall surely come in the morning. I am waiting for my morning. I know it will come. In the meantime, I continue to focus on the One that loves me beyond measure. The one who captures me with His grace all the time. The only name I know to run to in my time of need. The God who alone can hear my wordless prayers. Nothing can ever separate us. Nothing.

Shalom!

Wednesday, 22 April
Sometimes Don't You Just Wish God Would Hurry Up?

I am at the end of my work day and I am feeling a bit peeved (again!). You see, this is why I wish God would just hurry up already and move me on out of this season to the next one. C'mon Lord! I really do get it and I am sure that I can see now that most of what I am going through is my fault. Honest. I am sure. So let's move on? Please?

Just listen to me. Like someone once said, would you like some cheese with that
'whine'? OK, yes, I am whining. I am sorry Lord. I just cannot help it right now. I really am on some roller coaster ride. Is that what this season is all about? Teaching me how to roll with the punches? Teaching me how to endure? Teaching me patience.

I think it is all of the above PLUS refining my character. And knowing my old character..hmmm. Let's just say, I do need a lot of refining fire. lol! So go on then Lord. I know you know best. And even though am not feeling this whole season of lows at all, I am feeling that you love me anyways. So I will take it like a man..err. sorry woman. After all, I can do ALL things through your Son, my Saviour JC. Can't I?

But still Lord, could you just push me on a long a little faster....... please. Sorry, I was just trying my luck again. Well you did say 'Ask and you shall receive'

I wish you had just said it like it is - 'AND you shall receive it WHEN I SAY SO'

Shalom!

Thursday, 23 April
At The Rate We Are Going?

At the rate we are going, no matter what you eat or drink or DON'T eat or drink, you will die of one form of cancer or the other.

At the rate we are going, every person you see on the road will be a potential armed robber, ritual killer, ATM robber, 419 specialist, Pourer of acid in your face, Drugger of your drink, Rapist... in short every one you meet will be the enemy

At the rate we are going, human kindness will be a thing of the past cos we are all living in fear of the next man or woman. Or child. The little 'innocent' kid might just lead you to a doorbell that leads to your being raped and left for dead in an abandoned house somewhere in the hills!

At the rate we are going, people will soon begin to stash their money under their beds again (OK well maybe not) cos your house help might just be a thief or your steward the member of a gang of robbers!

At the rate we are going, getting married and staying married will be something only fools do. Why bother, just live together!

At the rate we are going, being married before having a child would be considered the height of lunacy!

At the rate we are going, a woman marrying a man would be the exception not the norm (OK maybe not but hey! it's my blog!)

At the rate we are going, people would rather trust a known 419er than trust their Pastor! (God Forbid oh! but it is true)

At the rate we are going, At the rate we are going......

You know what? I am done. At the rate I am going, I might just drive myself round the bend thinking of all the possibilities of how mad this world can get.

All I know is that at the rate we are going, ONLY those who know their God and hold fast to him, will have peace of mind. The days are evil. Beyond evil.

SO bottom line? Take Your eyes off the world and all the madness therein. Focus on the Lord Our God. He is Our Help and Our Shield. To be honest, He is the only reason for the Hope that I have!

Shalom!

Friday, 24 April
Pride Must Die (A Conversation With God)

Yesterday, as I drove home after our Thursday Worship meeting at church, I had a conversation with God. I had really felt him touch me during the meeting but as I sat there in the car I still felt like…well, just me. The same old me. This is, to the best of my recollection the dialogue:

Me: Lord, I know I came into your presence today but I still feel the same
God: It's not about feeling. It's about knowing and being confident
Me: Then how come I still feel the same.
God: Did you not hear me? It's not about a feeling. Just know.
Me: I really need your strength to go on Lord.
God: I have given it to you already. Flow in it.

(Pause)

God: So now I want you to call X
Me (scandalized): Why? X did not call me. Why should I call?
God: It shows you care
Me: But is it OK that X does not seem to care. I have received no call!
God: That's not the point. Just call. Demonstrate my love.
Me: But it's not fair
God: I did not say demonstrate fairness. I said demonstrate my love
Me: It's so hard. I cannot. I just can't do it
God: And you wonder why you cannot flow in my power. You do not have my love in you. My Love is Power
Me: But I love you.
God: How can you say that when you cannot even call X because you feel it's unfair? To love me is to love X. And this is a kind of love that enables you to rise above pain and hurt. It does not keep tab. Calling will demonstrate that you are walking in my love enabled by my power.

Me: So what's wrong with me? Why am I still like this?

God: Pride. You are still full of pride.
Me (stunned): Pride? I am not proud…am I?
God: Yes, for it is pride that makes you think 'how dare X not call me first!'
It is pride that makes you feel 'how dare they do that to me!'
But who are you really? But for me, who would you be?
What gives you the right to think you are ALL THAT and no body dare get on your wrong side?
My son, who is God like me, came to your world and was spat on. Yet He loved. Are you better than him?
My child, if Jesus could pray for those who nailed him to the cross.
So can you if you walk in my Love
But note one thing – My Love is not proud.
Pride must die.

As you can imagine I was humbled and shamed into silence. I made that call though I must admit I was relieved when there was no response. Yes, the flesh in me still needs to do some dying of its own but at least I called now! And X called back. And we spoke. And I scored a brownie point with God. But I was still stunned…so I AM proud??????

But it's all good, cos God also comforted me. He told me to just trust Him. Together we will continue to work on my issues. So good to have a God that, though he hates my sinful nature loves me to bits!

Shalom!

Saturday, 25 April
The Joy of the Lord

OK I have to admit. I am a bit stumped on this one. I have said it a thousand times and even used it to encourage other people who come to me for comfort or guidance. But today as I rode to the shops running the usual wifely and mommy errands in a state of near stupor, I began to wonder about this. 'The Joy of the Lord is my strength'. What does it really mean?

Does it mean that, as I know that I am God's child and He dwells in me along with his son Jesus Christ, I am joy filled? Is it the knowledge of this, the knowing of who I am 'in the Lord' that is supposed to give me joy and therefore make me strong?

Or is it the fact that God knows that I have given my life to him and am trying to live my life in HIM. The joy He HAS in this knowledge. Knowing that I love him and want to be like him. Is it HIS joy in me that is meant to be my strength? God is happy with me so I should be strong knowing this.

I am still thinking about it. In the meantime, I will buy both ideas. They make sense to me. I should be joyful and joy filled because I know that I am IN God and this should make me strong enough to face my life. Being saved and walking with God makes God joyful along with all the angels and this should make me strong. OK, I agree, I am probably rambling. But you know what I mean, Lord.

And at the end of the day, as I type this, you did hear my call; I asked you for this your joy to fill me little by little today. And I must say, as usual, you rose to the challenge. I am not a sour puss any more. What a day!

Devil? I really feel for you cos you are just a loser. Always were. Always will be!

Oh and scratch that! I do not feel for you at all!

Sunday, 26 April
So Where Are They Going?

As I ran my wifely and mommy errands yesterday, I was accosted by a young woman at Shoprite. She looked safe enough so I did not think she was about to beg or anything like that. It was her opening statement that caught me unawares.

" Madam, good afternoon, according to a UN Survey approximately, 165,000 people die everyday' (she may have said 165 million but who cares, thousand, million, the point is a lot of people die each day)

She continued

"What do you think about that? Where you think all these people are going?"

Honestly, until the last question, I really thought she was working for the UN though I wondered why she was not in some sort of uniform. But then the light switched on in my head and it dawned on me that she was 'witnessing'. The opening statement is just the 'hook' that is meant to engage the one to be witnessed to. This young woman was doing something we all should be doing. Something I want to be doing. Winning souls for God.

The truth is that loads of people are dying every day. The way I see it and I hope I am wrong, many of them are going to 'Ile Okuku' - The dark hot place. Why? Cos there are not enough of us out there telling them about the reality of life without Jesus Christ. This lady asked me something as we parted and after she had established that I was not totally 'lost'. She asked me ' Are you winning souls?'. I could not lie, I responded that I blogged about it but truly needed to be more active about it like she was doing. She simply replied by saying 'Please do Madam. God bless you ' and off she went. Simple. Please do.

Please tell people about Jesus Christ. Please tell them that Heaven is for real. That Hell is real. Please live your lives in a way that leads people to Christ rather than turn them off the whole idea. Please let people know the reason for the joy in your eyes. The smile on your face. The blessings you enjoy. The strength you have to carry on. The reason for your confidence. Just tell them. Be always ready to share with people the reason for your being. And if you are like me, remember that it is NOT up to you to make someone accept Christ. That is the job of the Holy Spirit. All God asks us to do is to go 'tell the world'. My bible does not say 'go tell them and make sure you convince them and they accept right there and then'. Does yours? lol! No really, it does sound funny but that is one of the things that has always put me off - the rejection that comes with witnessing. But we must get over it. Even Jesus Christ was rejected so who am I?

And as if to seal the deal on this just today as I checked my FB, a sweet friend of mine who is blissfully enjoying new mommy hood and I were chatting and she talked about the same thing. The importance of going out there and telling the world (that is that part of the world that is within our own circle of influence), telling them about Jesus Christ. Inviting them to reach out and take hold of His already stretched out hand. For indeed, God's hand of friendship is always reaching out to us... will you tell someone about it? Will you show someone the way today? Will you help just ONE of the 165,000 people that will die tomorrow make a choice for Jesus Christ?

Pls do.

Shalom!

Tuesday, 28 April
It's A Process

I just want to share a mail with you. It is a mail that a sweet friend of mine sent to me. I had sort of pushed my way into her life via a word God gave me for her. He basically asked me to tell her that He missed her. We shared. We prayed. We cried a little. Some time passed by and I felt led to poke my nose in her business again. 'How is it going, I asked?'. 'It's a process' her first mail said to me then. I understood without fully understanding. You know, it happens. But with this her second e-mail to me, today, I fully understand. And I fully empathize. I KNOW what she is talking about. It is a must share.

its a process, I told you
I didn't know what form the process will take
nor did I know when the process would be complete
but I learnt something last night
after our talk, our discussion
I went blank. Completely blank
for a few days.... wondering...
what am I going to say to a God
who's pissed off with me? (and right fully so)
I know what I've done and I'm not happy about it but he knew I would do, even before I
was confronted with the situation
every sin, every problem, every crossroad, every compromise
I have ever made and will ever make in this lifetime
is known to God. what do I say to him?

So I've been praying the prayer of the guilty,
asking for forgiveness and understanding
but the guilt doesn't go away
I recognize it to be a trial on its own,
the accuser never goes away,
telling me I'm too bad and too worthless and nobody's listening.

I learnt something last night

*I learnt that when I pray because I feel guilty, I WILL be guilty
but I last night I prayed because I missed God.
I started by saying God I miss you!
God we haven't spoken in a while and I miss you
Father, I want to catch up with you.
I know you've been seeing what's been happening
but let me tell you again what my issues are.*

*And I feel so much closer to him
than I did for a long time*

*its a process, I don't believe its ended
nor will it ever end, but its a process......*

Here is my reply to her:

*I love this. And you are so right.
Can I share this on my blog? I will not put your name or anything. (I usually don't use names anyway).*

Someone out there needs to be saying the same thing to God. Someone other than me.

Yes, me. since I spoke to you. I have been through hell and back. In ways you will find hard to believe.

I asked God why? Why? Why now? Now that I am trying to get my act together....

Thanks to you, I too now see, my walk with God is actually A PROCESS during which I will be refined little by little every day through highs and mostly through lows, very low lows (for how else can Christian character be built up?)

Bless you X, for sharing this...

MAY

Tuesday, 05 May
Voice of Mine, Thou Must Say Something

What?! I cannot believe I have not been here since last week Tuesday. The enemy has really been up to no good. Tell me, what else is new. Is that not his only job? Doing no good.

Anyway, I have not been doing too well and add on to that the fact that I had to go away to bury a dear uncle...yes. nuff said. I know Death is just the door to the next life and for us Christians, a very good life at that. But *na wah*, it is still hard to see a loved one being shoved into a box and placed under a pile of dirt. Silent. Dead. Gone.

And you know what. Life must and does go on. And quite quickly too. In fact almost to quick for my liking as I watched in amazement as people struggled for souvenir umbrellas less that 30 minutes after they had just been sobbing and snivelling for their dear departed relative. It was like please, the man is dead, it might rain tomorrow so move out of the way and give me my umbrella. He does not need one but I do. I am alive.

And indeed, as vexed as I am (OK not vexed just thoroughly harassed), I must agree with them. We are alive. We still have a say. We still have a voice. The question is what are we doing with our 'say'? 'Our voice?'

I am not the sort that would like to be up in front of a crowd but I do know that this writing of mine is my pulpit. These blogs of mine. They are my voice. The groups I chat on and exchange views on, they are my channels to the world. Via them I reach out to people, I say my piece. I preach my love, my life which I pray reflects my faith....I hope.

Dear Father in Heaven, guide me and my voice that we may both only reflect you in Jesus Christ's name. This blog was a bit rambly and just in case I have lost you, let me say it this way - You might not be here tomorrow, Make your today count for something. Let you voice be heard. Somehow.

Shalom!

Thursday, 07 May
Sleeping With the Enemy

I once heard Pastor E. A. Adeboye warn about praying that God should 'Arise and scatter our enemies'. It is a good prayer. It is also a dangerous prayer. For the enemy might just be 'you'.

I can identify with that and maybe you can too. Most times, we are not fighting enemies or wicked foes from without. The subject or rather the cause of our wahala lives within. For me, I struggle still with self control. But for the grace of God, I would 'spark' at every little irritation or annoyance. Errr, no I am not going to go on and enumerate all my foibles for you. Lol! All I am saying is - be careful to check yourself before you go into warfare against your enemies. Lest you be launching missiles at your own good self. That just won't do. Not one bit.

Shalom!

Friday, 08 May
God does Love us BUT...

People of God, I know God loves us. A LOT!
But I also know that God is Holy. VERY HOLY.
Me and you are the apples of his eyes.
He loved us so much that he paid the ultimate price to save our souls
But sister mine, brother mine
As much as He loves us. He hates sin.
As much as He loves us. His Heaven can tolerate NO unholiness.
No spot. No stain. Not even a speck of it.

So people of God, if you die today in sin
As much as He loves you, He cannot compromise the integrity of Heaven for you.
He will shut you out of heaven albeit with tears streaming down his face.
Now why would you let that happen?

Shalom!

Saturday, 09 May
Are You a Thinking Person?

The Yoruba have a saying that anyone who knows how to think will give thanks.
So are you a thinking person?
I find that most of the time, I must not be a thinking person.
It is true. If I was, then how come I am able to stay in a position of worry and doubt?
Forgetting all that God has done for me in the past
Which if I did remember, then this present issue will no longer loom so humongous (is that even the right spelling?)
No really, I am serious. I must be a non-thinker.
I must be one of those people who the moment God does some awesome thing in my life
I forget.
Cos if I did not forget. If I remembered. Then I would give thanks
And then I would kick that miserable shapeless
Yellow eyed demon of despair and worry
Off my back!
Yes I would!
So please do not be like me at the moment
Put on your thinking cap. Bring to fore, the memories of all that God has done in your life.
And rejoice confident that He can and He will do it again!
Yes He will!

Tuesday, 12 May
You CAN Just Keep On Going

I know life does throw you curve balls sometimes
But you can just keep on going. Cos God is an expert curve ball catcher
I know people can wound you and then rub salt in it for good measure
But you can just keep on going. Cos God heals all wounds and kisses them better

I know time can seem to just be a-ticking by and not taking you with it
But you can just keep on going. Cos God controls all time and all seasons

I know that sometimes things don't just make any sense and the world must've gone mad!
But you can just keep on going. Cos God knows the end from the beginning.
To Him, it's clear as day!

So my sista, my broda. You really can just keep on going....
Well at least, if you know this God I talk about. Like I do

But for him, I would be rolling, groaning, moaning, and despairing.
But I am not.
Instead, I am smiling, laughing, praising and rejoicing
Cos God helps me to just keep on going.
I just know He has got my back

Shalom!

Friday, 15 May
Of Frumpy Clothes and Head Gears

Boy oh Boy! Am I glad it is a Friday? Honestly, this has been one of my worst weeks ever. I mean it. Yes, this week I have had the worst bad hair 5-days and the worst 5-day wardrobe malfunctions. Actually, that is putting it mildly. My wardrobe did not malfunction cos that would mean that I actually had something in it to wear!!!!!

My oh my, I have never dressed so badly to work before and I just give God all the glory that I work for a company that just does not seem to worry too much if you wear jeans to work every single day! OK, well I did not wear jeans EVERY day but close. And as for my hair. Someone had to ask me why I seemed to cover my hair up so much. Once again, I explained that I just had not had the time to go to the salon last weekend and so I wore all manner of head apparel this week. From Gatsby hats, to turbans to pashminas of various colours tied around my head in various styles. I wish I can say it made me feel stylish. *Na wah*! Just made me feel frumpy. lol!

Anyway, like I told my MGM this morning, I *sha* made it to today and by the grace of God, I shall be re defining my look over this weekend. Ahhhhhh I really would like a 'me time' spa day but that will have to wait. For now, just a new hair do and some nicely dry cleaned clothes will have to do!

Shalom!

Monday, 18 May
I Am Home

I can see clearly now. Once again.
The horse and its rider are like wax before the fire
The enemies of my soul like dust in the wind
Oh, what a wonderful feeling to be light again
To feel free again. In my heart. In my soul

You know this world can be a very dangerous place
We all go about with masks. Looking A-Ok
But on the inside, not so, Not Ok
Grieving, screaming, and hating what we are dealing with
Yet knowing, deep inside, that it is our own self that we are hating on
For the enemy within is more vicious than the ones without.

But Father, Dear Father of Mercies. Father of Light
I thank you for your mercies, for your light
Mercy over my life. Light to find my way home.
Back to you. For real.
Now my outside reflects my inside.
Now, I am one and at peace.
With You.
With Me.
I am home.

Wednesday, 20 May
Shell-shocked but Merciful Like My Dad

One just must keep on looking to God. If I do not, I will actually become the wicked witch from the east! I am still in semi-shock that my dear trusted nanny and housekeeper who I thought was the next best thing since sliced bread has now turned out to be a common thief! You know, I was too sad to be angry.

Yes, this young promising woman who I actually used to give the key to my room to hold thinking the other younger nanny needed watching (how ironic) was caught with the proverbial hand in the proverbial cookie jar. And but for my aunt who came to visit, I bet you this would have gone on for yonks. Cos yes, I am naive and just too tired to put the zillion and one checks one needs to be able to prevent this from happening. But now, I guess I have to get less tired.

Long story short, young woman had been pinching my store supplies and hiding them away in her bags. Tins of sardines, corned beef, and bars of toilet soap (would a 3 year old eat soap? Oh, Ok to bathe him I suppose) She was taking them to her son, she said. Funny, this same son, I pay a 'salary'. He is 3 and stays with his granny. This same son, I send stuff of my own volition. This same son, she has asked me for things to take to him before AND I said 'no wahala'. So someone please tell me why this young woman still felt she needed to steal from me????

I am confused. This is why people are so mean to their staff and you go about frowning and tut tut tutting at them. For being so unkind. So mean. So heartless. Now I see that perhaps, they, like me, have been dealt this heartless Judas blow. Perhaps their kindness and Christian heartedness has been thrown in their faces so often that they feel no point. All are evil. All are rogues. Christ like compassion is pointless.

Alas, even if I wanted to, I cannot. My nature does not accommodate such. So I shall just be less tired and more vigilant. I shall just lock all the lockables and count all the countables. I shall just continue as I am, forgiving and believing that people can change. The young woman has been given a second chance as she rolled this way and that on the floor begging not to be let go off....

Who am I to not give a second chance? Me to whom a zillion chances have been given by a most Merciful God and Father....

Shalom!

Friday, 26 May
It's My Birthday and I Can Brag If I want to!

Ah hah! Yeah! Ah hah Yeah!
It's my birthday and I can brag if I want to x 2

Lol! Yes, you can tell I am in a splendid mood.
Cos this day, 41 years ago, my mom was about to or had given birth to me.
Yes, I took my first breath and have been breathing ever since.
Yes, so I can brag if I want to. Not about me. But about my God.
Yes, I can brag on my God who has kept me alive all this time

Yes, it is my day and I can brag if I want to
I can brag on my God who saw me through my childhood years
My teen years, my young adult years.
I have a God who has been the pillar of my life all this time.
So yes I can brag on Him if I want to cos He deserves it.

My God saw me through school, got me my first job
He has always surrounded me with good people and even the bad ones,
He made them work for my own good in the end.
So again, He is my God and I can brag if I want to.

You know, am so happy today and I could go on and on
But I will end by saying My God has given me 4 reasons to live life well.
4 reasons only. But even if these were the only reasons I had, I would still brag on him
My dear MGM and my three children. My 4 reasons. On this day as I turn 41,
I can brag if I want to cos God has blessed me with 4 reasons to do so.

It's my birthday I can brag if I want to
It's my birthday I can brag if I want to

Lalaalaalaalaalaa

Saturday, 30 May
Cappuccino Chocolate-chip Ice-Cream and the Love of God

Today was extraordinary. For one, I had ice-cream. I have not had ice-cream in ages. And for two, I had a gist-fest with a sista-divine of mine at one of the latest ice cream places in town and then we went on to order take away at Chocolate Royale. People of God, it's been a long time since I just sat and ate with a non-family member and talked about everything and most especially nothing. It felt good and I have promised myself to do it more as often as I can.

But I digress. The main hero of this blog is the ice-cream I had. Now, I am not really an ice cream person and when I do have it, it has to be chocolate. So usually I know what to expect. Chocolate. Plain and simple. People of God, I did not see this one coming AT ALL. As my friend said, at the taste of this ice cream, my legs turned to jelly. I was sitting down yet I still almost fell down. Yes, it was THAT good. Suffice to say, we were both speaking in various languages as we demolished the cold feasts before us. I suspect both of us will be thinking about it for a while to come. Not cos of the company (no doubt, that was good) but mainly for the ice-cream. Lol!

How I wish people would taste the Love of God in the same way and come away with the same experience. How I wish I could pass round a bowl of delicious 'Jesus Loves You' ice cream to people I meet and with one spoon-full, they too are convinced, that it is 'to die for'. As I sat in the car on my way home this evening, I wondered why it was so hard for us to see how much God loves each one of us. I mean a God that creates that kind of ice cream must be so full of love for me! Lol! Why we cannot say for real that we are His, if we do not act in love all the time. And how much better the world would be, how much better our lives would be if we lived a life of agape love. Even now as I type, I am still wondering. Nope. I have nothing. No answers.

But Lord, maybe one day, you will let me figure it out. However, I cannot help but thinking that perhaps you should have offered us your love with a side serving of the fantastic cappuccino chocolate chip ice cream I had today, Maybe just maybe, it would be easier for some....

P.S. Yes, if you live in Lagos, you need to be visiting the Ice-Cream Factory. It's on the OmegaBank Lane, Off Adeola Hopewell Street in Victoria Island. And the answer to your un-asked question is No. I do not know any of the owners/founders of this house of cold delights. I am just a well pleased customer!

JUNE

Tuesday, 02 June
Welcome To the Month of June

Indeed, it is a new month and I thank God. Sadly though I do not think June being the 6th month is the month of anything. As Christians, we tend to shy away from the number 6. Especially when it appears thrice in a row! Evil!!!! Poor number six, you had to go and be the number of the beast! I really would like to help you but I am stumped. Does anyone know what the number 6 represents that is GOOD?

But at least we know that June ushers in the summer and holidays and for those of you out there, the possibility of some sunshine. Packing away the heavy sometimes ugly winter clothes and bringing out the nice colourful pretty (sometimes, almost not there) summer clothes! People like to plan summer weddings. We love June babies. June brides, June, June....so it's not all that bad. It cannot be. You are here and so am I. And God is still on His throne. So it's all good!

Happy New Month!

Tuesday, 02 June
Solomon, Now Really, Tell Me Something.

I was listening to the book of 1st Kings today (and yes, you know am going to ask you if you have bought your Bible Experience CDs yet. Well have you?). Anyway, there I was in King David's room as Bathsheba, backed by the Prophet Nathan, came to report Adonijah and his self-enthronement as king. Yes, I was in my car but I watched as King Solomon tried his first case – the duel for the baby. You know these days, Lagos early morning traffic does not faze me. Thanks to my Bible Experience CDs, I am usually somewhere else. Anyway as I listened on and on, I could not help but wonder about what Solomon had done that was so captivating to God that He went out of His way to bless him so much.

No matter how smart anyone in this century claims to be, Solomon was smarter. No matter how rich, Solomon was richer. No matter how much discernment a man claims to have, he cannot beat Solomon! Why? What did he do that made him so special to God? Yes, I know he asked for wisdom but is that all? Just because he did not ask for riches and for all his enemies to die! (I had to smile here cos I know of some of our prayers that seem to focus on every kind of evil befalling our enemies. Hmm…I mean, this man got God to write him an open cheque for asking for something other than that – he asked for Wisdom)

You know what I think? And I believe I have heard Pastor Adeboye say it or perhaps it was my dear Pastor Eskor. Anyway, no matter. The secret to God's 'favoritism' so to speak over Solomon was in his thanksgiving and offerings. Do you realise how many offerings that man made to God in his lifetime? At one point, he offered so many sheep and cattle that the Bible says, the recorders were unable to take note. It became uncountable. He thanked and worshipped God with an almost reckless abandon (see 1st Kings 8:5).

So let's see, what is my equivalent of uncountable sacrificial sheep and cattle offered unto God? How does a modern day Christian emulate

Solomon? Get God's attention like he did? I believe it is so simple. I must simply be equally as reckless in my own form of thanksgiving, worship and praise of God. That means not being selfish, or self conscious or self centred or stingy when it comes to thanking God (and I think helping God's children when ever we can is also key. Prudent is good. Mean and miserly is not).

See *ehn*, Solomon did all that for God and this was even before He had given up His only begotten son for mankind yet. How much more appreciative of God should we be? For it was for us that the most High God came down to earth in human form and died a most shameful and painful death.

When last did you offer '20,000 goats and sheep worth' of praise and worship to God? When last did you just go before God with pure and unadulterated thanksgiving? No requests. No complaints. Just pure appreciation. When last was your worship to God so abandoned, you lost yourself in His Presence? Let's ponder on this a little. Methinks, therein lies one of the key secrets to being God's favourite.

Shalom!

Wednesday, 03 June
By The Way, Number 6 Does Stand For Something

Remember the number 6 matter we were talking about yesterday. Well I am actually reading a book now titled 'There Were Two Trees in the Garden' and if like me you have ever wondered about your spiritual schizophrenia then this is the book for you. It is opening my eyes to so much about why I still fall flat when I mean to be on the straight and narrow. I am desperately seeking to be like Christ. Yet most of the time I find myself more like.....hmm lets just say, not like Christ at all. Lol!

Yes, am laughing but it's not funny at all. One key thing I have learnt from this book now is that I will NEVER be like Jesus! (Shocking? Yes, I was until I read on). You see what I should actually be seeking is to have Jesus FORMED on the INSIDE of me. There is a difference. IF Jesus is formed IN me, then I will actually, For REAL, have his heart and then I will be equipped via His Spirit to live more like Him. I am still reading and I will gist you more as I go on.

The main reason I refer to the book is that it actually talks about the number 6. Yes oh. It is the number of Man. As per man was created on the 6th day. I guess it became the evil 666 cos you have one 6 for man, one 6 for the serpent aka the devil and the final 6 for the beast. The book did not say so, that's me just trying to figure it out.

But nope, nothing good spiritually about that number 6 oh! Still, let's keep looking. You never know.

Shalom!

Wednesday, 03 June
Such A Little Thing, But Oh! What a Huge Difference!

I have to share this with all the wives and mothers out there. It is so easy and you might even think 'Oh what difference would it make?' I promise if you do it sincerely and consistently, you will reap the dividends. I have been doing it for just about 3 weeks now and this is how I feel:

I feel happy that my husband knows how I feel about him better i.e. how much and why I love him so.

I feel blessed that my children can now know how much I love them and the zillion little reasons why they are three of my four reasons.

I am thrilled that when I am gone, my MGM and my children will have something to remember me by. No, it's not morbid. Its foresight! Lol!

Ok, I am sure you are fed up and are probably screaming "Tell Us Already! What are you doing? Lol!

Well, I opened a gratitude journal for my MGM. I make an entry into it every day even when he is away. My entries are little 'thank you' notes to God for something my MGM had done for me that day. Or for something I just appreciated more about him that day. Little stuff. Big stuff. I started placing this book open to the entry page on his pillow so when he comes in he sees it immediately and sits on the bed and reads it. Simple. Now, when he comes into the room after work, I see his eyes go straight to the bed looking for 'his book'. I shall not give you TMI but suffice to say, things have been 'sweeter' since then in all ways. Lol!

And then I opened another one for my children. Same intent as above. Except that I use one book for all of them. I even write for the youngest one who does not read it yet. When he grows older, he can and he will probably have a good laugh. But mostly, they will all know how and why I love them so very much.

So you see, it is so simple but oh so powerful. Try it. I got the idea while counselling a couple who were about to get married and we were talking about communication and how the lack of it is one of the biggest destroyers of relationships. At the end of the final session I presented the bride and groom with two special journals and gave them instructions on how to use it. They loved the idea and so did my Pastor's wife. And I thought hey! Why don't I do the same for my hubby?

And why don't you?

Monday, 08 June
The 'Crowd' In Church

I was listening to the story of the woman with an issue of blood this morning and how she pressed on ignoring the multitudes around her to touch Jesus. She was determined to get her healing and she knew she did not even need to engage the Man. She knew that this Man had so much power that just a touch of the hem of his garment would change her life forever. What faith! What understanding! What determination! Do you and I have the same? I wonder…

But you know what; this blog is not really about this precious woman. It's about the 'crowd'. Yes, the throng of people milling around Jesus that day. They too, no doubt had needs, stuff they would have loved Jesus to sort out for them. I am positive there were some other sick people in that crowd. Abi what do you think? Or everyone else, apart from this woman, just came to 'look at the bridge' as we say. Other people in that crowd must have come quite close to Jesus. In fact, that is why the disciples could not understand why Jesus was asking who touched him! I mean with all these people pushing and jostling, chances of someone leaning on Jesus were beyond high. But Jesus knew someone had touched him with a difference. Someone had touched him with POWER-ACTIVATING FAITH!

You know, the same thing happens in church all the time. We all go to church. We all go for ministrations and anointing services. But how many of us go with this woman's kind of determination and faith. We are like 'the crowd' just following. We are looking but not seeing. We are hearing but not understanding. We are right in His Presence but we never reach out to touch the hem of His garment. I mean we think we do but mostly we are just playing church. And trust me the one finger pointing out at y'all means the remaining four digits are right up in my own face!

So people, lets get our acts together. Let's go for every service we attend with a mission mind set. Let's be like this woman. Let's go to church ALL THE TIME with a clear goal – to reach out in faith and touch the

Master. In the name of Jesus Christ, we shall not be one of the mission-less-come-to-look-the-bridge-angel-of-the-Lord-is-passing-them-by kind of Christians! Amen!

We are 'in it' to 'win it' so to speak!

Thursday, 11 June
Provided? Prepared?

I do not know about you but I have always thought about Jonah being in the belly of the whale as his punishment for trying to evade service unto the Lord. God caught up with him and banished him to imprisonment behind fleshly fish bars under the sea. So you can imagine my consternation when, as I listened to the story on one of my Bible Experience CDs, I heard these words:

17 But the LORD provided a great fish to swallow Jonah… (NIV)

Huh? Provided??? Do you PROVIDE a punishment? I mean when you think of the word 'Provided' do you think of it in negative terms? (I checked the NKJ version of the Bible on line and it used the word 'Prepared' so I was still in the same state of bewilderment). I mulled and mulled over this and then I had another 'aha' moment.

Sometimes we find ourselves in hot water situations of our own making. Jonah was sinking to the bottom of a foaming sea cos He had run away from his calling. God then 'provides' a 'way of escape' for him to 'dry out and think about his life and figure out where he missed it and how to get back on track. Jonah could have just drowned to death in his error but God *provided, prepared* a great fish to swallow him so he could go through the process I just explained above. The whale was not a punishment. It was actually his 'salvation'.

I think Jonah knew this too and that is why his prayer while still in the belly of the fish was one of thanks. Listen.

5 The engulfing waters threatened me, the deep surrounded me; seaweed was wrapped around my head. 6 To the roots of the mountains I sank down; the earth beneath barred me in forever. But you brought my life up from the pit, O LORD my God. 7When my life was ebbing away, I remembered you, LORD, and my prayer rose to you, to your holy temple. 8Those who cling to worthless idols forfeit the grace that could be theirs. 9 But I, with a song of

thanksgiving, will sacrifice to you. What I have vowed I will make good. Salvation comes from the LORD

Yes, Jonah knew that God had brought his life up from the pit and had hidden him in the whale to dry out and reconsider his life. So we too must examine our current situations, if they are somewhat smelly and fishy – perhaps we too have 'run away from God and are going through our own 'Jonah in the belly of the whale' experience'. Perhaps God has just saved us from an even graver fate and it is for us to now do some self- examination, repent, re-align and then begin to praise God. Just like He did for Jonah, God will command our 'aquatic prison warden' to open up its mouth and vomit us out unto the dry land of 'right standing with God ready to move on in His will'. Shalom!

Monday, 15 June
June Blues…

We are exactly half way through June today. And I am exactly half way on my way to yelling vehemently at myself. Am not really in a good place right now though to look at me you may not know it. But then again, you just might. Seeing as I seem to be on a war path with my braids and I have not put on my 'face'.

I am just feeling a bit weathered today, that's all. After all, I am a woman in her 40s. Am allowed *o jare*. On the bright side I did have a nice Sunday yesterday with a nice GF coming to visit. I enjoy her company. She is nice and bubbly. I also bought hair weaves that am looking forward to rocking soon. Yes, the braids have got to go! I shall not tell you how much they were. All I can say is that like 'L'Oreal, they are worth it' and so am I dammnit! Sheesh I am even swearing so you know I **am** having an off day!

But God is good cos He is, as I type, allowing me to balance my mood swings. I think about my 5 year old and how he almost drove me mad yesterday. Then I remember how sweet he is and how he ticks me off and then tells me he loves me. And then I thank God am not in the US cos they would have smacked and ADS label on the child for me. I reject it! I think about my 12 year old and her never ending list of art supplies and the fact that am strapped right now (yes, I paid for the weaves with a post dated cheque!). Then I thank God she is so smart this daughter of mine and is a mini-mom to us all really. So I smile. I think about my oldest. I cannot believe he is actually taller then me. Imagine that. I still remember crying over him during his naming ceremony. Don't ask. Post-natal hormonal imbalance I guess. He is so into himself. Basically I think he is a tad selfish. Only looks out for number 1. But then I remember that he has this cute way of coming to hug my knees when he is frazzled or wants something! I like it. Even when I pretend he is being a blubbering pest. Oh and there is my dear MGM. He can be so 'out there sometimes' like he is not home for me. And then in a flash, am the best thing since sliced bread and he wants to spoil me and pamper me and buy the whole of wherever he is for me. And after 16 years to still have him to hold and to cherish is a good thing. On a scale of 1 to 10, my life is really at 7.5. And all the 2.5 points that make up the last coin in my bag of 99 coins??? Oh, please who cares? I am still more happy than unhappy.

So I don't care if all I can think of now are negatives and blahs BUT I know that I am blessed and that God is still my God. So devil, I feel for you. Cos you are barking up the wrong tree here. You need to go find someone who does not know their God cos eventually I will end this my pity party and move on. And get this, right now the music I am rocking at this 'pity party' of mine? They are all songs of praise!

Frustrating you eh devil? Good!

Tuesday, 16 June
So Can God See Me In Himself Yet?

A friend sent this to me and I just love it. Had to share it. If you have seen it before it is still worth a second read.

Malachi 3:3 says: 'He will sit as a refiner and purifier of silver.'

One woman wanted to know the process of refining silver. She called a silversmith and made an appointment to watch him at work. She didn't mention anything about the reason for her interest beyond her curiosity about the process of refining Silver.

As she watched the silversmith, he held a piece of silver over the fire and let it heat up. He explained that in refining silver, one needed to hold the silver in the middle of the fire where the flames were hottest as to burn away all the impurities.

The woman thought about God holding us in such a hot spot; then she thought again about the verse that says: 'He sits as a refiner and purifier of silver.' She asked the silversmith if it was true that he had to sit there in front of the fire the whole time the silver was being refined.

The man answered that yes, he not only had to sit there holding the silver, but he had to keep his eyes on the silver the entire time it was in the fire. If the silver was left a moment too long in the flames, it would be destroyed.

The woman was silent for a moment. Then she asked the silversmith, 'How do you know when the silver is fully refined?'

He smiled at her and answered, 'Oh, that's easy -- when I see my image in it.'

Isn't it just heart-warming to know this? It all for our own good all these trials we go through. It's to make us like God, our Father. And you know my favourite part? The fact that He is there with us watching closely over us ALL THE TIME. So we are never alone. Never!

Wednesday, 17 June
Do You Have a Minute?

Do you have a minute? Cos that is all I really need for this. It's a short one today. I just wanted to know if you have taken out time to chat with God at all today. The day is almost over I know but it is never too late. I get the feeling that He is waiting to hear from you on that matter you have been brooding over lately.

No, please I am not a *Woli-esse*. I just sense in my spirit that we women are bearing a lot of unnecessary burdens only because we are unable to find time to connect with the Lover of our souls. The power to live in this world is within our grasp. That is, the power to live 'victoriously'. Not just a 'how for do' kind of life. Trust me.

Go to Him today. Connect with Him today. On the way home. In the loo, under the dryer. As you get your braids done. As you make that meal. In Your spirit, connect with your Maker. Therein lies the power. Therein lies the release.

And you know what the funny thing is? God is waiting for you...He loves us so much that He is always waiting for us.....wow!

Shalom!

Thursday, 18 June
They Laughed At Jesus Too.

Sometimes being a Christian means people will laugh at you. It's mostly because they do not see things the way we do. They live purely in the natural. The things of the spirit do not mean anything to them at all and so when we speak in line with what we know is possible with God, they laugh at us.

I am not ruffled cos they laughed at Jesus too. Remember when he told the crowd to stop crying that the girl was not dead only sleeping? Yes, they promptly stopped crying and began laughing. Imagine. How blind must you be to laugh at the King of Kings?

Such blindness still exists today and we can only pray that God will open the eyes of those we love so that the light of the gospel of Christ can shine in through their eyes into their hearts and show them how hopeless they truly are in their earthly wisdom.

My main point today however is this. Stand your ground and do not let the derisive laughter of an unbelieving person discourage you. Jesus did not even have time for the mockers. He just faced his front and went ahead to claim the manifestation of what He already knew to be true in the spiritual - A girl who was alive! Glory to God!

Once you have prayed through and have that assurance in your heart about something. Begin to thank God and Praise Him until you see it come to pass. If, as you wait for it, people laugh at your confidence. Scoff at your faith. Don't worry, you are in good company. They laughed and scoffed at Jesus too. And we all know who was laughing last, *abi*?

Shalom!

Tuesday, 23 June
Daddy!

This note is to the Daddies (and to the moms that love them)
Cos I think anyone can be a Father. But it takes a real man to be a Dad!
Now or in the future so I hail all the Dads I know.

D is for **D**ude who rose and stepped up to the plate.
Fathers are the names on the Birth certificates.
Dads are the ones who are there and **DEMONSTRATE** love and Represent.
D is for the man who does not **DUCK** responsibility.
The man who is not **DAUNTED** by the task of rearing children.
The one who **DOES** not replicate his own negative past.
D is for the male who **DEALS** with the issues as they come.
The one who **DECIDES** that his role in the lives of his progeny is number one.
D is for the man who is able to **DESTROY** the lies of the enemy and **DISH** out the word of God when the enemy and the strange women come lurking.

A is for the descendant of **ADAM** who **ADMITS** that but for God he is finished.
A is for the man who is **ABLE** to show emotion and show his children that he too has a heart that feels.
A is for the man that God has ordained to be a lover to one woman, their mother. The woman God helped him find
A is for **A**BILITY to make wealth that God has given you. Just hold fast. It shall come. God does not lie.

And my man of God.
Father of blessed and prophetic children.
Trust me
You are

D - **D**estined for greatness
D - A **DOER** not just a Hearer

D - Like **D**AVID, you are a man after Gods own heart and
D - **D**EAR to the woman God has given you
And finally, my brother, my friend, you are
DIVINENLY inspired to **D**O Great things in this world.
All you need DO is tap into God. He is the Daddy of All Dads

I hail you all cos I know its not easy being who you are BUT God will help you.
May you enjoy now and always the joy of Daddyhood!

Happy Father's Day!

Shalom!

JULY

Thursday, 02 July
It's Half-time. Let's Take Stock. Let's Re-strategise

A sista-divine sent me this mail and I love it. I am sharing it here cos its sooooooooo wise. And this is the year of the wise. So read slowly, assimilate, meditate and get your wisdom on!

The first half of 2009 is gone and whether we like it or not, there is nothing we can do to change the result at half time. The half time break is a time for us to reflect upon the happenings of the first half. Some of us played well during the first half, scored vital goals and are leading the game. Others did not play so well and conceded some goals and are therefore losing.

Whichever position you find yourself, I have good news for you: It is the 2nd half that determines the final result. Every good coach understands the importance of good tactics. The half time break is a crucial opportunity to review the team's tactics.

Listen to what the chief coach is saying to you at half time: He says "I am giving you a new beginning; your latter shall be greater than your former. I will restore you to health and heal your wounds. Therefore, arise and shine for your light is come and the glory of God is risen upon you. Behold I do a new thing …….. (Can't you see it?), I will even make a way in the wilderness and rivers in the desert. "

No matter how many goals you conceded in the first half, u can equalize and still win the game. Remember that the best form of defence is attack. Go all out in this second half; attack the enemy knowing fully well that the weapons of our warfare are not carnal but mighty through God to the pulling down of strongholds.

Arise and let's take the battle to the gates of the enemy because the victory is sure. Maybe you have been winning; the second half is not for you to relax. Remember that the adversary goes about like a roaring lion seeking whom to devour. It is a time to double your efforts.

It is easier to fall than to rise. To maintain your victory, you must step up the attack. Know that the devil will never give up on you; he'll keep trying to pull you down. Let us take up the sword of the spirit and keep attacking the enemy so that we can have a convincing victory at the end of the game.

In every game, it is important to study your enemy and know his tactics. What weapon has the enemy used to keep u down in the first half? Who are the enemies' attackers that must be marked out? It is a time to have a sober reflection, look deep into your heart. Identify your weaknesses and ask the Lord for strength in that area- He said His strength is made perfect in your weakness.

If the devil's attack on you has been fear, bind that spirit of fear in the name of Jesus Christ our Lord. Confess the scripture that says God has not given us a spirit of fear but of love, power and a sound mind. Get the strength that you need from the word of God. He will give you the winning strategy for the remaining part of this crucial match. I see you rejoicing in victory at the end of this match called Year 2009.

Don't you just love the blast of positive energy you feel after you read this! And the best part is you can share this with all your football crazy friends and they will get it! Lol!

Happy 2nd Half!

Shalom!

Saturday, 04 July
God is a Vigilante

I am so careless. Yes, and it is unbelievable. Because I know better.
But Glory to God, cos He is never caught unawares. He is never caught napping.
Even if I am.
My testimony is too cool to be true but yet it is.
I was living with the enemy and knew it not,
In fact I cosy-ed up to the enemy and was so happy with her.
Yet only my downfall did she plot
But Praise be to my God, The One who knows all things
The One who sees the hearts of men. And women
He saw and knew the heart of this woman. This wicked girl
This child who decided she would bite the finger that fed her.
Long story short, God fought for me after opening my eyes
After shouting that which He had been whispering.
Words I had been hearing but ignoring.
At last God just got fed up with me and in the end, He arose!
And all became clear. The things done in the dark were revealed in the day
Praise the Lord! He scattered my enemies. His enemies.
My sister. My Brother. Pay attention to God. He is always speaking
Because He is always vigilant.
Always watching over us.
Try to listen and to Act
But rest assured that should you miss it. Not hear it.
Our God Is A Vigilante.
He is on top of the matter.
As long as your heart is His, he will continue to scatter
Your enemies. His enemies.
Hallelujah!

Tuesday, 07 July
Goodnight Michael. Rest Well. At Last

I could not watch the Memorial Service. Regardless of my 'minor fan' status, that still would have been too much for me. But my son, knowing me very well, dubbed it for me so once I get over it a bit, I can then watch it on my own. And not along with the rest of the world. The global mourning would have been too hard for me. I knew I was right as I came down to serve my mgm his dinner and caught sight of Paris Jackson saying her goodbyes....aahhh too much. Too sad. It's funny how now I see that indeed his death had hit me harder than I thought...funny.

So anyway, I join the rest of the world in saying 'goodbye' to you Michael Jackson. There is no doubt in my mind, that you were an icon of humongous proportions. But you have, by your life, shown us more than ever, that the rich also cry.....that the world is really a loving place to everyone...it just needs to wait for you to die first.... that parents should really let their children be children regardless of their talents..... that money or fame cannot buy happiness......that people can really be misunderstood....that all we really need is LOVE.

I confess to being one of those that just thought you had 'lost it'. Yet I know that your music will continue to sell for years to come. Yet I know that I will be sighing heavily every time I hear or read about you. Yet, I now confess to being one of those that know that you will truly be missed. By people of all colours, creeds and ages.

Good night Michael Jackson. Good night. Rest Well...At Last....

Monday, 13 July
A Toast to My Kind of Friendship

Not everyone is a good friend. In fact, not everyone you meet can be a good friend.
I am one of those. I am not a very friendly person to be honest. Though people think so. I have my moments. I love people don't get me wrong but am not good at a being a friend in the traditional sense of things. Visits, phone calls, chats that go on for hours, sms messages at least once a day. Once again, don't get me wrong, I can do all of this BUT that's not me being your friend. That's just me being.....well, sociable... mere social exchange.

For me being a friend goes beyond that. Being a friend means that even when all of the above do not happen, there is no controversy that I care. That you are important and that out of sight is most definitely NOT out of my mind. Some of the few people I count as real friends today are people who I have not even spoken to in the last 3 weeks or so. But I know beyond knowing that should I need help, a shoulder to cry on, an agreement in prayer, a listening ear, I know that I can call on them. And you know what the best part is? We never skip a beat. It's like we spoke the day before. Our friendship transcends calls and visits into that continuous continuum that neither can frustrate.

For me, this is the sort of friendship I am comfortable with. I am not into the friendship that requires. That demands, that takes note. I am more of a free falling, 'see you when I see you' sort of friend. No strings. No games. No by force stuff.

I may be wrong but this is my cup of tea and am sure it will not be to everyone's taste but hey! That's me oh! I am an intro-extrovert. A funny mix of 'leave me alone' and 'come dance with me'. I can take company or leave it. I love to laugh and I love people BUT I also love my space and my company. Why am I on this subject right now today? Well cos I just went through some stuff recently and two people understood the above so well. When I said, I was going off to be alone. They did not take it personal. They understood. When I said I would not take calls.

They did not balk. Through it all, they stayed away, yet supporting. They kept their distance. Yet I knew they were praying. I salute them today. My Ms. Bardot and my Praise Jam Leader. Not all people will grasp it. You both did. Thank you. I salute you! I thank God for people that get me.

I salute my kind of 'True Blue Friendship!

Thursday, 16 July
Becos of God

Sometimes I wonder how God manages to tolerate the world and all the sin in it.
I am sure things are infinitely more seedy and torrid than they were back in the Sodom and Gomorrah days. And yet He does nothing.

Oh! I am sure He is not just sitting there turning a blind eye. Knowing God, things are happening. Just that I cannot see them. And I want to. Or do I? Perhaps, I better be careful cos if justice does fall, I might find myself beneath its iron axe head!

I really want to live a holy life pleasing and acceptable to God. I know He loves me ANY HOW I am and it is just my sin and waywardness He hates but yet the bible says IF I love HIM then I will do his <u>will</u> and <u>keep</u> his commandments. Yes, that is what I want to do. Prove to Him that I love Him. That He did not kill His son for me in vain. So...

Becos of God, that sin that so easily besets me? I shall fight it, Flee from it.
Becos of God, when I want to scream at my housekeeper, I shall be still, be quiet
Becos of God, when the TV lures me away from time with Him, I shall drop the remote kia kia!
Becos of God, I will be thankful, praise-ful, worship-ful, love-ful. A fool for God!

Yes, He has done so much. He is so much. I must run this race to Him. I must. I must.

Becos of God!

Friday, 17 July
Life is a Gift

A good friend of mine just sent this to me. I have known her for a little over 3 years now and from the first time I laid eyes on her I was taken in by her……hair! She has the most incredible hair ever and I always told her so. But beyond that, she always had and still has such a calm gentle way about her. And a great sense of humour. She has been through some stuff that most of us will never be able to understand. She is a Survivor. She inspires me. This message she sent is so INSPIRATIONAL, I had to share it. It hit me at the right moment. A word from above. Read it slowly. Think on it deeply. Act on it passionately. Live it daily.

If you actually get this in your mail, then know you are also someone who has impacted my life directly and there is nothing else in the world I want right now than for you to live a happy and content life. It's not 'how long' but 'how well'. It's not what we have or don't have. It's who we are deep inside and who we have touched in love. These are the things that matter most. The things for which we will be remembered.

****

THERE WAS A BLIND GIRL WHO HATED HERSELF BECAUSE OF HER BLINDNESS. NOT ONLY DID SHE HATE HERSELF BUT SHE HATED EVERYONE ELSE, EXCEPT HER LOVING BOYFRIEND. HE WAS ALWAYS THERE FOR HER AND SHE SAID THAT IF SHE COULD ONLY SEE THE WORLD, SHE WOULD MARRY HER BOYFRIEND.

ONE DAY, SOMEONE DONATED A PAIR OF EYES TO HER AND THEN SHE COULD SEE EVERYTHING, INCLUDING HER BOYFRIEND.

HER BOYFRIEND ASKED HER, "NOW THAT YOU CAN SEE THE WORLD, WILL YOU MARRY ME?" THE GIRL WAS SHOCKED WHEN SHE SAW THAT HER BOYFRIEND WAS BLIND TOO, AND REFUSED TO MARRY HIM.

HER BOYFRIEND WALKED AWAY IN TEARS, AND LATER WROTE A LETTER TO HER THAT SIMPLY SAID. "JUST TAKE CARE OF MY EYES DEAR."

THIS IS HOW THE HUMAN BRAIN CHANGES WHEN OUR STATUS CHANGES. ONLY A FEW REMEMBER WHAT LIFE WAS LIKE BEFORE AND EVEN FEWER REMEMBER WHO TO THANK FOR ALWAYS BEING THERE EVEN WHEN TIMES WERE PAINFULLY UNBEARABLE.

LIFE IS A GIFT

TODAY BEFORE YOU THINK OF SAYING AN UNKIND WORD - THINK OF SOMEONE WHO CAN'T SPEAK.

BEFORE YOU COMPLAIN ABOUT THE TASTE OF YOUR FOOD - THINK OF SOMEONE WHO HAS NOTHING TO EAT.

BEFORE YOU COMPLAIN ABOUT YOUR HUSBAND OR WIFE - THINK OF SOMEONE WHO'S CRYING OUT TO GOD FOR A COMPANION.

TODAY BEFORE YOU COMPLAIN ABOUT LIFE - THINK OF SOMEONE WHOSE LIFE HAS ALREADY ENDED.

BEFORE YOU COMPLAIN ABOUT YOUR CHILDREN - THINK OF SOMEONE WHO DESIRES CHILDREN BUT THEY'RE BARREN.

BEFORE YOU ARGUE ABOUT YOUR DIRTY HOUSE, SOMEONE DIDN'T CLEAN OR SWEEP - THINK OF THE PEOPLE WHO ARE LIVING IN THE STREETS.

BEFORE WHINING ABOUT THE DISTANCE YOU DRIVE - THINK OF SOMEONE WHO WALKS THE SAME DISTANCE WITH HIS OR HER FEET.

AND WHEN YOU ARE TIRED AND COMPLAIN ABOUT YOUR JOB - THINK OF THE UNEMPLOYED, THE DISABLED AND THOSE WHO WISHED THEY HAD YOUR JOB.

BUT BEFORE YOU THINK OF POINTING THE FINGER OR CONDEMNING ANOTHER - REMEMBER THAT NOT ONE OF US ARE WITHOUT SIN AND WE ALL ANSWER TO ONE MAKER.

AND WHEN DEPRESSING THOUGHTS SEEM TO GET YOU DOWN - PUT A SMILE ON YOUR FACE AND THANK GOD YOU'RE ALIVE AND STILL AROUND.

LIFE IS A GIFT, LIKE IT, ENJOY IT, CELEBRATE IT, AND FULFILL IT.

****

To everyone who has ever been there for me in one way or another. I say 'Thank You'. To the Almighty God, The I AM that I AM, that I am able to call Daddy, I stand in awe of your love for me. Thank you for keeping me to see this day. I should be dead. I really should be. But in your mercy, you said 'No'. Forgive me Father, for rubbishing the work Jesus did on the cross for me. I am so sorry. I love you Lord! Help me to live a life that proves my love. In Jesus Christ name, I pray. Amen!

Saturday, 18 July
Two Men and an Awakening

I am hot and sweaty as I type this. Just back from the market. I cannot tell you about my fiasco with the driver cos I will just get mad and I aim to stay cool calm and collected for at least......24 hours.

I have three pots boiling away on the stove and I just had a thought. I miss my mgm but more than that I miss my first born son. I miss my two men. Thank God I still have my youngest man and my only princess with me. Wonder what I would have been like by now if that was not the case. And they have only been away for a little over a week. Amazing. Once again I learn that those who bug you the most are the ones you tend to also miss the most if and when they go away. Indeed my mgm and my first born son are those who bug me the most in a good and bad way so to speak. I miss them so.

So as I am waiting for my beef to boil. As I prepare to make my afang soup, my soul is awakened to the truth that is 'Family'. Nothing like it. I love my mgm and my first born son and right now. I just miss them both. Nevertheless, I am so so grateful to God for this opportunity He provided for them to have this superlative bonding experience away from nagging wives and sisters and a stupendously irritating yet adorable 5 year old brother. I suppose they love us too, regardless.

Come home soon people so we can nag and irritate you some more. It's only cos we love you!

Sunday, 19 July
The Psalm 112 Christian

You probably have heard of the Proverbs 31 Woman. Well, the sermon my pastor shared with us today can almost be tagged 'the Psalm 112 Man' or as I prefer, 'the Psalm 112 Christian'. Who is she or he? Well....I will be sharing that with you later this week. This blog was really just to wish you all a nice week ahead. What ever you do, where ever you are, however you feel, remember that God loves you with an everlasting love.

AND the devil hates you with an everlasting hatred. It should be easy to figure out whose side we want to be on.....but alas by our choices, we tend to side with the very one that seeks only to destroy us.

This week, May God himself give us the grace to side with Him. Much better. Much safer. Much wiser. Now and in the hereafter.

In short live like a Psalm 112 person. Why don't you read it up before you read my blog?

Give yourself the head start!

Shalom!

Tuesday, 21 July
The Psalm 112 Christian

You know how we all (women that is) are always being told to emulate the Proverbs 31 woman. I think, as Christians, we should all aim to be a Psalm 112 person. I got this revelation from my pastor's sermon on Sunday. Let me break it down short and sweet. A Psalm 112 person:

Fears The Lord
Delights in the Lord
Is Upright and Righteous
Is Gracious and Compassionate
Is Generous and Lends freely
Conducts his/her affairs with justice (i.e. fairly without fear or favour)

And because He does the above, A Psalm 112 person:

Is blessed
His generations to come are blessed
His children are mighty in the land
Wealth and riches are in his/her house forever
Even in darkness (like that of credit crunches!), light dawns on him/her
Good comes to him
No matter what, he/she is never moved by circumstances
He/She will be remembered for good forever!
Has a secure heart. Is never afraid of bad news
He/She will, in the end, look in TRIUMPH over his/her foes.

I mean, what's not to like?
I don't know about you, but I think I want to be a Psalm 112 person.

Prayer Point: Almighty God, My Dear Heavenly Father, I thank you cos you are God of a million chances. Thank you for keeping me alive till this day to grab another chance to be who you have called me to be in You. As we step into this week, help me to be a Psalm 112 person. It is clear to me that this person loves and wants to please you. That is my hearts desire also. Lord, give me the divine enablement. Help me Lord! In Jesus Christ's name. Amen!

Tuesday, 21 July
Career Woman? Great! But Read This and Be Wise.

Personally, am not so career minded as to let a nanny/housekeeper take over my home. For me, it is just sheer laziness that is the problem. In my early years of marriage I wanted to be 'Martha Stewart'. Cook, House girl. Nanny. Sex Goddess. Mommy. Laundry woman. Sister. Friend. In short, anything my mgm wanted or I thought he wanted I tried to be. After over 16 years in the game I realise that all my mgm wants is good quality sex! So now, my motto is if someone else can do it, I will pay them to do it. The small energy I have left after working from 8am to 5pm and struggling through Lagos traffic, I shall save it to deliver on the sex front.

BUT I sort of know where to draw the line even with that. And reading this, I am going to even close some other gaps I know exist in terms of taking care of my mgm and children as well. Yes, oh, you have to be wise unless you are no longer into your relationship. However, there are some of you out there. You KNOW yourselves. You really want to take your career somewhere. That's not a bad thing but please read the true life story below and get your wisdom on oh! There has got to be a balance. May God Almighty help us all. Just thought to share. It is long BUT I assure you, you need to read to the end!

Two years ago, 41-year-old Margaret Mwangi (not her real name), a senior manager in one of the largest banks in the country, thought she had it all. Already a Masters degree holder, she was a year into studying for a PhD in financial management and had won several awards for her outstanding performance. She was earning good money and had extensive contacts. But as she rode the wave of her success, she forgot to channel the same effort and energy she directed at her career towards her husband of 14 years and three children.

Margaret would be up by 4 a.m. to get ready for the day's numerous strategic meetings and for mandatory 30-minute jog around her upmarket neighbourhood.
She would leave the house at 6a.m., as her husband and children were waking up to prepare for the day. Thanks to Martha, the efficient and

capable house-help she had had for eight years, Margaret knew that her family was in good hands.

Martha would prepare a healthy breakfast, ensure that everyone's clothes, including her husband's, were ironed and laid out and that their shoes were polished.

Given Margaret's busy schedule, including her daily evening classes which ended at 8p.m., she usually got home at around 9 p.m., tired to the bone. By then, the children were in bed, having had supper and completed their homework with Martha's help. In Margaret's mind, she was a good mother and dedicated wife since she ensured that her family was well taken care of.

But due to her constant absence from home, her once close and loving relationship with her husband faded, to be replaced by a cordial one, devoid of emotion and passion. Their conversations were perfunctory and usually, after asking about each other's day, she would take a shower, have a quick meal then collapse in bed, exhausted, with things that needed to be done at work the next day going in her mind.

She could not even recall the last time she and her husband had been intimate, but this did not really bother her. According to her, all marriages lost the initial fire they had after a couple of years. After all, hadn't her friends confessed that they were going through similar experiences?

That's why Margaret was shell-shocked when her 45-year-old husband announced that he was marrying another woman last year. But nothing could have prepared her for the bombshell that he dropped shortly thereafter — the other woman was Martha!

How could he do this to her after she had worked so hard so that they could all have a good life and a secure future? It is not like he or the children had been neglected – they lived in a clean home, had healthy, wholesome food everyday and led organised lives, she argued, as she tried to come to terms with the shocking news.

But when her husband pointed out that it was their live-in house help who did all these for the family, the argument instantly fizzled out.

During the last five years of their marriage, Martha had practically usurped Margaret's roles of wife and mother. She cooked for and served the man of the house, washed, ironed and laid out his clothes and dutifully cleaned and polished his shoes everyday. She even made the couple's bed, as well washed and changed the linen because Margaret often left early in the morning and returned late at night.

But more important, Martha had raised the couple's three children almost single-handedly. When they were young, she would wake up in the middle of the night to lull them back to sleep or warm them a bottle of milk because their mother would be too exhausted to do it. And when they started going to school, she walked them to the bus stop, picked them up in the evening and helped them with their homework.

"How then can you claim that you are my wife and mother of my children if someone else has been doing what you should be doing?" her husband had retorted when she asked how he could embarrass her by having an affair with their house help right under her own roof.

Not ready to live in the same house or share her husband with Martha, Margaret walked out of the marriage with the children. Although she can offer them the comfortable life they were used to, re-learning how to be a mother to her children is proving very difficult. The older two, a boy and a girl, are teenagers. Sulky, disobedient, and disrespectful, they are constantly getting into trouble at school. The other, now eight, is clingy, teary and has not stopped asking when they will move back home to "daddy and auntie".

Margaret recently learnt that her former house help, a single mother of two, had given birth to a baby girl, who had been named after her husband's mother.

A word they say is enough for the wise woman. Well unless, your relationship with your husband and children does not mean a whole lot to you...

Shalom!

Tuesday, 21 July
Call Upon Me – by Pastor Bemigho Omayuku

I love this book for a number of reasons.

1. It is about prayer and if there is one thing I want, it is to be a Prayer

2. Its author, Pastor Bemigho Omayuku or 'Pastor B' as lots of us call her, is one of my favourite people on earth. And my spiritual role model when it comes to prayer.

3. It is a simple easy-to-read book that demystifies praying. Simply put, prayer is about talking to God. It's about a relationship with the God that loves you.

And I loved reading it so much that I got a few extra copies and am prepared to give them out to the first 5 people who ask via this blog. Err, sorry, you have to live in Lagos and be prepared to come get it! I know, not fair but in real life, there is no real FOC matter. There are always some hidden charges. Lol!

Anyway, if you cannot come, look for the book in any good Christian bookshop. Laterna Bookshop, on Oko Awo close (off Adetokunbo Ademola Street, Victoria Island, Lagos) would be a good place to start.

The book is also available outside Nigeria as it was actually published by Winepress. So simply Google it and find out where you can get it near you.

Wednesday, 22 July
My New SALT Rule – That I May Be Wise in Speech

I talk too fast. Over the years I have tried to slow myself down a little but during the Digging Deep Service we had in church yesterday, I had a light bulb moment. My problem is not speaking too fast. My problem is speaking **too** much AND without thinking.

Being quick to hear and slow to speak has never been my strong suit. But the time has come to address this flaw. Yes, I think it is big enough to be granted the 'flaw' status because the good book says it clearly in Proverbs 21:23 that he who guards his mouth and tongue saves his soul from trouble. So basically, when my mouth runs wild and my tongue lashes out without thought or consideration, I am more or less destroying my own soul with MY OWN hands! *Lailai!*

As my Pastor preached and as we dug deeper into the Word, I just listened. Ashamed. I was guilty on all counts. Speaking without thinking. Talking too much. Making rash promises to man and rasher vows to God. In short, I was foolish. And trust me the Bible's opinion of a foolish person is not pretty. I mean, read these samples:

Proverbs 17:12
Let a man meet a bear robbed of her cubs, Rather than a fool in his folly.

Proverbs 26:1
As snow in summer and rain in harvest, so honour is not fitting for a fool.

So I aim to remove myself pronto from the camp of the foolish. And step one is to begin to bridle my tongue (for yes there are still many other ways to be biblically foolish! God will help me). I have asked God to come and stand watch over my mouth. No more verbal diarrhoea. No more foolish talk and jesting. There is no rule that says I must respond even BEFORE the other person has finished speaking! Here is my new 'art of conversation' rule - S.A.L.T:

S: STOP & listen actively first. Think about what you want to say for a second.
A: ASK yourself, does it help/hurt; build/batter; add/attack; clarify/crucify
L: LET it go once you know Jesus Christ would NOT say it.
T: True wisdom is sometimes demonstrated by saying NOTHING.

I think if I practise this SALT rule, my speech will 'always be with grace, seasoned with salt…' Colossians 4:6. A veritable fountain of life as it should be if I say I am a woman of God.

God Bless you Pastor Seye Kosoko! Mercy Place Parish Rocks! Shalom!

Thursday, 23 July
What If Her Dream Was For Real?

My one and only princess jolted me this morning. She told me she dreamt that the rapture had taken place last night. I said to her thank God it hadn't cos for sure I was not ready and would have missed it. Believe it or not, I was actually laughing at myself and was quite cavalier about the whole thing. Then it struck me! How could I be so foolish? (Ouch! that word again! The word 'fool' is translated as 'asiwere' in yoruba and it means 'a stark raving lunatic'!). And really, only a stark raving lunatic would take the matter of eternity so lightly.

And as if that was not bad enough, a good friend then sent me this mail early this morning. For me, God is speaking. How about you?
****

Greg woke up suddenly one night and saw a strange light in his room....
The problem is that the lights are off he saw the clock; it was 3.30 in the morning
Okay...so where is all this light coming from??

He turned around and saw something very strange...
His body was half way through the wall (??!)
He immediately pulled it out and sat down to see if he's okay
This seems strange to him...HE tried to push onto the wall, but his ARM GOES THROUGH. He heard a sound. HE turned to his brother's bed to see him sleeping
He was really scared of what was happening to him...so he tried to wake him up.... but.... he doesn't reply!!

He went to his parent's bedroom. Tried to wake up his mother...and father...just wanted somebody to react to him...but nobody did.
He tried to wake his mother up again...she woke up this time...she got up ... but didn't communicate to him. She was saying "In Jesus Name" again and again

She woke his dad up saying 'get up, man, I want to check up on the kids.'
Dad replied in disinterest. 'It's not time for this, let me sleep and by God's grace tomorrow I'll get to that'

But she was insisting. So he woke up. Greg was THERE. He was screaming 'Dad, Mum'...!' Nobody was replying. He held unto his mother's clothes to grab her attention but she didn't recognize his existence. He followed her till she got to his bedroom

They got into the room and turned on the lights...it wasn't making any difference to him anyway because there was a strong light there. He then saw the strangest thing in he had ever seen his life. HIS OWN BODY.... on his bed.

He was trembling...how can there be two of him? How can that person look so much like him? . And what is he doing on his bed????

He started hitting/slapping himself to wake up from this nightmare... but it was too real to be a nightmare. Dad said, 'See the kids are sleeping. Let's go back to bed. But mother wasn't at all confident...she went to the person sleeping on the bed and said 'Greg, wake up!! ... WAKE UP!!'

But he wouldn't reply. She tried again and again.... but no reply. Then he turned to see his dad weeping. He had never seen his Dad cry before. The place was shaking with the screaming.

His brother woke up..."What's going on?" In a very sad tone , with tears rolling down her cheek, mother replied 'your brother's dead! Greg is DEAD!!'

He went to mother and said 'please mum...don't cry. I'm right here look at me!'
But nobody's replying to him. WHY??

Greg turned to Lord Jesus Christ and asked Him to wake him up from the nightmare! Quickly following his fear was a voice saying:

"It is appointed once for a man to die and after that is the judgement"

Suddenly two creatures held his arm. They weren't human!!
He started screaming, "Leave me ALONE! Who are you and what do you want from me??" They told him they were his grave's guards'. He responded 'but I'm not dead yet! Let go of me!!' I can still see, hear, touch, and speak. I'm not dead!

They replied with a smile: "You humans are fascinating! You think that by dying your life ends, while in fact life on Earth is a small dream compared to the life after; a dream that ends at your death."

They started pulling him towards his grave...

On the way he saw people just like himself, each had two guards like his.
Some were smiling, others crying, others screaming.
He asked the guards 'why are they all doing that?'

They replied 'these people now know their fate...some were in ignorance so they shall go to Hell. 'And those laughing are going to Heaven'

He quickly replied: 'what about me? Where will I go??'

They said 'you were at times a good Christian, while other times not. One day you obey the Lord Jesus Christ, the next you disobey Him. And you weren't clear with yourself and your fate will remain so: lost.'

Greg replied, shaking: 'SO! AM I GOING TO HELL??'

They said: ' God's mercy is great, and the journey is long'

Greg turned to see his family carrying his dead body in a coffin. So he ran to them.

He said: 'Pray for me' but nobody replied..
He went to his brother and warned him. 'Be careful with what you do in this life... don't be a fool like myself!' He was really hoping that they could hear him... The two angels (guards) tied up his soul on top of his body.

He saw his relatives pouring sand over him and at that moment He was hoping that he would be in their place... that he could turn to his Lord Jesus Christ and do as much as He wanted for him. That he could ask for forgiveness and once and for all repent of his sins that angered Him... but unfortunately he couldn't.

He shouted ' People, don't let this life tempt you! Wake up to the truth... one day you will DIE, and you never know when or how. 'He hoped for somebody to hear him. Nobody there did but **YOU, yes you reading this now, you can hear him. Save yourself!**

Smile to others; forgive them when you have the power to punish them. Lord Jesus forgives those that forgive others. Let God guide your life, not Satan. Read the Bible regularly and let the Holy Spirit be your role model in life.

Work in this time bound life for your salvation in an eternal one.
****

Hmmmm....people of God. Once again, a word is enough for the wise.

Shalom!

Friday, 24 July
The Centrepiece

When you walk into my living room, I think the first thing that strikes you is the black glass spiral-shaped table in the middle of the room on a rug. First of all, it is black and shiny. Then it is glass (you are like, are there no children in this house?). Finally, it is an eye catching even if odd shape for a table. It just seems to draw attention to itself. Regardless of where you stand in that room, you are constantly drawn to this shiny black 'what kind of table is that' object. It has become the main focus, the centrepiece of the room.

As a Christian, this is what God should be in my life. The centrepiece. I should reflect Him so beautifully that people are drawn to me. I should be 'eye-catching' cos I behave 'oddly' in a world that does not 'get' being holy. Regardless of my situation, need, state of health or wealth. No matter what. Where ever I stand in life, God should be my number one object of desire. He should have my undivided attention and focus. He should be The No. 1 priority. The No. 1 relationship out of which all other relationships flow.

Just like I am always on alert when the children are messing around in the living room, in the fear that one of them will run into the glass table and break it (or themselves for that matter!) In this same way I should be guarding carefully, fearfully the 'Centrepiece' of my life. Nothing. No one. Should interfere with my relationship with God. And if anyone or anything bumps into me, the God who lives in me will act as a buffer. I shall not be moved. I shall keep my eyes on God, the pillar of my life. He is unshakable. And unlike that centre table in my living room, He can never break! Praise His name! So how about you? What is the current centrepiece of your life?

Your marriage? Or your desire to be married?
Your financial situation or Health?
Maybe it's your desire to hold your own child?
Or perhaps some 'wayward' child or sibling or parent?

You need a job or admission to school? Or you may even be dealing with some form of addiction?

My sister, my brother, take your focus off all these and fix your eyes on Jesus Christ. In Him lies the answers to ALL of the above and any other issue of life. Invite him into your life anew. Spend time talking to and listening to Him in prayer. Study His Word more. Praise Him and Worship Him. This is what I plan to do and I encourage you to do the same. I believe that as we focus more on Christ and begin to enjoy a more intimate relationship with Him, the angels will set off on assignment to take care of all our issues. Remember Peter, when he took his eyes off the storms all around him and fixed his eyes on Jesus Christ? Yes, that's right, he walked on water.

And you know what? For me, even if my issues remain, I will still count it all joy to be closer to my God. Cos at the end of the day, none of these so called issues will matter. All that will matter is where I will spend eternity. And in eternity, I shall not need 'stuff'
Shalom!

Sunday, 26 July
Jesus 'The Fall Guy'

Church was good today. And as usual my favourite part, praise and worship took me to another level. I am so thankful to God for life and being able to offer thanks, praise and worship to Him. It is indeed an honour and at those times, I feel more alive than any other. It was during our worship as we took Michael W Smith's 'Above All' worship song that God began to speak to me.

The end of the song talks about how Jesus Christ took the 'fall' for me. He was crucified and laid behind a stone. He was rejected and laid there dead and all alone. Like a rose trampled on the ground. And all this for who? For me. For you. Jesus took the fall. He paid the price so that I could go free. Scot free. You too.

I was THAT important to God that He counted me worthy, ABOVE all, of such a sacrifice. He thought of ME above all else and took that fall for me! As God spoke to me in the midst of this worship time, He began to ask me how come I was unable to think of Him the way He thought of me. How come I could not place Him ABOVE all the issues in my life? How come when a choice had to be made - His way or the world way - I went the world way? How come when push came to shove, I did not take 'the fall' for Him? It was a long conversation between Father and Child, Lover and Loved, Saviour and Saved. As worship came to end, I rose from knees, having made some fresh commitments to Him.

I am going to place Jesus Christ ABOVE ALL this week. He took the fall for me. The least I could do is say 'thank you' by living a life that will not rubbish such an awesome and incredible act of love.

Shalom!

Monday, 27 July
I Am a Morning Person

Yes, finally I am sure about this. You know how you take some of those 'self-discovery' questionnaires and you are asked 'are you a morning or evening' person? I always struggled with that cos I figured I was a bit of both. I love the newness of each day that mornings bring. But I also love the sleep that evenings bring. Every morning was a brand new start, a new gift from God. Yet the evenings gave room for self reflection. Work was over by the time evenings came. But with mornings, oomph! Came another day of work, and on and on. So I never could make up my mind. A.M or P.M?

Now I know for sure. I am a MORNING person and you want to know why? I find that my head is clearest in the mornings to the things that matter most. I have such clarity on the wrong I engaged in or got trapped in the day before and am ever so sorry and repentant. You see, as I take a bath, get ready for work and begin my commute to work, my thoughts are collected. God and I are talking and I see clearer. I stand surer. I feel committed to relationship with God IN THE MORNINGS. I am like TODAY, I shall shine my light bright for Jesus Christ!!!!

But there is something about the day when the 3.00pm mark strikes the iron. This is me personally now. The first few hints of weakening surface. That 'for sure, I will not miss church this evening' stance of mine begins to waver. Oh just one extra hour watching 'E News' cannot do THAT much harm. And on and on it goes. The evil suggestions from the camp of the enemy gain power over my mind as the day draws to a close. I don't like me much at these times. I see now that I operate at a level below God's provision in the evenings. No wonder it's called the kingdom of darkness...darkness comes as evening approaches..... *abi? Na wa!*

BUT guess what? With this understanding also comes much power! Cos NOW I know. Ignorance kills. Knowledge empowers. The eyes of my understanding have been opened so now I can begin to cover my mind in the blood of Jesus Christ BEFORE evening falls. In advance, I can now take into captivity EVERY evening evil, unholy suggestion that takes me off my divine path. In the morning, when I am strongest, I will lay an ambush in advance for them. And God has assured me, that victory is mine cos I am an Overcomer.

So what are you? A.M or P.M? And why?

Tuesday, 28 July
Hang In There

Please read this and assimilate the truths it offers you and I. Let them sink deep into your soul. A dear friend in far away Dubai sent this to me and I told her I would share it on my blog.

It spoke to me. I pray it speaks to you too.

Whatever it is you do in life,
Try to remember that nothing is too big to achieve
And nothing is too small to ignore,
Hang on in there, even if it's with the last thread,
It is well.

You may be on life's path
Not having an idea how and when you'll get there,
The most important thing is that you have a sense of direction,
All you have to do is to take each step one at a time,
And you'll get there.

The idea behind life is about meeting people,
The beauty of life is loving people,
The essence of life is about making impacts,
The joy of life is leaving footprints in the sands of time.

Have a wonderful relationship with God,
And know where he wants to place you in life to function,
For without him,
You are nothing.
On your journey through life,
Absorb everything you hear,
But choose what you want to believe.

30 July
Making Progress in the Wrong Direction

Proverbs 4:10-12
10 Hear, my son, and receive my sayings,
And the years of your life will be many.
11 I have taught you in the way of wisdom;
I have led you in right paths.
12 When you walk, your steps will not be hindered,
And when you run, you will not stumble.

I would usually always associate the word 'progress' with something positive. Wouldn't you? It does connote a sort of 'getting better, moving higher' kind of vibe, *abi*? So I thought oh!

I have recently learnt however that it is very possible to make progress well...negatively. In the wrong direction. Bear with me and read on a bit.

Suppose I board a taxi and ask the driver to take me to Ikoyi. Now I am new in Lagos and I don't know the route or anything. I am totally at the mercy of this merry driver whistling as he drives and trying to make small chat with me about the nonsense government and bad roads. I try to ignore him, completely oblivious to the fact that he is not facing Ikoyi at all! In fact, all things being equal, I will find my self in Surulere in another 20 minutes!!!!

Now, I DID board the taxi 15 minutes ago. Taxi was making progress, avoiding potholes here and dodging mad 'okada' riders there. In spite of the traffic, we WERE moving ahead, getting closer to the final destination. The WRONG final destination! I was making progress alright but in the wrong direction. You get it now? Hmmmm, so do I?

And sometimes in life, I think we find ourselves on this same kind of journey and only God can help us by 'opening' our eyes and helping us to realise that we are heading towards the 'Surulere' of our destinies.

Meanwhile He had planned 'Ikoyi' for us (all due respect to the Surulere people oh!) But we get so caught in the chatter of the 'taxi drivers' in our lives, the people or situations that drown out reasoning and bar us from paying attention....the people who, because they don't understand what we are about, want to 'force' us to live a life that they are comfortable with. They want to drive us down their own understanding of 'our' road.... in the wrong direction.

But praise God! He allows U-turns. Today, chuck out that taxi driver taking you no where fast. Get Jesus Christ in the driver seat of your life. Talk to Him. Tell Him where you want to go. But trust Him enough to know that HIS plans for you can never be wrong for you. His is the Master Voyager. He has your whole life's itinerary all staked out. With Him, you can never end up in the wrong place. Never!

Shalom!

Friday, 31 July
The 7th Month, going, going…

You know July is the 7th month of the year. We Christians see the number 7 as the number that connotes perfection. For us, July is meant to be a month during which we focus on God more in a bid to work with Him, Jesus Christ and the Holy Spirit as they 'perfect' the areas of our lives that need a divine refining touch.

Me, I am in a good place as this month closes and I thank God for that. I feel….how shall put it? Like am finding my balance again. I am cleaning up my act (again!). Toxins are being flushed out, physically and spiritually. I am letting go of unforgiveness. And there is nothing like that to throw a desperate woman seeking to be Christ-like off balance. Trust me, walking with God and unforgiveness are like trying to sip hot cocoa after feasting on an ice-cream. Eugh! Just thinking about it sets my teeth on edge. The two just do not go together.

So, as I was saying, am being taken back to that place where I belong. No one dragged me down that mad road but myself and only a God like the one I serve would even bother to come fetch me. Back to Himself. Back to the right road. Back to making positive progress.

It's a nice way to end a month of perfection. It's nice to feel connected to a force higher than one. Its mega nice to be alive today. Had a fantastic prayer meeting with the women of my church. My MGM and I managed to scrape together the fees needed for our 3 children (*God, na you biko!*), had a nice chat with a colleague today about childlike faith in God and then a good friend/mentor is around. Yes, I am on a high! I wish I could bottle it up and sell it…..Its true what they say; the best things in life are actually free!

Oh well, the least I can do is wish you all a lovely week ahead. And congratulate you on making it to the end of another month. Look out August! Month of New Beginnings. Here we come! And we who know our God are fixed on doing exploits to the glory of His name! Amen!

Shalom!

AUGUST

Sunday, 02 August
Top Tips For The First Working Day of August – God and Exercise

Yes, tomorrow is the first working day of August. Monday

For some bizarre yet exhilarating reason, I am happy.

Yes, excitedly happy. You see, I hate Mondays. Honest, it was just not one of my days at all. But today, I am in a good place about tomorrow being Monday.

And you wanna know why?

I have been thinking about it myself and though am not super sure I think its cos
One, I am happy with where I am with God right now. Trust me, this is a major deal clincher or breaker for my state of mind.

Two, I am actually looking forward to, by the grace of God, living a crucified life minute by minute. Yep! Any time I see the old me trying to come down from that cross where it was crucified along with my saviour Jesus Christ. I am nailing it right back. As far as I know, dead people cannot sin! So if am walking on the wide road, exhibiting fleshly traits, then that old self is alive and well. Rara o! By the Holy Spirit power in me right now, I am fighting back. I am keeping you dead, dead! You hear me, old self you?

Three, I am happy because of the happy endorphins that have been let loose in my brain via a gruelling workout in the gym this evening. Now I believe all the hype. Exercise, as painful as it is, can make you happy.

I think there are some other reasons but I shall not bore you with those ones. The three above are my top ones.

So, assuming I was your Shrink and you had a thing about Mondays. I would have two words for you: God and Exercise. Get some! Now.

Happy First Working Day of August!

Shalom!

Tuesday, 04 August
Very Randomly…

My shoulders feel like lead. My sides hurt. My arms don't belong to me. Yet, I feel, strangely *good*. Yes, actually very good as a matter of fact. In spite of the fact that the *old* me climbed down from the cross well well yesterday and I was not able to nail her back before she threw a fit. Yes, in spite of that I will continue to encourage myself with the bible verse that says the rod should not be spared to the spoiling of the child. Let's just say the child shall not be spoiled in Jesus name. Amen. Old me is safely nailed on the cross again. I am in a *nirvana* of my own making. Heady potion this God and exercise concoction I am taking!

Anywho, my only princess just got off the piano having just rendered near perfect pieces of some truly lovely songs. She is quite good and is beyond driven. I cannot remember being that driven about anything when I was 12 years old. Except maybe why everyone in my class had had their periods barring me. Oh, the things we wish for when we are naive and young.

Work was good today. I love my job. Would rather not be working but if I must, then this is it. I have one of the best Supervisors on planet earth and I am not trying to flatter him (for one I doubt he ever surfs the net so chances of him reading this are next to nada). It is just the truth. The ambiance in my office is superb and its the first job I have had where my BP did not rise when I first started! So I salute my boss and my team-mates. Here is to you all!

My son is off to school in 24 days. Yes, as only a mom would do I have started my count down. I am not sure how I will survive but away he must. Spread his wings and learn to fly far away from the nest…*nah wa*, I still remember pushing that child out into this world! Now, he is 15 and off to boarding school for the very first time. Ah!!!!! I will survive!

OK yes. You are right, I am just babbling away randomly about nothing and everything. But really is that now what life is sometimes? A series of random events connecting the hours of the day together…Yes, me thinks so BUT if we pay attention and look closely, as children of the most High, we can see his divine plan for us still working its way out.... or don't you agree?

Yours randomly,

DNW

Wednesday, 05 August
Pray Along With Me? (An all-in-one prayer based on Colossians 1:9-14)

Dear Heavenly Father

You know I love you and all I really want to do is live a life that pleases you. So dear merciful and loving father:

Help me to know fully what you want me to do concerning EVERY situation in my daily life NOW and always.

Lord, give me great wisdom and understanding in spiritual things so that I will live the kind of life that honours and pleases you in EVERY way. I am a woman of God with so many roles. I need wisdom to navigate life and play all these roles, as you would want me to. So help me Father as only you can!

Father, please give me the grace, the divine enablement to produce fruit in every good work and grow in the knowledge of who you are. I want to know WHO you are. Not just WHAT you do. Draw me closer to you with each passing day!

Father, strengthen me every single day with your own great power so that I will not give up when troubles come, but I will be patient.

Finally Lord and Gracious Father, help me to always be joyful, giving thanks to you who has made me able to have a share in all that you have prepared for your people in the kingdom of light.

Thank you so much Lord for freeing me from the power of darkness, and for bringing me into the kingdom of your dear Son.

Help me to walk continually in the knowledge that the Son paid for my sins, and in him I have forgiveness so the enemy can no longer mess with my mind and make me feel condemned. I am FREE!

Father I thank you. Thank you for who you are in my life. Thank you for hearing these my prayers, which I have raised to you in Jesus Christ name.

Amen!

This, people is going to be like a prayer mantra for me from now till the end of 2009. Join Me? Hope so!

Shalom!

Wednesday, 05 August
A True Friend of Jesus

What a mighty mighty breathe of fresh air for Christendom! For once, a good report about someone who claims to be born again. Let me share with you this fantastic report.

A colleague was on her way to Ikare for a friend's wedding. On the way, the car they were all in, mostly women, I must point out, had a flat. It was late. It was getting dark. Just as they were trying to fumble around with the puny little spare tire they had, a car drives by.... and then stops! Out comes this man and he offers to help them. Of course, at first they were scared as you can well imagine but then he assured them and long story short, this guy helped them change the tyre. A stranger helping out a group of young ladies in the middle of nowhere for NOTHING.

Along the way, as he conversed with them, they found out he was a Christian and the founder, I believe, of a Face book group called 'Friends of Jesus'! The only thanks he required of them? 'Next time you are on face book, look up my group! Awwwwgh bliss!

Who can blame one of the girls in the car for being so sure that should they dial his number, no one would pick it? He could not have been for real. He had to be an angel!

Shalom!

P. S. Yes, I will be joining 'Friends of Jesus' on FB shortly.

Thursday, 06 August
Prayer is Really Just A Conversation with God

A nice young lady sent me a mail today. She lifted my spirits and in turn I tried to share some stuff with her. The most important bit was about being prayerful. My favourite quote on prayer is the one that says a 'Powerless Christian is a Prayerless Christian'. So simply put. Yet so vitally true.

This is one of my KISS blogs. I am going to <u>K</u>eep <u>I</u>t <u>S</u>hort and <u>S</u>imple. I just want to say that I know that sometimes in fact most of the times, our lives do not cut us any slack at all. There is barely enough time to get the job done so how does one carve out time to pray???? To spend time with God?

The truth of the matter is we just HAVE to. But for God, where would we be? Who would we be? So at some point, we need to make that call and say, hook or crook, this time of the day is sacrosanct, its me and God time, and that's it.

Now, in the meantime, this is how to look at it and this is what I shared with this blest woman of God.

Just see prayer as one long drawn out daily conversation with God. From the moment you wake up chat with Him about your day, share your plans with him as you shower. Bring matters that come up during the day to him for help. Thank Him for the job, ask him for help to deal with that cranky boss, bless his name for the strength you have to work and the intelligence he has given you, ask Him to part the red sea of traffic for you so you can get home on time to the family he has blest you with. Thank you Lord for my wife. My husband. My children. Lord about their fees, I am trusting you for that. Make a way where there seems to be no way.... and on and on it goes. Before you know it, it becomes second nature and you are actually praying WITHOUT CEASING.

So for all of us who know our prayer lives need a bit of boost; this is a good place to start. Get the conversation with your Father in heaven going today. Now. Trust me God loves jist too.

Shalom!

Saturday, 08 August
Reflecting Backwards

I feel like turning things on their head a bit today. Yep! I am feeling good like that. Plus which 'its MY blog and I can do what I want'! heeeheee.

No really, I think this will do all of us some good. This is the month of August, the 8th month of the year and mostly we have been looking at this year a la the cup is half empty and praying that the cup will get full before the end of 2009. True, there are things I am still looking to God for BUT today I choose to examine the past 8 months with my 'its all good in the hood' spectacles on! I am in what you would call a 'blessing counting' mode.

Now lets see...this year...

1. I have taken concrete steps to improve my general health status. Fixed my impacted wisdom tooth. Got some fillings done. Trust me. I hate the dentist so doing this is a big-ticket item. My keep fit routine now includes walking up 16 floors once a day at work, 30 minutes of treadmill or dance aerobics plus another 30 minutes on all sorts of contraptions meant to either firm up my arms or tummy at least 3 times a week. For me, this is a ++++ achievement!

2. My first-born son finished secondary school! Hurray!

3. My only princess finished her first year of secondary school. Hurray x 2!

4. My last-born son 'graduated' from Nursery school! Hurray x 3!

4. I started blogging!!!!!

5. In spite of my housekeeper issues, my house has not fallen down and am still alive...and so are my children!

6. Barring a few anxious illness moments, my children have been mostly happy and healthy and extremely noisy.

7. My MGM and my first-born son had a serious 2-week bonding experience in China recently. That is the highlight of my year so far as a mother.

8. That bring me to the zillion of zillions of kilometres my MGM has travelled in the past 8 months. Land, Air, Water. You name it. H has travelled it. And he has come back safe each time. Now tell me you don't have a similar testimony. We all do.

9. I still have a job and a good one at that and though things are tight sometimes, I have not had a single month where I did not have just enough to tide me over till the next pay day. AND, for the first time in a looooooooong time, I am saving as well! Now that is ++++++++++ for me!

So reflecting backwards, I have much to be grateful for and am sure you do too. I could sit here and begin to wonder about ALL THE OTHER STUFF I had on my TO DO list for 2009 that I have not done or that have not happened. But I shall not. I refuse to do that today. 2009 is not over yet and see all that God has done for me. I trust Him. Yes, He has never failed me....

Yes oh! I am sure I will be driving before the end of 2009! Lol! And yes, I will be swimming too!

How about you try it? Reflect backwards and see if it wont make you feel better...

Shalom!

Sunday, 09 August
My God. My Mother

I recently reactivated my IPhone to aid and abet my drill in the gym. It got 'lost' for a long time and I just found it again (I shall not bore you with that tale. Suffice to say that someone thought it belonged to her!). Anywho, as I was saying, I had forgotten how good the music I had on my IPhone was. Real rocking music to lift your spirits and get you stomping on the treadmill or along the pavements. Real good stuff but my favourite gym buddy is Kirk Franklin and his songs 'This is It!' and 'Jesus' from his 'Fight of My Life' album.

This past weekend, I was stomping along the streets building up a nice sweat and about three quarters into my 7000 steps when the words of the song playing caught my attention. Mind you, I had probably heard it many times before but this time I 'heard' it with my spirit. As I type right now, the exact words fail me but it goes something like this 'Zillions are calling your name, but you still hear my voice'

Let that sink in a little.

Do you realise that there are a million people like me, like you, calling on God every second of every hour of every day? Do you ever wonder how He copes? Sometimes, when I get back from work, I am met at the door by all three of my progeny, excited to see me and all three of them trying to talk to me AT THE SAME TIME! Please! I only have a pair of ears and one brain! And after surviving the traffic home, this brain of mine can take only so much information and it has to come ONE at a time and slowwwwwwly! lol! But that's me, I am only human.

But you see our God is a better-equipped 'Mom'. Yes, for me, God is a Mother too. Even though we refer to Him most of the time as Father, I see God also displaying the attributes of a loving, caring Mother. AND He is able to listen to ALL His children at the SAME time.. He has no problem doing that at all. Praise God! And He does it in zillions of different languages too!

Does it not just blow your mind that God knows and recognises each of our voices? Sometimes I get confused and call my first-born son by my baby son's name. In fact, I could go through all the names of my children before I land on the right one! In fact I have been known to 'what's your name again' them on occasion. Lol!

But God? No! Never! He never mixes us up. He knows each of us by name. He recognises our different cries just like a mother can recognise the sound of her own child crying on a playground full of children. I was watching Oprah today and she was talking to Jenny McCarthy about 'Mother Warriors'. All mothers have that warrior instinct in them. The one that turns a gentle woman into a fiery tiger when her child's safety is at risk. I think we get this from God. After all He is the Warrior of warriors, the Mighty Lion of the Tribe of Judah. Yes, God is my Father but He is also my Heavenly Mother who knows me by my name and will go to any extent to protect me.

And you.

Shalom!

Thursday, 13 August
Ah-Sholly-Babes!

I actually have a number of things floating in and around my mind. Stuff that I was going to blog about but this one has climbed its way to the top.

I tell you walking is a good form of exercise but I have found that for me, it is also a time when my thoughts go on different journeys. Yes, sometimes they go ahead of me into the future. Sometimes they mind themselves and stay with me in my 'today' (especially if I decide to blast loud music into my brain! It just stays with the music! Lol!). But sometimes, they take me back down memory lane. Yes, I love to walk now and as I set out, I wonder 'where will you take me today, oh ye thoughts of mine?

In recent times I have been thinking about my family members and some issues I am trying to work with God to sort out. So I was not really surprised when during one of my last walks, my thoughts took me to my sister. Hmmmm, yes she is my sister but she is also my 'first child'. Not sure anyone can take this away from us. Ah-Sholly-Babes! This is what I used to call her all those years back (I used to call her by her full Yoruba name too but I will not put you through that right now). I tell you she was the cutest little thing you ever saw. My thoughts were nice and warm and fuzzy and as they took me back in time, the kilometres just seemed to melt away...

I was 12 years old when Sholly Babes was born. She was my pride and joy. Honest, from the first day I laid eyes on her, she became the joint property of my parents and myself. I remember it so well, it was in my Form 2 and I had just gotten home for the Christmas holidays. I knew she had been born cos her birthday is in September but this was the first time I was going to get to see her. It was one of the happiest days of my young life. I was happy for me and I was happier for my mother. Indeed, her 'joy had been restored'. I also remember the first photo we took together. I was standing next to the Christmas tree. I don't even know where that photo is but I remember how I looked in it. I was a proud 'mama'. She was beyond adorable.

You might not be able to understand how I felt about this baby and sometimes even I do not get it but looking back now I see why God made it so. God indeed does see the end from the beginning. He planted in my young heart a quantum of love for this child that surpassed the regular sibling love. And Sholly Babes loved me back just as hard. At the end of every school term as I prepared to go home, I usually would daydream about only one thing. Of course I looked forward to seeing my parents and my brother. But my fantasies were mainly peppered with images of this little chubby baby running out to meet me screeching as only babies do ' Baaaaaalaaaaaaaa'! She would jump at me literally throwing herself on me and from that second till I went back to school, she was my little sidekick. That was the highlight of all my secondary school holidays. I can say with a respectable level of pride that it is thanks to me that she now has this awesome mane of hair. I spent holidays concocting all sorts of hairstyles for her. I basically 'used' the poor child's lovely locks to learn how to weave hair!

Over the years, we grew up but our feelings did not change at all. In fact the bond only grew stronger. I can safely say there is nowhere I have been that Sholly babes has not been. I was like Mary and she was my little cute lamb. Everywhere I went, she was sure to follow. If a place hosted me, it hosted her. She slept with me on my university hostel bed in Uyo; She bunked with me on my postgraduate bed while I was doing my masters in Ibadan. She shared my NYSC flat with me in Calabar and she co-habited with me in the BQ I lived when I started working in Lagos. It was almost as if I had a child. And I believe when my mgm started thinking about marrying me, he must have factored her it to the deal. Lol!

Thankfully my thoughts wanted to keep me happy so as I poured sweat down the road, pumping my heart, they did not let me dwell on the fact that life eventually made me this child's mother for real so to speak. My thoughts were kind. They just skimmed over the fact that we lost our mom when she was just 5 years old. Quickly, they moved me on to how we survived all that life threw at us in those hard times. They made me remember how my mgm would carry her on his shoulders when she got tired of walking. Which she actually did not find funny at all! Like me, she thought he was 'too yellow'. Lwkm!

My thoughts were funny as they reminded me of our many laughs in the Minna kitchen back in the day. The *orisirisi* meat pies and concoction fried rice meals I made her eat. She was usually my number one cheerleader. Except for the cornflakes saga! She did not want to eat it a.k.a 'wasting' and I basically forced her to along with a nice dose of the 'there are children in Somalia starving to death' spin that only mothers can do so well. I don't know who died and made me the Queen of Sheba!. Actually, that would be my mother, she died and left this child in my care! Yep it never occurred to me once that the child still had a father. After all, he was 'just' a dad! What did he know?

Ahhhh, my walk was over and as I rounded the bend towards my house, my eyes glazed over with tears of gratitude to God. We had come along way. All those years ago when she went off to live far far away, I thought my heart would break. One cos I was not there to say goodbye. Two, cos I was like 'how will she cope without me? Three, because I felt, at the time, that life should have played itself out differently. But then I was not God. He knew better. It has ALL worked out very well. Very well indeed! Sholly Babes is all grown up now and getting set to get married. Imagine. My baby. A grown woman. A beautiful, confident, exceptionally talented and beyond smart African Goddess.

If there is anyone I can tell 'all' to, its my Sholly babes. She never judges me. Always believes me in. Always. And I believe in her too. I guess I cannot really call her my baby sister anymore but the truth of the matter is that, in my heart, she will always be my baby sister. Sholly babes! Aburo, *I wo wa o jare!*

Here's to you girl!

We showed them!
No, actually, YOU showed them!
Truth of the matter is, GOD showed us all!
Praise His Name!

Friday, 14 August
Reach Out and Touch Caroline Johnson. Please!

Oh that our hearts will be touched by the plight of this woman and moved into action! DNW

Thursday, August 6, 2009
Save Caroline Johnson

Caroline's husband put this on facebook. I thought more people should see and read this...and hopefully help!

TO SAVE CAROLINE JOHNSON FROM LEUKEMIA (CANCER OF THE BLOOD) - As written by Tony Johnson

We write with sincerity of heart, hoping that after you have read this letter, our good Lord will enable you give. We are a family of 5 (five) and have been married for over 7years; blessed with 3 Children, my wife is a Christian actress currently showing on air. (Heaven's Gate as UJU) and I am an architect by profession.

We are members of THE POTTERS HOUSE CHRISTIAN FELLOWSHIP CHURCH - Adeniyi Jones, Ikeja Lagos, Nigeria. We had plans, hope and aspiration like any other good citizen of Nigeria would, until my wife was diagnosed to have leukaemia, i.e. (cancer of the Blood) in October 2008, when she was 5months plus into the pregnancy of our 3rd Child (Oluwatise Johnson).

Initially the cancer was diagnosed at a Private Hospital at Surulere in Lagos, but we were referred to the Lagos State Teaching Hospital (LASUTH) Ikeja.

There she was on admission with the pregnancy but a dilemma to save my wife or baby was managed with multiple blood transfusion and treatment until her pregnancy was 7months 1 week when she suddenly fell into labour, but we thank God both mother and child survived on the 17/12/2008.

We thought all was over, since the doctors initially thought she had an acute anaemia, but four weeks after delivery my wife's immune system and blood level dropped to 9% PCV and fell almost into a shock, then further investigations were carried out including bone marrow test (aspiration and biopsy) and she also had multiple transfusions.

It was then the doctors gave us the news that my wife has ACUTE LYMPHOBIASTIC LEUKEMIA TYPE 1 also known as (CANCER of the BLOOD)

Since then, she has been through chemotherapy treatment and blood transfusions hoping that it would help contain the cancer cells. But now, further investigations and tests including bone marrow transplant were advised by the doctors at LASUTH to be done abroad in INDIA. (Please feel free to request backing documents).

A lot of our life-time savings have been spent on hospital admissions, treatments, drugs, investigations, tests and scan. We have currently spent over 2.5million naira but that's just a phase of the treatment. We are currently seeking your help to support in raising funds that will help us travel to India for further investigations and to carryout a bone marrow transplant summing to a total cost of $50, 000 (fifty thousand dollars). (Eight million five hundred thousand naira)Currently, we have a total collection of "One million one hundred thousand naira" from Families and friends.

I would sincerely appreciate your donation and support towards saving my wife from this dreaded disease 'Cancer of the Blood'. I wish that every one who reads this would help with at least N10, 000 and in a short while we will hit the target to quickly evacuate her from Nigeria to India please do not look at the huge amount as that will scare u, just as little as u have will go a long way.

I honestly hope that by midweek we can consider to fly her out if we can raise about 50% of the total cost.

A lot of people want to know how to get money to me from UK and USA. Please kindly feel free to call me on 08023139587 and email me on tonyjohnson@savecarolinejohnson.com.

Unfortunately, our two older children Omolayo 7 and Imisioluwa 4 struggle to understand or accept what has suddenly happened to their very loving and argyle mother.(We both trust God for His perfected miracle, we feel led to take this step as time is running out as well as our personal resources. Please in whatsoever way you could help Caroline, please do.)

We have set up an account at GTB bank for those that would simply like to help out through funds transfer. All donations in cheque may be written in favour of "save Caroline Johnson" GTB 206-179570-110

May the good Lord stir your hearts to help and hold back the forces of sickness from you and your family. Amen.

Caroline before *(sadly the photos are not showing but she is just s pretty pretty woman and I loved how she captured the plight of UJU on Heaven's Gate! DNW)*

Caroline today *(this picture has ABSOLUTELY NO RESEMBLANCE to the real Caroline! DNW)*

If you can, please help.

May God be with her

Please just see this a sowing a seed into her life and into yours as well. As we help this dear woman, may the Lord keep such away from our homes and families in Jesus Name. Amen! DNW

Shalom!

Monday, 17 August
God Is Just A Whisper Away

I am still pouring sweat as I type this but had to get it out of my system. Indeed our God is just a whisper away. Today I experienced this truth in living colour. There I was, one of the zillions of others at this embassy! I tell you, I would rather have been a million trillion miles away but how for do. One has got to do what one has got to do for one's children! Back to my point.

So many things could have gone awry today. Some my fault (forgot my yellow card!) Some no fault of mine whatsoever (the ATM/POS machine did not work!) But I am here to tell you that each and every time I just breathed a prayer to God to have mercy on me. I told Him how He was worthy and how my life was a testimony of how merciful He is. AND I had no problem with this continuing to be so at all. And I am here to tell you that God answered each and every one of those whispered prayers. I thank Him from the bottom of my heart. He has been so good to me. To my family. So faithful. I do not know how to thank him. But I shall continue to try. With every breath I take.

So you do not know how to pray? You may want to try whispering. It's a good place to start.

Shalom!

Tuesday, 18 August
If God said it, He meant it. He will do it

I have been meaning to share this for a while now but other stuff kept cropping up. But today, with all the other testimonies flying around, it just seems like the perfect day in the end.

I am not sure what God has in mind for me. All I know is that I have given him carte blanche over my life. Wherever He leads, I shall follow. Simple. Stress free and I do not need to think or over obsess about the matter. If God says it, I shall just do it. If He likes, he can sit by and let me fail. That would be HIS problem. And since I was young and now I am over 40, I have never known my God to have a problem! So nuff said on that matter.

Anyway, the above has not always been the case. I was running as far away from being of any use to God as possible. As far as I was concerned, the most I could do for God was manage to go to church, get married in a church, take my children to church (which was major considering MY parents never took me to church) and if possible, arrange it so some church or the other buried me. After all, I was not a BAD person per se. Although it appears a number of people believed I required salvation cos all through life especially in University, there were people who would try to drag me to one SU meeting or the other. I went along and always managed to 'escape' before every thing became 'spooky'.

After my Masters in UI, I came to Lagos to look for work. I was living with an Uncle of mine. My favourite one actually (no offence to the others, love you too but you know how it is). Anywho, he used to run a house fellowship in our house and one day, Lord have mercy, the house fellowship leader 'saw' a vision about me. He said he saw me standing before a crowd of people, preaching the word of God. Just close your eyes and imagine my reaction. Me? Miss God-just-dont-try-me-i-know-you-are-up-there-and-almighty-and-stuff-but-please-just-leave-me-alone? Preaching the word of God? Yeah right!

But ladies and gentlemen, I am here to tell you that God meant it! I stand to testify that more than 18 years later; Gods word over my life came to pass. In spite of ME. On the 12th of August, 2009, for the first time in my LIFE, I stood before a group of women and tried to get them to choose to be a woman of God ON PURPOSE. God helped me cos I know that could NOT have been me that day. But that's another story entirely. So what am I trying to say to y'all? Simple. IF God has told you something directly or indirectly. If He has spoken a word over your life or some situation you are facing. Trust me, it shall come to pass. Sure enough. Why? Cos God is not a man that lies. IF He says it, He means it and He WILL do it.

Shalom!

Wednesday, 19 August
Being Like Christ... A Good Place to Start

I do not know about you but am feeling sort of 'urgent' about life. Like 'Mistress Mortality' has gotten all dressed up and come to live in my house. I know am not THAT old that I should be obsessing about death but I also know that I DON'T KNOW what God's deadline for me is. Yes, I do pray for a long life and left to me I will be at all the 3 weddings of my progeny. And all the first 3 naming ceremonies at least. Oh and of course, before all that, all the 3 graduation ceremonies. Like any other mother, I want to be around and healthy enough to fully participate and comprehend what is going on in the lives of my children till they have children of their own.

But what IF THAT IS NOT GOD'S PLAN FOR ME? If you look at the life of Jesus Christ, he only lived 33 years on this earth and look at the impact he had, IS STILL having. Why? Well I believe it was cos he purposed in his mind to do his father's will. He did ONLY what God told him to do. All that Jesus Christ did pointed back to God. His life was a pure and unadulterated reflection of His Father in Heaven. His thoughts, his words, his deeds, they all were in line with the will of God. Are mine? Are yours? Are we living to please God? Or just ourselves? Fear not, no show of hands required.

As it is now, I have outlived Jesus Christ by 8 years now. If I die tomorrow, would I have lived a life as legendary as Christ? True, I probably cannot do that but God will not be upset with me for trying my best. Even Jesus said it himself that I would pull off greater stunts than he did. Imagine that. Imagine the potential in me as I sit here on this PC. Yet, if care is not taken, I shall die without using this potential. How miserable!

I was singing along with my buddy Kirk today and I agree with him about something and I think it is a good place for us all to start. A place to begin making our lives impactful in this generation. It is in the place of trying to be the Jesus Christ that people see. The truth of the matter is, we might just be the only Jesus Christ some people would ever get to see. You know, if I could just do that in the coming days and weeks and months to come, I think I would be making some headway on living a fruitful life to the glory of God. I would be on my way to being a true woman of God. I will be on the right path towards fulfilling my *numero uno* purpose.

Yes...I think I might have something here.... being the Jesus Christ that the world sees...every day, in every way. It sounds easy but I am wise so I know it will not be a piece of cake. NEVERTHELESS, being the desperate woman that I am for all things Christ like, I am gonna give it my best shot.

Join me? Hope so!

Shalom!

Thursday, 20 August
The White Horse Came Calling

.... And took my loved one away. Yes, I am beyond grief stricken but there is something I must share with who ever reads this today. I really want to just lie down and have a good good cry but this seems a bit more constructive. For one, already done that. For two, I have two 'cry police' around me aged twelve and five. One will join me in my tear fest. While the other will yell 'mommy, DON'T cry! It's OK!' Neither is pleasing to me right now. Regardless of how cute it sounds.

So I have come here to 'breathe' and to share. Its a very short sharing though and then am going for a walk. I believe there is a lesson to be learnt from all that God brings my way. The loss of a loved one is no different.

So what was I meant to learn from the white horse coming down here and whisking my person away? Dear Lord, what is all this about? What would you have me learn from this earth shattering experience? One that I was not in any way prepared for when I spoke to my person just last Friday? What could I possibly learn from this? You want to know what God said? He said to me, loud and clear:

'Be READY like he was ready'.

So dear one reading this right now, please live your life now so that YOU will be ready when your white horse comes a-calling. The only thing sadder than losing a loved one is not being sure where they were going to end up. Please live so your loved ones will be sure. Please. Losing you will be sad enough as it is.

So for me, I am drowning in waves of grief but every once in while I come up for a gulp of joy filled air when I remember that my loved one was for sure HEAVENBOUND. Glory to God!

Shalom!

Friday, 21 August
Let's Not Forget This Time Around

I am extremely aware of how much love is flowing in my family at the moment. Its so nice and then again it is so sad. Why? Cos we just lost one of ours. Why does this happen? Why do we all of sudden remember to love one another and reach to each other better in times of grief. Actually, I sort of get it. At times like this you want to just reach out and hug someone and let him or her hug you back. You are crying inside and you want someone to reach down into your soul and heal the gut-wrenching ache away from your breaking heart. In return, you do same for them. So here we all are in my family at the moment reaching out and expressing love for one another in any which way we can.

This is not a bad thing at all. And you know what? I am not even surprised in this case cos this particular guy was so caring. He cut across all the generations in our family and left his imprint on us all, from the oldest to the youngest. So yes, am not surprised that even in death, he is managing to foster family love and joined-up-ness. But people of the world, may I say one thing today? OK, two things actually.

One, lets not wait till someone dies before we express how we feel about the people in our lives. I have made some hard commitments to myself about this and I have mapped out some hard-core actions to be taken in this regard. There are some many so many things I would have loved to tell my person. I never did and I never can (actually I believe he can still read so I still will sha!) However, I would have loved to tell him while we were both still on this side of eternity. What am I saying? Pick up the phone. Send that email. Make that drive over there. Send that SMS. Go tell that person, those people, that you love them. Tell them how much they mean to you. How they have impacted your lives. Please do it. Today. Now. Yes, NOW!

Secondly, mi familiglia, my peeps, the people that the 'Crown has used wealth to beat' we have lost one of the 'love' kingpins of our family. If there was one thing he showed us it was how to love and care for people. And how to love God most of all. Right now, he is inspiring a lot of outpouring of love amongst us. That's fantastic. Let's keep it rolling rolling. Don't let it die off as time begins to heal our wounds. Cos the truth is that time will do that. Soon, the pain will not be so sharp anymore. So today, while it still bites, make a note to tell someone in the family you care and appreciate them. He never forgot us, was always reaching out to us...

This time, let us too, in remembrance of him, not forget ourselves, let us keep on loving one another *tangibly*

Shalom!

Friday, 22 August
Taking A Break

Breaks are good. Sometimes we need to take breaks. Coffee breaks. Lunch breaks. Power nap breaks. Even grief breaks. Yes, today am taking a break from my grief. I have jumped out of my mind and faced my body and told myself to let it go for a while. Let the sadness go, just let it slide.

I am a wise woman and I tend to obey my inner voice more these days. It comes with age. Mature ears are able to block out all the juvenile noise and tune in to the voice within. The voice of reason. The voice of a force higher than I. The voice of God. Yes, I like to listen to my God. And today, He made me change the channel. There are so many channels to my life right now but I managed to pause at a good one today. The channel that was showing my older son getting ready to go off to A level school.

I must be dreaming it cos I still remember pushing that child out into this world. Was that not just yesterday? Was he not just starting playgroup just now. Tell me I am dreaming cos I am sure it was just this morning that my mom-in-love and I stood crying at the window of his playgroup class. I am not sure which was sadder. Two women crying or the poor 2 year old child crying as he adapted to the reality that was school. Alas, I am not dreaming and those visions are beyond old as that 2 year old is now a semi demi grown man. Yep! My son is leaving the nest for the very first time. He is so happy and excited that all my mommy fears and anxieties melt away just watching him and listening to him go on about the school and his new friends (ones he made during all the interviews). Indeed, I am blest. To give birth to a child, have him survive the first 15 years of life and excel academically is not a given AT ALL. I bless the name of God for it is not to him that wills or to him that runs but to the LORD that shows mercy. God has indeed been merciful to me and my MGM.

So today as I took a break from the pain of losing a good man, I can rejoice in the Lord cos right before my very eyes another good man is in the making. Yes, my son is about to launch into another phase of his life. One that will surely, by the grace of God, prepare him to be a very good man after God's own heart. In Jesus Name. Amen!

And I use my son as a point of contact to all the sons of anyone reading this right now. May your sons too be sources of blessing to you all. May your baby sons live long to the glory of God. May God's hand of favour and protection be upon all the sons in your family. May your sons be filled with the spirit of God, the Spirit of excellence! May they all have the mind and stature of Jesus Christ. In Jesus name. Amen! As the Lord lives, all our sons will be wonders to their generations! Amen!!!!

Shalom!

Sunday, 23 August
My Uncle Abiye!

My Uncle Abiye!

The very first time I met you, I was about 8 years old. I opened the door and there you were! This tall, funky looking guy in blue dungarees, a pair of elevator platform boots, and a red handkerchief tied round your neck (I can't remember what colour shirt you were wearing but I know it was loud to match everything else!) To top it all, you had long permed hair and the longest fingernails I had ever seen in my life! And as far as I was concerned, you were the coolest guy I had ever laid my eyes on in real life. As if you couldn't get any cooler, I looked down from the balcony of our flat to see what car brought you and believe it or not, there parked in our compound was the biggest Harley Davidson bike I had ever seen. My Uncle Abiye was one of the biker boyz of the University of Ife. I know, knowing him today, you will never believe it. My Uncle, a rough rider! *Na wa*! I was trying to share the above memory with Moni, your daughter, my cousin during her recent and first trip to Nigeria since she left age 3. She just stared at me with her mouth wide open in utter disbelief at what I was describing. Hmmmm, yes, Uncle changed a lot over the years. For the better. Yes, he just got better.

I believe we had a special bond just like the one you had with my mother (in fact she was the only one able to convince you to get rid of that death trap of a bike! And you named your first daughter after her) and over the years, you were a constant in my life. I looked up to you and in some ways I wanted to be like you. You studied Modern Languages at Uni-Ife. I wanted to do same but Jamb score *no gree* so I settled for French at another university in the South South. You loved to write and here I am a blog junkie! So the fact that I love to write too is pretty much established. You were always there to congratulate me and be proud of me for every achievement, every milestone. I remember my mom used to always tell me that you were her favourite brother in law. As I grew up and began to experience your love and concern myself, I soon understood why. You were a loyalist to the core. You didn't care what we did or did not do, your belief in us was always rock solid. I remember all your letters to me as I grew up. 'Hi Mum!' would always be the opening line. I never really asked you why you called me that. Who cares? I loved it. It made me feel special. Sadly, as I grew older and got married, this term of endearment changed. You gave me other new ones like 'Madam Ajala, the Traveller' to 'Mama Akan' to ''Dear Beloved' and so on and so forth.

In our family, you were a quiet mover and shaker; a bridge. Many people will not know how often you helped out, reached out to members of our family. But I know cos I was usually the middleman. I used to wonder how you managed it cos, at these times, I knew you were no longer working for the Nigerian Foreign Ministry. I knew things were not that easy for you over there in the US. BUT still you would always manage to send something. That's just the way you were. And I bless God for the wife God gave you. My Aunty Anire, what a woman! I am not sure how she tolerated me all the time I lived with them in Ikoyi. I was such a brat. Not a big one but a brat all the same. But as far as I know she never complained about me. And if she did, my Uncle never let on. I remember some years back talking to my Aunty and actually apologising for all my rubbish behaviour while I lived with them. She just laughed. Yes, that's just the way she is too. Tolerant, Loving and Forgiving.

You had the best sense of humour. I just loved how you would say the craziest thing with the most deadpan look on your face. Everyone would be cracking up and you would be there looking so innocent as if 'what's funny?'. Yes, in your hey days you were wild and one thing is for sure, when you gave your life to Christ, you did it with the same amount of fire as you rocked your life before. It was an all or nothing situation with you, your Christian walk. There was absolutely no grey areas. Nope, you were clear on that.

To me, Uncle Joe, (yes at some point, I began calling you Uncle Joe along with everyone else) you personified what a true Christian man should be in all your roles. I will miss all your e-mails! Oh Uncle! I will miss you so much. Losing you is one of the saddest things that has happened to me in my entire adult life. I cannot even begin to imagine what your brothers, my dad and my uncles are going through right now. You were more or less the youngest. This is not the way things are meant to go but like they say, the good ones die young. I cannot begin to understand what your other nieces and nephews, my cousins; my siblings are feeling at the moment. I know you so I know that each of them also will have a memory to hold on to. No matter how old. No matter how young. Oh Lord have mercy, what could be going on in the minds of your children? I cannot even go there. Too hard. Too sad. Especially cos I too know what it is to lose a parent...too early.

I am marinating in sadness and the only thing that gives me a sliver of joy is the fact that I know without a shadow of a doubt that you are resting with our Lord and Saviour Jesus Christ. I know God will reward your labour of love towards me and mine by keeping Aunty Anire, Moni, Tutu and Ope in the secret place of His tabernacle now and always in Jesus Christ's name. Amen!

Uncle Abiye. Uncle Joseph, I am so sorry for rambling like this. And I do hope this has not been too mad a letter for you to read. I really just want to let you know how much I love you. Thank you so much for helping me even after you died. Yes, the news of your death broke the 3-month cold war that was going on between my dad and I. Remember I ranted about it in a mail I sent to you recently. Typically you ignored all my rants and promised to help ease the situation once your book sales took off. I felt so lame once again cos you did not even try to take sides. You just went straight for the solution and how you would play a role in it. Imagine that. Still being a bridge.... even in death.

Yes, I love you. Your whole family loves you. And to live in the hearts of those who love you is not to die. So you are not dead. You have just gone on to rest with your Maker till we come join you.

So, see you later Uncle. See you later!

A bientot!

Tuesday, 25 August
How Would You Live If…

You had just a few hours to live?

Walk with me a minute. Let's imagine that you find out you have only 36 hours to live. Don't mind me, I could have chosen 24 hours or even 48 but I just felt like being odd so I chose 36 hours. Yes, you go to the Doctors or your favourite Woli and you are told that the 'light out' bell is going off for you in one and half days. What would you do? How would you live those last hours?

Hmmm, let's see if we can do a mock up

Moment of discovery: You faint/Cry/Scream/Stare in shock at the bearer of these evil tidings and try look into his/her eyes to see if this is just some nasty joke. It is not. He/She is dead serious. Pardon the pun!

30 minutes after Discovery: You are still sitting there in the doctor's office or the Woli's church in a daze. Mind you, the clock is ticking. Yep! Time waits for no man, even one that has just 35 hours and 30 minutes left to live.

1 hour later: You manage to get up and decide to go and inform your significant other or others. You all wail some more together. They ask God why? They suggest seeking second opinions. Then you all wail some more. In short, you are just there wailing away precious time. Understandably so anyway. But still time is a-wasting…

OK, let's stop imagining now. Mainly cos I have no plans of taking you on an hour by hour account of the life of this person but please, am I being silly to wonder why this person just does not get on with the act of living, albeit for just another 36 hours. What's my point exactly?

Not sure really but am just a bit confused with people today. Everyone has been sending me such comforting words assuring me of the fact that my dead uncle is resting with our father in heaven. Yes, I know that and it is one of the things that makes me feel a tad better. My confusion lies in the fact that if indeed we believe this to be true and we are in fact living our lives as real Christians then please someone tell me why, the above information of one's imminent departure from this earth to go and meet our Maker is SUCH MIND BLOWINGLY EARTH SHATTERING NEWS.

Is it that we just say we believe in Heaven but we really don't. Or we believe it but do not want to go there YET? Or is it (and I fear this is really the truth for many of us) that we do not want to die because we know we will not enter through the pearly gates? Cos we have not been 'walking our talk' so to speak. I don't know. I am just confused. It just seems that for people who claim to be living for a God we love, we don't seem to be in a hurry to go meet Him. Why now? Perhaps it is that we still have much work to do over here. I guess so and I have no issues with that. God knows how long each of us has. All I am saying is that while we do our best to live good lives here and enjoy all that God wants to give us for the time He has allotted to us, we should always bear in mind that THIS life is just temporary. This is not really where we belong. We are passing through. So THAT time WILL come when we will have to leave this earth and go home. It is up to you to decide if you want that home to be breathtakingly wonderful or teeth gnashingly horrible. Blazingly hot or pleasantly perfect. Joy-filled or Pain-full. Smiles or tears.

You decide that by how you live. Its that simple. OK I agree, sometimes it is not that simple. That's why it has to be a Grace-assisted. Tap into the grace. We all need it to enable us 'walk our talk'. So that when death comes a- knocking we do not resemble the totally confused person we tried to imagine at the beginning of this blog! Actually, I wonder why he was not chuffed a little. At least he was getting advance notice!

Shalom!

SEPTEMBER

Friday, 04 September
East, West, Home Really IS Best!

Was it just seven days? It feels longer to me. I loved South Africa. Nice place. Met some really nice people especially the cab driver that took us round most of the time. He was nice even if a tad too chatty. Sometimes you just want to be left alone with your thoughts you know? He had no sensors active on this point and not even guarded silence seemed to put him off. Yes, SA was a fun place to be for seven days but not sure I could have taken it for more time than that.

Hold on! Don't get me wrong. Nothing to do with the place or the people. I had gone there to drop my son off in school and that was mega hard for me. Especially cos I had to make like it was not. I had to be the 'Man' so that my son could in turn be the 'Man'. We had struck a deal. I would not launch any water works so he in turn will not embarrass himself by keeping me company!

All is well that ends great. He settled right in to the regime of the school and I know that God has launched him off into a new interesting, eye opening, and horizon expanding experience of a lifetime. We went to say good-bye to him the day before we left for home and he introduced me to some of his new friends. Such a lovely mix of young people from Kenya, Mozambique, Namibia. How awesome is that? So I am happy. So OK I spent almost all of the nights crying all the tears I could not get a chance to cry in the daytime cos the 'cry police' were still on active duty you see. So at night, when the moon came out and the eyes of the cry cops had succumbed to slumber, I sat at the desk in the lovely room we were staying in and stared at my face in the mirror as I wept to my heart's content. Yes, I missed my son but when I remembered that I would get to see him at Christmas, then I switched my grief channels and cried for my uncle. Him, I don't get to see at Christmas. He had gone home to be with the Lord. To see him, I need to make sure my heavenly visa is always valid.

So that's what I have been up to the last seven days. Its good to be home. Its good to belong to a God that bears one up on eagle's wings safe and sound from point A to B. I don't know about you but when I am sitting in a plane zillions of miles above the earth, all the technology holding that plane up does zilch for me. I need something...someone more substantial to hold on to. And that's God oh! Yes, he calms my nerves. There is nothing like divine protection. Nothing. And you know what? East, West or even South of Africa is good but my home is better. I am happy to be back.

Shalom!

Saturday, 05 September
Please Come Spook Me!

My mother died 23 years ago and for most of the first 5 years I prayed and prayed she would appear to me in dreams and visions. At some point I even got mad at her for not doing so. Did she not love me enough to come spook me? How come I hear stories about other people 'seeing' their loved ones in dreams and stuff? Did it mean my mom did not love me enough to want to come spook me? I eventually got over that phase and once I do remember actually dreaming about her and she was teaching me how to carve a chicken. Hmmm Trust Mumsie, she had to make her apparition a practical lesson in home keeping.

But you know I really would not mind being spooked by the ghost of my mum and now my uncle. I actually welcome it. I would love for you both to appear to me once in a while and reassure me or something. Yes, I would love to see 'dead people'. You two. I hate to whine and whinge but if you could take time out from being with Jesus and come show your faces to me, I would be ever so grateful. I promise not to be scared. You are two of my favourite people and you spooking me would be very welcome. Honest.

So Mom, I am sure you are so pleased to see Uncle Abiye and both of you are busy catching up and all but do spare a grieving soul a minute. Please come appear to me. I wont be scared. I won't cry. I will really just love to see you both one more time. Once in a while. So do come spook me. I promise I won't be scared.

Sunday, 06 September
I'm So Spectacularly…Blue

I hate to admit but am actually sort of enjoying being blue. It's warm and comforting and is trying to snuff the joy out of me. Arrrghhh! I know I should kill it before it kills me but alas right now, I lack the impetus. The will. The desire. The energy. As we say round here, *'I don tire o jare'*. Maybe when I wake up in the morning, I will be able to dip deep into my being and throw off this designer jacket with the misery detail and anger buttons! And I am sure it is made of real fur too, which is double evil. I would love to put a 'Lol' right there but that would be lying. Cos am not about to laugh at all.

So here I am 'the lady singing the blues' and am sure as you are reading, you are trying to fathom why this is so. What is wrong with DNW? Now, that is a brilliant question and the answer is even more so. And I would love to share but since I really do like you for coming to visit my blog I shall spare you the details of it all. It's a Pandora's box of emotions, feelings, situations, actions, non-actions, etcetera, etcetera that it is best I keep the lid firmly down.

At times like this, there is only person to turn to and that is the ONE who made the crazy, mixed up, sometimes cool, sometimes nerdy, hot tempered, funny, mixed up…oops said that already, person that I am. If He does not get me, then I am sunk. But as He would have it, He does get me. Better than I get my self. Yes, so rather than bore you or scare you with my stuff, I am off to talk to God. He knows best. And the best part is, His services are free. No shrink fees to be paid!

Shalom!

Monday, 07 September
September – My 'Celebrating Family' Month

I made a promise to myself when my Uncle died last month. I said, never again will I be caught unawares by death anymore. What do I mean by that? It's like this. I never really got a chance to tell my Uncle how I felt about him. Now he is gone. And all I can do is write him letters, tell anyone who cares to spare me a moment or two what he meant to me and light a candle for him on the anniversary of his death every month (yes another promise I made which I will BGG keep). But the thing is I had ample time to tell him all of the while he was alive and I missed all those chances. Not again. Never again.

So now, I still have family alive today. Some of them I know a whole lot and have a whole lot to say to them. Some of them, well, not too well and can probably not say much and that's fine. But for those who are close to me and with whom I have shared memories no matter how small. I plan to tell them and tell them NOW what they mean to me. How I feel about them. For some, it might be another long letter. For others, it might just be quick short note. The length should not be relevant but the contents. So *Mi Familigia* wherever you are, I shall be in touch shortly. You will read it in your mail if I have it or it shall just be posted here on my blog so maybe someday, somehow, you will get to read it even if I am gone on to meet my mother and my uncle and my pastor and most importantly my Jesus.

There are some truths that are unshakeable and one of them is this - Family Is Important. Treasure Yours.

For now, Shalom!

Tuesday, 08 September
Ronkus Babes – The Lady With The beautiful Eyes

Hey Ronkus Babes!

Fear not, I am not picking you first cos I think you are going to die! God forbid. And neither am I for that matter by the special grace of God. The truth is this is going to be quite random. As the Lord leads so to speak. You came to mind quite quickly I guess cos you just had a birthday and I have just been gazing incredulously at your '29 on the 29th' birthday album. I see how grown up you are and I marvel. One cos that means times has flown so quickly and two, cos that means I too am getting old!!!! Lol! Once again I tell myself 'age is just a number' *o jare* and it is as they say 'mind over matter'. If you do not mind, it will not matter.

Why am I doing these letters to *'Mi Familigia*'? It's quite simple. I want to let my people know what I remember about them. I want you to know how I feel about you. What you mean to me. And I want to tell you all this stuff NOW. Not later. And trust me I am not being pessimistic or morbid nor am I trying to spook you. Far from it. I just want to say 'I love you'. It's that simple. And you are under no pressure whatsoever to reciprocate. Of course that would be fab but that's not what this is all about. This is about me letting the people in my life know what's in my heart and mind and soul about them! From time to time I will come and refresh the letters cos life does move on and we are making new memories every day.

So now that I have explained that out of the way, hmmm, let me see when was the first time I laid eyes on you! I think it was a foto actually that I say. My mom had gone to the UK and had visited you guys. I think it was someone's birthday. Could it have been Uncle Joe's? Anyway, if I cannot remember, neither will you cos you were much younger as I recall. But the foto I see is a group foto and everyone is standing round while the celebrant was cutting a cake. In my mind's eye I see this little girl looking sulkingly but ever so cutely into the camera. Already one could see that your 'eyes' would be the main focus of your face. They were and still are gorgeous. To this day, I can still hear your mother calling you '*Kongba* eyes! or '*Soyoyo*' cos you were so fair and lovely to look at. I think it drove you mad and that's what made it so funny every time! Lol! But it is true *sha*. You have the largest and loveliest eyes I know in our family. Actually apart from Tutu and his seemed to have gotten smaller as his macho-ness increased!

You were always so quiet though. Like a true Adef, you did not talk much but I could always feel your eyes following me around when ever I came to visit in Yaba or you guys came over to our place in Ijesha. And then once in a rare moment, you would smile...Ahhhh, what a sight to behold. I am so glad you are all grown up and do it more often. It really lights up that lovely face of yours. I remember before you went off to the UK back to school, you came to spend some time in our place at Tafawa Balewa. You were so easy to have around cos you just minded your business, reading or watching telly quiet as a mouse. I really like you and the girls cos for one, you always laughed at my dry jokes and I loved to hear you laugh so I always tried to crack more and more horrible jokes. Gosh! I am sure you guys were tired of me.

Like I said, I am doing this just so that you will know that I love you deeply and even though we see rarely and talk ever rarelier (just pretend it is an actual English word!), I care plenty about you and all my other cousins out yonder in diaspora. It would be nice to sit down and gist and chat about this and that and nothing at all but as time and distance may not permit that, this here blog is dedicated to you!

To letting you know that I am proud to be your cousin. I am proud of the woman you have become and are still becoming. I am proud that you are a Christian and know what's up. I am super proud that you are waiting for the right man to come into your life. I get the impression that you will not settle for less than the best as God ordains it. And that is mighty mighty wise. If there is one thing you MUST never be is desperate (well only like me, for Jesus Christ *sha*!) but not to marry. *Lailai*! I am praying for the veil to fall of the eyes of the mighty good man (MGM) that God has ordained for you. Sometimes, the enemy covers their eyes so that they cannot see the Ruths that God has kept for them. So I know that today, that veil of covering is falling off the eyes of your

Boaz and he will begin to shine his eyes now now and he will see you in Jesus name. Amen! I cannot hear you!!!!!! *Eh hen*, that's better. You need to be shouting the 'amen' in vernacular. Not in Dublin phonetics! Lol!

My prayer for you is that you will become ALL that God has destined you to become. You will be a woman after God's own heart. A blessing to your husband and a mother whose children will be made for signs and wonders in Jesus name. Amen! I pray that God will ring fence you now and always. That He will hide you in His secret place forever and that as you make up your mind to serve and obey God 200%, you will continue to eat the good of the land in Jesus name. amen! You will not die but live to declare the works of the Lord in the land of the living. That God will bless you with a long life of contentment and fulfilment and you will see your children and your grand children and your great grand children in Jesus awesome and peerless name! Amen!

I also pray that you will always remember that I, your cousin *ni tooto* loves you. That you can and must call me if you need a listening ear. As you well know, I was not the wisest of young married women (or actually I hope you do not remember me running to your house from my matrimonial home and then being promptly sent right back a day later! Your mom was something else!) but I have learnt some hard lessons along the way and I pray that none of you, my sweet younger ones have to travel that same road again. Of course you will travel some new ones of your own but what's the point in me being foolish if you cannot learn from me???? You catch my drift? So call on me or mail me or sms me. These days there are so many ways to get across. So promise me you will use one of them if you need to talk. As the song goes, 'If you need someone to talk to ya! Call me!'

And finally, may the Light of God shine continually and ever so brightly through your lovely eyes, the windows into your soul! I hope this meets you well and I hope that it makes you feel chuffed cos that's what writing it has done for me. There is nothing like sharing love, it warms the heart and lifts the soul!

Mwaah!

Wednesday, 09 September
Ekaette

It's funny that as I started this, this is the name that comes to mind. I never call you this at all. It's actually Nana that calls you by this name (she would just say 'Eka' though). I usually just call you by your English name with an exaggerated drawl. I picked you next just cos. Well just cos. You are my sister in law or sista in love as I have recently picked up from another sista divine. I have blogged about my in laws before and I think it is quite clear I have been blest as per the family I married into. Yes, indeed God just knew that with me and all my issues, I did not need any added in-law wahala! So he sent me the Nelson family. And you, Audrey, in your own way have made that true.

I remember the first time we met. I believe I was serving in Calabar and you came to do 'the Lord knows what'. I think you were on holiday or something but all I know is that you and my other brother in love, Perry and his then girl friend, Nnena and Jerry maybe came to see me where I was serving. Mind you, I might be getting all this wrong and we had actually met earlier but this is what sticks for me. The visit was over and you were all going back to your Uncle's house I guess and we were all gisting as we walked down the lane of the Army Barracks towards the main gate. You were wearing a long skirt and blouse and had tied your scarf hausa style. Funny what the mind retains. In my head, this was my first real sighting of you even though I had seen you loads of times but just in photos.

The early years of my marriage were rocky and sadly you witnessed and sometimes got caught up in all the *melée*. I felt sorry for you at times cos it really was not your *wahala* but you would always try to help. It just was not fair *sha* and I would usually feel bad and sorry for you. But at other times, my word. I was so jealous of you. Yep! I actually quite disliked you cos in my messed up and immature mind, your brother loved and loves you so much and I wanted him to love me too JUST THE SAME WAY. Crazy huh? Even saying it now makes me feel so naked but truth must be told. You were all the things I was not. You spoke your mind all the time. I just let my feelings fester. You had what

I considered to be wonderful relationship with your mom. My mom had upped and died and left me. Sheesh you would think it was her fault. And mind you, your mom was doing quite a good job of making sure I didn't feel like a motherless child. But you know, when the mind wants to mess with you. It messes with you real good!

But you know, I just could not understand what on earth you both could sit in your room for ages talking about on and on and on. Lol! Boy was I just a fool in those days. Anywho, I have over the years gotten over all of my mixed up emotions about my mgm and his relationship with his family. You now as you grow up and come to a better understanding of yourself; you are able to see things from a different perspective. Thank God! To be honest, I think you won me over when you never ever complained all those months you became our 'by force' nanny when I did not have one and had to go to work. I left AK with you for God knows how many months. And I loved you for it cos you did not have to do it. You had your own life and were looking for a job and planning your future. You did not come to our house to be the nanny! But you did it and you never complained. At least not to me.

I was happy for you when all your plans to go to the US fell in place cos I felt your frustration when no job seemed to be in the offing after all the interviews. I still smile when I remember you recounting some of the experiences. I cannot begin to describe how hard I laughed when I found out you were marrying your hubby. And I am sure you know why. I have never heard so many 'no, its not like that' in my life! But time has proven, it was and is a good match. I also still remember that humongous white teddy one of your pretenders gave you one valentine's day or was it your birthday. I believe AK inherited that and then passed in on to Ima who I think was actually scared of it at first. It was that big!

Distance has been an issue since then cos the US is not just next door you now but still I have sort of always known that should I need you, I could come calling. At one of the lowest times in my life, you stood by me thousands of miles away and you may not know it but it helped.

You are smart cos I don't remember you ever bad mouthing the parties involved and I loved you for that.

I remember when I came to have Aniekan and you were feeling poorly. I remember you driving me all the way to the shops to do my shopping even though you were not at your best. I will never forget that. As you got a bit better, you would spend time with Nana and I in the kitchen telling us stories from work. My favourite till this date is the 'Pencil and your Boss's head' story. Sometimes, I had to hold myself back from laughing out loud cos you just kept telling me the same stories over again. It was hilarious. Especially cos you would always start by saying ' I don't know, I have probably told you this story before!' Of course, I would just smile and let you ride on. You are one helluva of storyteller!

But you know when my favourite time with you was? When you visited Nigeria for the first time ever since you left. Remember the hours we spent jisting in the salon while you were getting you 'do' did? I loved that time and will cherish it for life. I cannot even remember all that we talked about but I just know I was at peace with the world and had no care on my mind. Who says that mindless chatter is not good for the soul.

I am so proud of all that you have achieved. Leaving your good job in a bank to go back to school to study something so totally different from your first line of study. All the reading and all those medical exams. I am amazed and thank God for blessing the work of your hands. I thank God for the hubby he gave you and the children he has blest you with. You had a goal and worked towards it with such focus and I marvel all the time and relish telling the testimony to people. In short, my dia sista in love. I am happy we are family via me marrying your brother. I am proud of all you have done, you and Lolade. I pray that God will ring fence you all in Jesus Name. I actually believe the sky is just the beginning for you cos you are a beautiful, smart woman and once you decide what you want, you go for it. At least this is my impression. Just move as close to God as you possibly can and hide your family in His care. As for me, I am here and am looking forward to seeing what you set your mind on doing next!

God bless you Audrey. Mwaah!

P. S. It just occurred to me you might now know what this is all bout. In brief. September is my family month. I am writing members of my family that have made even the smallest impact in my life. It is sort of in honour of my Uncle Joe. Him, I did not get a chance to tell. I shall not be caught unawares again. And no, I am not saying you are about to die! God forbid. Neither am I by God's grace. But, you know we never get round to expressing our feelings and gratitude to the people that matter to us and I think that's important. So I may need more than one month and that's fine but I aim to make sure that those who mean something to me know about it.

My prayer is that we live many more years and I can have many more memories about you. That would be fantastic. All I will have to do is come update this here letter. Love is evergreen and so is this my blog in your honour.

Thursday, 10 September
Mummy Silifa – My Aunt of Inestimable Value.

This is going to be abit dicey cos I cannot imagine how you are going to get this but I trust that my dia 'Banco' will find a way to get this across. Mummy Silifa (as my last born calls you), Hmmmmm, I am not sure I can actually put into words what you mean to me. When I was much younger I was your little handbag. I would go everywhere with you. You were my mother's baby sister and you lived with us most of the time. In fact, I think you were to her what Sola is to me. When Mom and Dad lived in Kano, you were there with them. When they moved to the States, you went to live with them there. I still remember a little how they used to tell of how you boarded the plane to the US unable to speak a single word of English! Thank God you did not end up in Mexico!

I don't remember a whole lot about you from our lives in Tallahassee but there is not one part of my life in Nigeria that can be written about that can exclude you! Aunty Silifa. What a gem. You were and still are so so pretty and I remember whenever we went out, we would never go the whole way without some car stopping and offering you (and me) a ride. Men were hot for you and I got to get all sorts of treats from your many pretenders! lol! Now that I think of it, you were probably using me as an alibi of some sorts! Lol!

Do you remember all those lovely art works you used to do when we lived in the states? You are so gifted and I think my dad still has some of them hanging in the house till this day. My favourites are the peacock and the lovely picture of the African Jesus Christ hanging on the cross. Anyway, you channelled your creativity into hair dressing eventually and opened up your own salon. Silkcare Hairdressing Salon. It was in Maryland and the highlight of most of my weekends and primary school holidays was going to stay with Aunty Silifa! I used to love standing around the salon watching you and your girls fix hair.

I remember travelling home for your wedding and being one of the bridal train. I remember till this day, the *ankara* we wore and how I struggled to walk in the *iro* and *buba* I wore. It was my first time of ever going to the village and my first time of ever tying an *iro* round my waist! Both experiences were quite unnerving to say the least! But what I remember most is how beautiful you looked. I am till this day quite chuffed when I remember how people used to say I looked like you.

How I wish you life's story could have been as pretty but indeed you have endured some hard times but I admire you so cos you are a survivor. NO matter what life has thrown your way, you have stood up to it. Mom was always so protective over you I know how eager she was to see you have your first child. And I remember how devastated you where when she passed on before Banco was born. I have never seen anyone express grief the way you did that day in Calabar. Never. Till this date, I know this is one of the most painful parts of your life. I know. And I agree with you. Its mine as well. But hey look, we are still here and I am sure Mom is happy to see that Banco is such a guy and doing so well in school and that you, in spite of all, are such a rock for me and her other children. I am quite sure you would tear a tiger apart if it means protecting any of us. You are so committed to our well being and if you have spent thousands of hours praying for yourself, then I am sure you have spent double that time praying for me and my siblings. That is just the way you are.

Aunty, for all your love and concern over the years. I thank you. For all the trips across Nigeria to see me where ever I was, I thank you. Remember, even when I was graduating from school in Uyo, you travelled all the way from Ibadan to support me. And till today cannot understand why I decided to dye my hair purple to mark the event. Trust me, neither can I but it seemed a good idea at the time. Lol! When I was doing my Masters in Ibadan, your house was my weekend hideout from all the stress of that. You would take me to church and I learnt so much from going to church with you. It was a totally different experience but I loved it. The Head Pastor so impacted my life by her obvious dedication to God that I even mention her in my MA Thesis. Every time you took me to see her, she just always looked so peaceful, So connected to God. And even though I was still in my rah-reh days, I knew that when I started following God well well, that's how I wanted to be! Lol! Thank God for His mercies!

I do not think there is one single major move of my life you have not prayed and fasted over. Every step of my life, I would just have to call you and tell you about it to hear " *A fi sadura. Ko is problem. Baba a gbo ti wa'*. And you did put it to prayer and God did hear you. For indeed, I have had a good run on this life so far. It's not been all honky dory but I am without a doubt thoroughly blessed. I think my MGM realised quite quickly that you were the 'mom' he would have to deal with! In fact, I think one of the first family visits we made as a couple was to see you in Ibadan and you gave him a nice talk a.k.a. warning about him being nice to me or else...Lol!

I have three children and you have come to bath all of them. Apart from Nana, no other woman has come to stay with me for long periods. Giving up personal time and life to come and help me out. You are from such a different time and had a different way of doing things and handling situations and I remember so many times, I see you biting your lips cos you feel I should be doing something different. But in your wisdom, you always hold back. Always letting me be me in the hope that life would be my best teacher and that I would learn from my own mistakes. I love you for that. And yes, mostly, I have not turned out too badly even if I say so myself. Lol!

My prayer is that you will reap the fruits of all your labour of love in our lives and Banco's life too. I pray that you and Uncle Dapo will live long, happy lives in spite of all the enemy's plans. You are a beautiful, kind; caring soul and you deserve so much more out of life. God is not mean, I know He sees it and knows it. And best of all I know He will do it. Thanks for always being there to take care of Grandma for all of us. You are doing what I know mom would have been doing where she still alive. Thank you so much!

If I had a magic wand, I would wish for so many things for you. More children cos you loved us so much and I know you would kill for Banco. But God knows best. I would wish for loads and loads of money right now and set up one of the best salons in Ibadan just for you cos you are talented and have not yet had the chance to show it. This makes me feel so so bad and so so sad but I pray to God for the chance to still make this good for you. I would wave my wand over your head and restore you to 100% health. I would make you whole again. But no I do not have a wand but you know what I have? A mighty mighty All-powerful God. A truly wonderful God who is Omni-*gbogbonkan*. Yes and He that is God of ALL things can do all of the above for you!

So I leave you in his care and trust that He will continue to be merciful to you. I know you and deep down in your heart, all you want is for us all, your children, to be happy and content. And we are on our way, Aunty. So please relax and enjoy as best you can. By God's grace, the best is yet to come! In your life and in ours. I had to add that cos I know that if Sola, Tokunbo and I are not OK, you will not be either. That is just the way you are. You love us like we are yours. And trust me, we love your right back.

God bless you! *E pe fun wa* in Jesus Name! God keep you safe and sound now and always

I love you my Aunty of Inestimable Value!

Thursday, 10 September
There is No One Like Our Nana!

This is actually the second letter I wrote after I made up my mind to start doing these pseudo tributes. I was so frazzled at the time that the first two were direct letters to the people. It was like I NEEDED to let them know quick quick what I wanted to say. Now, they know and am at peace.

I decided to put it here cos I really want to keep all these love notes in one place and my blog is turning out to be one of my favourite places in the world to be. And maybe one day, I will do something with all these blogs, especially the ones on my family.........

Dear Nana

How are you? I trust that all is well with you and everyone over there. God has been good and we are all fine over here too. Apart from all the katakata in the banking industry from which God , in his mercy, has been shielding us as well, we are all doing great. Thank God. AK is great and off to school on Wednesday. Ima and Aniekan are fine too and will be back in school in the second week of September. I am also currently on vacation trying to get AK ready. Henry is fine and just got back from a business trip now now. So, to the glory of God, all is more or less fine.

Nana, am not sure if *awon* Lolade have heard or have told you. My uncle Joseph was shot fatally sometime last week. I am sure you remember him, My favourite Uncle who lives in Greensboro, NC. It is so sad and we the entire family are completely devastated. Especially after we just lost a young cousin earlier on this year. It has been so hard for me this year cos so many people seem to be dying around us. First my cousin, then Joe Placid, our friend from UniUyo, then Uncle Boy Blues and now my uncle. I am in a real state especially as I don't have a US visa and am going to miss the burial. But God is still God.

Why am I writing this letter to you. Well you see as God will have it I spoke to my uncle a week before he died and I am so thankful for that opportunity to hear his voice one last time but still I did not and cannot remember ever really telling him how much he meant to me. I felt so sad about that and have made up my mind that it will not be the case ever again. I am taking steps to make sure that everyone who means something to me knows it NOW. Yes, all the people who have made concrete differences in my life. People like you Nana, you must know that I love and appreciate you dearly.

Yes, no list of such people will ever be complete without your name on it. You are one of the human angels in my life and I could never ever thank you enough for the role your played in my life and the lives of the children God gave Henry and I. Till today, Ak and Ima still talk about you and I feel kind of sad for Aniekan cos he is the only one who has not really had a taste of the 'nana love'. I remember one of the first things you promised me when we met. That I would never have cause to say 'how i wish my mom was alive'. And you kept your promise. All in all, and in spite of the little spats we had now and again, you made sure that if I was ever sad about not having my mom around, it would not be because I lacked 'motherly' care and love per se. And for that I thank you from the bottom of my heart. I always tell people that God sent you to me for a reason. You were just a saint in disguise and sometimes I am sure Henry used to wonder if you were his mom or mine!!!!! I remember all the secret conniving and hiding to do this and do that so Henry will not know or find out. I also know you and the children had the same plans and tactics which you all used to hide stuff from me!!!!! Lol! (laughing out loud)

So Nana, as I do not want to make you read any long epistle, I just want to end this note by saying you will always be in my heart. I truly appreciate all you did for me, for always being there. For me, all in all, you were the quintessential mother in love. I love you from the bottom of my heart and my prayer is that you will live a long and healthy life to see ALL the fruits of your labour of love. And my aim is to find a way to remind you of this fact from time to time. But never again, will any of my loved ones take my by surprise again. No, by the grace of God! Never!

Mwaah!

This letter does not actually completely capture the role this woman played in my life. I remember my sister and I talking about it and we used to have a joke about it cos we were so sure she was not 'for real' or something. How could anyone be THAT nice and concerned? I talk about her some more in an earlier blog titled 'Rare Breed of In-laws' (http://diaryofadesperatenaijawoman.blogspot.com/2009/03/rare-breed-of-in-laws.html) which I wrote sometime ago. Some people are just angels walking around in people skins! She is one of them.

Thursday, 10 September
My Aunty, the Mamandant

This was my first letter out......I remember crying so hard when I was typing this cos it was right in the thick of hearing about my uncle. What a time. I still cry every time I think about him.... I know the tears will soon stop falling but the love I have for him, the way I miss him? That will never ever stop. All these letters are in your honour Uncle cos you were always one to stand for family.... In my own way, I am standing up for my family now... yes, standing up in love!

My Aunty!

You know this uncle's passing has hit us all so hard. But it is just like Uncle to still be working in my favour even in death. Yes, there is so much I would have loved to tell him but cannot really. But I will not make the same mistake again. And I am starting with you.

I am not sure there is any other female in my family I admire more. I don't want to write an epistle today, all I really want to say is THANK YOU. Thank you from the bottom of my heart for all you have been to me, all you have done for me, all the worry you have gone through for me and all the prayers you have said on my behalf. I thank you.

For all your clothes I stole and for all the bags I 'borrowed' from your wardrobe. For always being ready to rise up for me and go the next mile for me. One would have thought I was your daughter. Actually, I am your daughter as that is how you took Sola and me. I thank you.

Thank you for counselling me and teaching me in those early years of marriage and for dragging me back to my husbands house those times I ran to you. Thank you for not allowing the enemy to rob me of the joy of a good happy marriage. Thank you for helping become a better woman, wife and mom. I thank you.

Aunty mi, my dear Mamandant, I could go on and on but for now I will stop here. You are such an inspiration and I share your testimony with reckless abandon with those who I feel need to hear about being a strong woman of God. A mover and a shaker. I tell them about you. I tell them about your beautiful daughters and son. I tell of how you managed to move them all out in the nick of time as if you knew what was coming. But indeed, God has always got your back. He has always been on your side. Always. And we all, your children, basked in that abundant love.

Aunty, I love, honour and respect you for who you are to me. You are a strong pillar in our family and we all know it. I take time out this day, as I remember my Uncle whom I loved so much, to cherish you. I wish I could have told him too how I felt about him. But I thank God for the opportunity to tell you.

I can only thank you but I know my God will reward your labour of love towards me and all the rest of us in our family and beyond.

God bless you Aunty. God keep you . God shine His love upon you now and always in Jesus name. Amen! I look forward to a time when I will be able to truly truly thank you in kind. For now, please accept this my humble lover letter. You are truly a blessing to me and mine.

Yours ever so sincerely

Wednesday, 16 September
No. Not Really.

I honestly feel like going back to work should not be my reality. The dream that I was living when I was on holiday? Now, that should be my reality. Barring the death of my uncle and my first-born going off to school, it was heaven in a cup. And I sipped away blissfully. But like all good things, even a good cuppa a heaven must come to an end!

No, not really. That is the answer to the question you might be asking. The 'so are you getting over your Uncle's death? question. I am not sure I will ever truly get over that. I soothe myself by going to light candles on his memorial website every once in a while. It does help. So simple a gesture yet so powerful.

No not really. This is also the answer to your other question. The 'Is it getting easier not having your first born son in the house? That is for sure, not going to be easier anytime soon. I pass a jar of peanut butter in the stores and my eyes well over. He loves it you see, peanut butter and now so do I (not eating it, but just seeing the jars in stores) cos it reminds me of him. My first born son. He is having loads of fun and learning and meeting people so as a mother I have pushed my issues to the back burner and learnt to bask in the joy of being a mother whose child is well and safe even if he is not in my 'very before' as we say over here.

No, not really. Once again, this is the answer to your last question. The 'have you run out of relatives to honour on your blog? Please bear with me for it is true I have not posted any in a while but its not for lack of kin. More due to lack of zen. Yes, permit me to say that I have not had my inner zen or is it yen? In short, since I went back to work, I have not been able to crack out the inner peace I need to sit still at my beloved PC and blog to my hearts content. I miss it so but trying to remember what it is I am meant to do at work (yes, I actually had to think quite hard to remember the password to my PC!), is so hard right now that all cerebral energy is spent by the time I get home. This is not the kind of fatigue that my beloved blog can deal with. This kind needs one thing only. My bed!

And you know, if you are a mom in Naija that I do not get to get my bed that easily. There is homework and mgm meals and pretend trips to France to organize and of course how could I forget, there was the matter of the screaming yelling only princess I had to take in a mad panic to the Emergency Room after one of my wardrobe doors and the mirror on it decided to unhinge itself all over my two progeny. All I can say is 'In your face! Nick! Once again, you have failed. Me and mine have got angels on our shoulders!

So all in all, this short note (by my usual standards) is just to assure you that I am still here, madly, tiredly, happily, relievedly and thankful to Godly so. I will be back soon to hail some more kin and kith. Just bear with me for now…

Oh, before I go. I must share something with you: You have suffered enough. God says its time to settle you. So do not give up NOW. Just hold on. God is up to something. Trust me. I got this message in my mail this morning and I am hanging onto to it for dear life. Cos boy oh boy, do I need a Divine Settlement.

How about you?

Shalom!

Sunday, 20 September
Mi Padre – No One Like You

First of all let me just say it upfront now. There is NO way I can ever capture in this or any other blog what you mean to me. *Ko possible rara*. But I will try *sha*. My Papa! What a relationship we have. What a life we have lived! I hail you from the bottom of my heart. Cos wrong or right. Good or bad. Loud or quiet. One thing is for sure. You have ALWAYS got my back. You have always been there and I thank you for allowing me to know this for sure. Unquestionably.

My first memory of you is one of my childhood favourites. My brother and I are in the back of the car as it drives along under the moonlit skies of Tallahassee. We are going to pick mom up from work or school or something. And I am asking you, like I am sure I had asked you a zillion times before. 'Dad, is the moon following us?'. Lol! Every time, you would tell me that it was not but just looked like it was. Obviously I did not believe him! Lol! We would pick up mom and drive back home and for me; it was some sort of daily nocturnal adventure. I have memories of you going to work, dropping us off at the nannies house, taking us to school but I will not write much about all that. Yes, I would rather talk about how I was sure you were the Ruler of the whole world. Yes, from when I was 5 years old till the end of my teens, I was convinced you were the hottest male on planet earth. Now, its not like once I got to Form 4, you suddenly became ugly. No, let me explain. First of all, you were and (to be honest, you still are) such a handsome handsome man. And I was in love with you myself. And I was also in love with all the seniors in my school who oohed and ahhed when they saw photos of you in my albums. Lol! Yes oh, my school mothers were into you big time. To be honest, as I grew older and wiser, I realised this was a good thing and a bad thing. But we are not going there today.

I used to love going on the road with you. I remember once we went on a road trip and for the life of me, I cannot remember what we went to do in all the places we visited - Ado, Akure, Ikerre and Ibadan I think. For me, it was just fun. I do recall making the acquaintance, for the very first time, of one of the ugliest creatures I have ever met. Its some kind of awful grasshopper that looks like its wearing a masquerades' robe. It's not green but some irritating multicoloured mix. Yuck! Just thinking of it makes me slightly ill. Anyway, I remember you laughing at me cos I refused to get out of the car after that! I really planned to sleep in the car until you told me they go into hiding in the night. Phew! Travelling with you was fun back then especially cos my phobia of travelling had not set in. I guess I just felt safe like that with you at the wheel... I think my baby sister tasted a bit of this thrill with you as well. Cos she too has logged in a lot of road miles with you!....................

...I am back writing this after a 2-day break. The truth is this is a bit hard for me to write and my *ogboju* is not working at all. So, pardon me, but I must stop before I drown the keyboard with my tears. Writing this reminds me of my mom and then when I manage to get over that, it reminds me of my uncle.... and when I get over that, it makes me think about my brother and then how much I miss my sister. And when I run out of things to cry about, I just still cry tears of joy and gratitude for the life I have lived as your dota...I think I will give this a break for a while. I will come back and try to finish it later, hopefully.

For now, I do hope that at least you will know that I love you Papa, always have. Always will. A part of you lives on the inside of me. I know you did your best to be the best father in the world to us. Some things are just out of your control. What can a man do? I pray that God will keep you strong so that you can see the fruit of your labour in ALL your children...I must stop now... I must. This is such a happy blog.... but for some reason, it just makes me cry uncontrollably. So I give up.

Wednesday, 23 September
Not By Blood

Yes, we were not related by blood but I feel like her kin. Yes, she probably knew more about me than I knew about her but I still feel a strong connection to her somehow. Aunty Yinka, the lady who was ever smiling, ever ready to welcome us with a warm hug and a sincere 'how are you?' The fact that I was in the medical made it quite obvious how I was most of the time, or how one of the children was doing, but no matter how down I was feeling, Aunty Yinka always made me smile and feel cared for. And it only took her a minute or two to achieve this. Yes, in the time, that I would sign in the register, she made me feel like a loved child. Funny thing is that she made a whole lot of people feel the same way. What a beautiful loving soul. For real.

Yes, we are all sharing similar stories about her now. How she knew all our children's names. How she would always wave or blow us kisses as we passed by. How she would make time to talk to our children whenever they came in. All my children know her and now we are all mourning her. For she is gone. Aunty Yinka has gone home to be with Papa God.

Aunty Yinka, this month is my Family month. I am trying to use it to honour my family and somehow, you fit right in. From the first day when I came in for my pre employment examination till the last time I saw you through the elevator doors when you gave me the thumbs up and a wide smile, you were good and kind to me. I never got a chance to tell you. Once again, death has cheated me. But its OK, I know you can read this now and all I want to tell you is that, though we were not blood relatives.... I will miss you like one. I will miss you like an Aunty.

Aunty Yinka, sleep *o jare*. Rest now from all life's cares...You touched a lot of people. A whole lot of people are numbed by misery now but I managed to remind myself that if you were here, you would not want us to remain like that, you would be going around, tapping all our shoulders, rallying us, cheering us up, having us smile. Having us live on.... so I shook myself and managed to smile as I remembered our times together working on Travel for Life, preparing for the HR song - Joined Up HR - do you remember? Yes, I will think on these...and I will smile. Cos I know that is what you would want from me. From us all.

Ciao Aunty Yinka. Till we meet to part no more. You were such a gem. I know God will give your family the fortitude to bear this loss. In Jesus Christ's name. Yes, He will reward your labour of love towards us all, your non-blood nieces and nephews!

Mwaah!

Sunday, 20 September
Live. Love. Laugh

This is my new Quarter 4 mantra. Live. Love Laugh. I like it so much cos you can build on it and make it yours. But this is how mine goes.

I, the Desperate Naija Woman a.k.a *Mimobioluwa,* QB or simply Bola, have made up my mind to:

- Live my life to the max making each day count for something
- Love my God with all my heart so that I can love others more unconditionally
- Laugh out loud ALOT. Its the best long life tonic I could ever find and...its FREE!
- Don't you just love it? They are so simple yet so profound. So lets move away from living 'La Vida Loca' and give more depth to our lives as we move to the end of 2009 by living 'La Vida L3'!
- What? You are not feeling my own L3? No sweat, why not build your own L3 mantra using the building blocks - Live, Love, Laugh. The bottom line is that you just make your life count for something.... good.

Shalom!

Thursday, 24 September
Sometimes Words Just Won't Do. (a birthday poem to my one and only Ah-Sholly-Babes!)

Yes, sometimes words just won't do
And this is one case where that holds true
For, my dear Aburo, how can I express
Why my hearts skips in my chest
At the very thought of disappointing you
At not being there enough, or making you blue
I know, yes I can almost hear you shout 'No way!'
But alas my dear Aburo, these fears weighed heavy one me some days
And even now, I could never really tell you
Because, my dear, sometimes words just wont do

But you know me, I will always try my best
Especially as you are about to lay your 28th year to rest!
Who am I that God has been so good to me, to us?
To keep you all these years, in response to my trust
I can only praise His name now
For you my baby sister, have shown how
When one holds on to God for all things
He never fails one, He is the real deal.
Even for Him, how can I capture His love for me and you
For real, sometimes words just won't do!

Ah Sholly Babes! It's your birthday!
And I guess what I am really trying to say
As you celebrate this glorious day
Is that you mean the world to me
And when I count my children, I don't count three
I don't care what they say, we both know
That you were and will always be my numero uno
Yes, my number one child cos life dealt us those cards
And, you know what, like I told you before, we played hard
We had God on our side, we laughed, we cried, but still shined!
And you my dear Sister, you make me so proud.

And since, now, I really am lost for words
I am going to steal shamelessly from my church
Cos sometimes when words just wont do, when you are in a crunch
You can just burst forth into song:
(Pretend you can hear me singing)

Happy Birthday! I am saying I love you
God be with you till the end of time
And may He say 'Well done'

And with that my Aburo, all I can say is
Iwo wa o jare!
Carry go! Rock your day like you know what's up!

Sunday, 27 September
Farewell 'For Now'

I will not bore you with the horrors of my trip back from my hometown. Nor will I harass you with tales of how difficult it was for me to see so many old relatives. My dad's friends who, like him, are much greyer and much more wrinkled than I remember. Time has taken its toll on them. But that is not what this blog is all about. No, its not about how much love they still have for me. They were genuinely proud of what I had become and who I was. Amazing. Most of them had not seen me since I got married 16 years ago. But that is not what this is about.

This blog is about my uncle's commendation service. That is what the programme said. We are in my hometown of Ikerre Ekiti to commend his soul to the hereafter. I dreaded going for this for two reasons. One cos it meant I would have to travel by road. I hate that. Two because it meant that I would have to finally let go. Cos for sure, it would bring closure. Closure I did not really want. I wanted to hold on. I did not want to say goodbye. I have been enjoying not having closure.... Worrisome but true.

I arrived as the Reverend was about to begin his sermon (of course I got there late thanks to not being able to find my way being as there was no signs to guide me along the way...but that is another blog which I am not even sure I will tell). I quickly sat in the seat my dad had reserved for me. He looked at me from his seat , his eyes asking me where my mgm was (that too is another blog and I am sure I shall not be writing that. Suffice to say that the banking world never sleeps. Even when you are on your way to say goodbye to an uncle in law). I whispered something about 'bank, call, had to go back. will join me' and he nodded his understanding.

Anyway, I continued listening, on this day, the 26th of September 2009, as the Reverend spoke on about living a life worthy of heaven, of honouring my uncle by living as he did but even more importantly about honouring God by living as He, God had called us to live. Holy.

Then he said something that resonated with my soul. He said, 'so as you all have come here to say fare well to you Deacon Joseph, for now, let us thank God for the life he lived...' I jumped in my seat. For now? FOR NOW! Of course, these good byes were not final. They were FOR NOW. I would get to see my uncle again. I would get to see my mom again. Yes, I would.... IF I lived a life that got me to heaven.

And indeed, that is what he was talking about...living a life now so that if you have lost loved ones, your goodbyes too would only be FOR NOW...

I am going through a really hard time now even though I try to mask it. I loved my mom to bits and my uncle was so close to her. So losing him is like losing my mom all over again. Its taking its toll on my YET will I thank the Lord. All I can do to make me feel better is to encourage anyone who may be reading this blog. If you are really a Christian. Check yourself. Are you living a life that will grant you access to heaven? Are you sure that if you lost a loved one, you could truly believe that you would see them later? Could you bid them farewell FOR NOW?

Shalom!

Thursday, 29 September
Kayuze!

That's what I called you. But your name is Kayode. And you were my first cousin. You are my first cousin as far as I know. You were the first cousin I met. I lived on 26A Saratu Street, Agege, Lagos and I still remember when I met you for the first time. Its funny what the brain remembers. I cannot even believe I remember the address of the house I lived in as a child. Yes, I do. Amazing. I also remember you. This cute little baby that came and invaded my space way back then in Agege. This, Kayode, is my blog in honour of you. You are the first cousin I actually met. You were a baby then. And I made my self your 'by force' nanny. I was 8 years old.

Your mum had come to visit us in Agege. You were just so adorable. I told my mom I wanted to sleep in the same guest room as your mom. Why? So I could be close to you. I wanted to take care of you and I did. I am not sure how come I knew what to do but your mom slept through the nite as I took care of you whenever you woke up at night and I was glad to. God only knows how I managed that cos I had to wake up and go to school the next morning.

Suffice to say, I loved you like my own. I think this is why we have some kind of bond. All your sisters took their time to understand me and love me. But you? No, you were free with me and my mgm right from the get go. Kayode. I don't know where you are now with your life. But know this - I love you. Cos you are the first cousin I laid eyes on. And took care of. In the middle of the night. I was 8 years old!!!!!!

I am looking to God Almighty to guide you in your life. I am trusting Him to lead you in the right direction. I am holding on to him to make your life sweet cos you are such (as far as I remember) a sweet person. I remember wondering how come you, the boy, were so much easier than your sisters. They were a tough bunch. But eventually I think I won them over too. I am a typical Adef. We are not very expressive unless we love you to bits. Kayode, I love you to bits. I don't care if I have not spoken to you in years. I don't care if I have not seen you since you left Naija. I don't care what you may think of me now. All I know is that I want you to know that I remember that as a baby in the middle of the night, many years ago, when you looked up and saw my 8 year old face, you stopped crying. And even my 8-year-old mind understood how special that was. You made me feel 'wanted'. I thank you for that Kayuzee.

May God be your Guide. Listen to Him, Kayode. He is speaking. Don't be led by any other voice. Listen for God. He is waiting to speak to you. This is not a final note. It is live. I shall update it as I go along. But for now my dear Kayuzee, don't doubt my love for you and for all your sisters. I love you all. I love your mom. I love you dad. You know why? Becos they have always loved me. Unconditionally.

Be true to your self. Love God with all your heart.

I love you and always will. I remember you as the first baby I got to watch over in my life.

Shalom!

Wednesday, 30 September
Go Blakky! It's Your Birthday!

Happy Birthday!!!!!!!!!!!!!!!!!!!!!!!!!
Before you start, you know you cannot even vex with me cos I am not the one that gave you this nickname – Blakky Shadow! Your mom did. And I actually think she was the only that got away with calling you that. But since this is my blog and I can do what I want, I have given myself a one-day pass to address you by that special nickname Lol! (Btw, does she still call you this?)

Happy Birthday Fadeke! Many Happy Returns of the Day! Long Life and Prosperity! Hip Hip Hip! Hurray! Happy Birthday to you! Happy Birthday to you. Happy Birthday! (Pretend you can hear Stevie Wonder singing this to you and not me. Yes oh, much easier on your ears!

Anyway, it is only natural that my next 'Remembering *mi familiglia*' blog should be about you. A sort of special B-day pressie as you celebrate another year. Glory to God! I thank God for your life and for the wonderful young lady you have become. Yes ke, you must be wonderful with a mom like your mom and a cousin like me. Lol! Sometimes I go onto your FB and am not sure if I am dreaming.... You and all your sisters have all grown up so much and even though it makes me feel terribly ancient, I am always filled with awe at how faithful a Father God is. He has kept you all ALL these years. How can we ever thank Him? For what He has done, is doing and is yet to do in your life? I guess we cannot but we must keep on trying. *Abi*? Yes o!

I am not sure who the quietest is or was but even if I thought that was you (although I think it is Funke) I have a feeling that you may have changed a lot. But maybe I am wrong. I do know though that when you smiled, it was one of the whitest, brightest smiles in the family. There is nothing like the contrast of pearly white teeth against chocolate dark skin. And the looks have just gotten finer with age. To God be the glory!

Anyway, you know I have no plans of flattering you beyond the facts. So all I have said is all I know from the little time we shared together. I am not sure when we will see again but one thing for sure is I will see you on your wedding day by the grace of God. No matter when that is. Yes oh! I plan to make it for all of your weddings!

So my dear I pray you have a lovely day tomorrow. You are an Independence baby so you are a special *Naija pikin*! I pray that God fills your heart with a peace that can overcome any thing Life throws your way. I pray that, as you walk in obedience to God, you will eat the good of the land to the fullest.

You are a Princess, daughter of the Most High God. Walk it. Talk it. Live it. It's your birthright.

May you live as long as you like as ordained by God.

May you have the things you like (in keeping with God's wishes for you) for as long as you live. In Jesus name! Amen!

Go on; rock your day like you know what's up! (don't ask me about this. I made it up one day and I just love the way it sounds!)

Mwaah! And if you close you eyes and keep real still, you just might feel my e-hug all the way from over here!

OCTOBER

Wednesday, 07 October
Dead Light

Dead Light
Dead Light?
Can light come from death?
Can death bring forth light?
Apparently, light can.
Apparently, death can
For I see, how in my life, the light still manages to shine somehow
Even when I know that death lurks within, I cannot lie, no, not now

You see, I don't boast to have any Gifts of the Spirit
But that's fine cos what I really want are the Fruits of the Spirit
Love, Joy, Peace, Patience,
Kindness, Goodness, Gentleness,
Faithfulness and Self Control,
As my Father's child, His offspring
How can I liv,e none of these truly offering?
Who am I fooling, displaying them in the congregation
When, at home, my nanny, my driver, live in confusion!
'This our madam, is she really a Christian?'

To be honest, while I worry about what they think
My real anxiety is what God sees when He looks at me
I know you love me Papa, even before I loved you
But if you are truly in me, Life of the world?
Why do I feel so unlike you, so fruits of the spirit-void?

I promise you, if you see me today and I smile at you. It would be a smile masking a whole lot of sadness, pain, fear and thankfully hope. I really cannot tell a lie. I have, over the last 4 to 5 weeks been living with a morbid fear that I was going to fall down and die a sudden death Or go to bed and not wake up. No, am not joking. And no, its not just cos people I care about have died in recent times.

True, you may have spoken to me recently. And yes I may have laughed and gisted merrily away and all that but trust me, I have no need to come here and lie to you. I don't have time for that. If I am writing it, then it is true. If I did not want to share it honestly, I would leave it in my heart. I don't have to come to my blog and lie. Just cannot see the point in that. So yes, I have been living in fear.

Very unchristian like. I know. Very unfaithful-ful like. I know. Very not-holding-on-to-God's promises-like. Really, I know! My knowing all this could not stop me. I sat in the back of my car this morning and thoughts spilled over themselves in my head. What was wrong with me? It's like my mind, body and soul had all ganged up to wage a war against me. And the creepiest part is this. I was the one orchestrating it all. Yes, I was….no, I AM the enemy of my very own self. Or perhaps, I am letting the real enemy of my soul, the devil, USE me to destroy me? But is that not so easy? To blame it all on the devil? It is but heck! I will blame him anyway. Cos like a dear sista said to me, 'he is a goat. A brainless goat'. And while I recognize my culpability in this my self-made inferno, I know nothing bad goes down without him having a hand in it.

But I digress. Today is the 7th day of October 2009 and I cannot begin to tell you how many times, since 01 January 2009 I have told God I was sorry. And that is just one year. I have been alive for 41 so do the maths! If I were God, I would delete my phone number right now. But thank you Jesus, cos God is not me and am not God. So still, God loves me so boundlessly. But do I really love God like I say I do ?

Why do I do the things I do? The good that I do to people, am I sure it's for God? Or do I just do them cos I want to feel good? Want people to think I am good? Nice? It must be for those shallow reasons cos if it was to please God, I should know by now that God is not really interested in my good deeds if my walk with HIM, my one on one walk with Him is tainted by sin. So if I continue to do that which I know hurts God then all the other stuff I do must just be for me and what does that get for me in the end? In the hereafter? So people think I am a saint and I end up in hell! *He eh! Wahala wa oh*! Sweet Jesus, Lover of my soul, have mercy on me!

So I sat in the back of my car with all these wild manic thoughts jumping from one side of my brain to another. Its funny the thoughts you can have as you try to apply your make up in the back of a moving car. I wondered how I had gotten so good at doing good, sounding good yet being downright bad? I wondered why God loved me so much that He continued to place a hand over my nakedness. I wondered how long He would continue to do that? To continue to allow dead bring forth light. I decided that I did not want to find out.

Yes, I decided that this life I am living. My life you see and my life you don't see. They need to match up. Cos at the end of the day, its what you don't see that will seal my eternal life. The part that only God sees and He is what matters… So off I go, me and my manic thoughts, throwing myself into the loving merciful arms of God. I know He will help me sort this out. He is good like that!

Shalom!

P. S. And please do me a favour. Do not sit there trying to figure out WHAT my issues are! Look within your own life my dear one…neither of us knows what's coming tomorrow…let's fix ourselves. Let's be ready. Today.

Friday, 09 October
God As Ammunition

Yes, a day ago, I was wallowing around in my own miry clay. Rolling around with death and darkness. I was, as Bishop T D Jakes would put it, lying there, broke, busted and disgusted with myself. But then, with one word, God turned my mourning into dancing again. He lifted my sorrow. I cannot stay silent. I can sing cos my joy is back. Yes, I know, this is not exactly how you remember the song but I am sure you catch my drift.

Women praying together is 'jazz' you know. It's a special kind of *juju*. I tell you. I am so glad that I did not let how I was feeling make me miss our Women of God prayer meeting on Thursday evening. So glad. Now don't get me wrong. I am not saying I am BACK but am saying I am standing strong in the Lord and in the power of His might. Yes, I have picked myself up from the pity party floor and latched myself on to the word God sent to me. In Psalm 149 verse 4.

My loving and most tolerant father told me that He takes pleasure and delight in me. Regardless of how I feel about myself. He loves me. That He will beautify the humble with salvation. He, she who is able to come before Him with a contrite heart. Truly sorry and ready to turn away from sin. He, she, will He give victory. He will help me win. He will help me overcome. He will save me.... from myself.

Isn't it just awesome the kind of love God has for us? I felt so sinful and lost but its like God arose, scattered all the enemies plaguing my mind like dust before the wind, He melted them like wax before a fire and scooped me up from off the floor into His loving arms. *Ha Baba*! A zillion tongues could not express my gratitude. My relief. My calm at this moment. How can I thank you o Lord! How can I praise you?

I guess I could never thank you enough but I know I will keep on trying.

I am humbled by your love. Please Lord, every day, just fill me anew with YOU. Fill me anew with Your Spirit. That's the one way I have come to realise to fight this battle for my life. Filled with the Spirit of God. Armed with God...on the inside of me...

Sunday, 11 October
A Listening Ear. An Understanding Heart. A Pastor B

I left church today with a headache. That should not be abi? But that's my lot today. As I type this, am doing a bit better but the reasons for the headache remain, partly.

Reason one. Teaching Sunday school to nannies is nerve racking. Today, I got to a point where I was like ' forget this!' Not their fault. It was mainly cos the children from one of the classes were not effectively engaged and were running wild all over the place. It got in the way of my concentration and being as I was teaching on 'Patience' and Self Control'.... well I had to be patient and self controlled. God has a sense of humour you know!

Reason two. As I cut behind the congregation to go through the back hallway, I was accosted by one of my favourite people in the world. Pastor B. I was walking with my head bent thinking, trying to figure out how to get my nannies hooked, wondering how many different languages I would have to speak to get this day's lesson across when bam! There she was standing in front me with a smile. I love this woman to bits but right at that point in time, I did not want to see her at all! But at the same time, I was so pleased, so glad she was there, standing in front of me. Do you know the feeling?

Pastor B is one of the very few people in this world I can REALLY be me with. I am not sure why but I have never been able to, nor have I actually ever tried to tell her anything but the reality of what is going on with me. She brings out 'the truth' in me. Yes, she inspires me to speak only my reality. Only my real-ness. Its like there is something in me that recognises that there is really no point hiding from this woman. I feel she loves me to the point that being or acting any other way in front of her is like 'stealing from myself'.

Don't get me wrong, I have some fantastic sista divines that support my daily walk as well and I know they have got my back too. But we lean on each other for mutual support. But sometimes, you just want to lean on someone and not have to worry about having to give anything back.... cos you, yourself are tired and weak. You need to rest in the arms of God and you do just that as He wraps His arms around you using the human body of someone like Pastor B.

I was not really going to blog today as my head is still pounding but as I sat here recollecting my discussion with her this morning, I realised what a special person she is. At least to me. There are very few people in the world that have the ability to inspire people to be real with themselves. Someone you can open yourself up to without any fear of being judged. Someone who believes in you no matter what. I think every person should have a 'Pastor B' in their lives. Someone who truly listens and truly understands you. From the heart.

This is to you Pastor B...from my heart.

P. S. Yes, I know the ideal is for this person to be your wife or husband... but really life sometimes is just not a straight line like that.

Thursday, 15 October
Enough!

Is it a poem? Or a prayer? Hmmmm, a little bit of both I guess. But one thing for sure, what ever this is, it came from my heart... This is dedicated to anyone, any Christian who has ever had the urge to yell! To shout! To scream.... at themselves! Cos, you know you are in a place you have no business being in your walk with Jesus! Join me, lets scream 'Enough is enough'! Like Ms. Bardot says, God will answer us! He is a prayer and shout answering God!

That's Enough!
Do you hear me?
I say, enough is enough!
I need to get tough
On my flesh, I need to be rough
Cos, my soul, my eternal life costs too much
I cannot sit by and scoff it off
So, indeed, enough is really enough!

So Father, my sista tells me, reassures me
You have a listening ear, and a heart that feels for me
So grant me grace O Lord, help me!
In your strength, by your power, I can free me
From this bondage, this cage that holds me
I am better than this, I am royalty!
So to this task master, I owe no loyalties
Ah, yes! Hear O Mountains, and seas underneath
This woman has had it, she will be released
Cos, she is coming out.
Cos Enough is enough!

It's enough!
O mess become a Message!
It's enough!
You test, become a Testimony!
My Redeemer has done the work, its all history

I am walking in His victory
Today, Now, This Moment, That is my reality!
I claim it, its mine.
God said it, Jesus died for it, and I believe it
So it's mine!
Cos enough is ENOUGH!
In Jesus mighty name.
Amen!

Saturday, 17 October
In The Meantime, You ARE Enough

There are so many struggles we go through as Christians and for me, the chief has been trying to get myself to that 'holiness level' that I know God has called me to be at. Lately, this has more or less robbed me of my peace and joy. And today, I realised that THAT could not be God's plan for me. Yes, he has called me to be like him and YES, he does not like the 'sin' in my life. BUT, He loves me still and NEVER turns from me (like I had begun to think).

Yes, the devil had simply found one more way to mess with me. To make me unproductive. By freezing me in place in an ice mould of negative sin-consciousness. It does not make you repentant. It just makes you sick of yourself. So sick that you want to just give up. Do nothing...

Hell NO! (Just pretend you did not read that)! I refuse to do that.

In the Meantime...

In the meantime, just do what you can.
Don't wait till you have ALL the money you need.
Don't wait till you have all the qualifications you want
Don't wait till you are as holy as you know you should be
Don't wait till whatever it is you are waiting for shows up
You are here right now; so just do what you can
Now, with what you have.
Trust me, it is enough.

I have just now realised one more trick of the enemy
It's making you think you don't have enough
Are not ready enough
Are not good enough
Cannot quote scripture enough
Or find the Bible passage fast enough
Have not saved enough souls,
So you just sit there, frozen in place, doing nothing

When the life in you is really all you need
To do something. Now. Today.
Trust me, it is enough

Yes, for now. In the meantime
YOU are enough.
YOU can do something with that which you have now. Today
It is enough.
Don't let the devil feed you his lies.
He knows that should you stand now, today, his victory dies
He knows that what is in your hand now, today, is more than enough
So he does all he can to make you believe you are not good enough
But you ARE!
Trust me, you are good enough.
So don't worry that you still struggle with this or with that
Yes, don't fret if you did not pray enough, or that your praise was a bit flat
God still loves you and wants you to shine for Him now
So go out there, yes in the meantime, be all you can
For this race we run is not a 100 metre dash
It's a marathon and along the way, sometimes we will crash
But the failure is not in the crash my dear friend, you see
Failure is in NOT getting up, NOT pressing on doggedly
That's when you fail. When you give up. When you lie there overcome
But tell me, do you not know David, the Murderer King?
In spite of his failures, his sins, God still considers him the best of kin.

So, in the meantime, permit me to repeat myself again and again

You ARE enough!
You ARE enough!
God says so, and believe me, that's ENOUGH!

Sunday, 18 October
Only You!

(If you know this song, just sing along with me now. As you do, cast your mind back to all the things God has brought you through. Seen you through. All the battles He has fought for you. The blessings He has rained on you.

You will have one awesome worship experience, I promise. There is nothing like worshipping God via the absolute road of total and absolute gratitude. God is enough. No doubt about it. Have a wonderful week ahead. Shalom!)

Only You, are HOLY
Only You, are WORTHY
Only You, are WONDERFUL!

There is NO ONE else like YOU
Ever Faithful, Ever True
Oh My LORD
My Heart, my Life
is a Testimony!

The choir of my church ministered with this song today and I tell you I was singing along weighed down by my thoughts when God pumped up the volume in my spirit and got me to really 'listen' to what I was singing. Don't get me wrong. I absolutely LOVE this song and was singing it from my heart. At least I thought so but my heart was loaded with all my stuff. And my stuff was blocking the ears of my heart from hearing what I was really singing. Am I making sense? Anyway, in an instant, I got it.

ONLY God. ONLY God. ONLY God. Is holy.
ONLY God. ONLY GOD. ONLY God Is worthy. Wonderful
ONLY God. ONLY GOD. ONLY GOD is ever true. Ever Faithful

So me looking to Man (i.e. any man or any woman) to be any of the above is really futile. ONLY God can be these things to me. And I should only look to God. He will not disappoint me. For the stuff I was carrying around in my heart, these were the exact words I needed to hear.

Maybe same rings true for you.

Friday, 23 October
Being A Woman of God – Totally Surrendered to His Will

I was just at my desk at work trying to close out some stuff when the thought dropped in my heart quite clearly that I was to post this on my blog. It would never occurred to me to do so ordinarily but I trust God, He knows someone needs to hear this message today. I have stopped second guessing God. He says 'Jump!' I ask 'How high Lord? How high?' This is more or less the word I shared with the women in my church on Wednesday (yes, I know, I don't know how that happened but God is not really in the business of choosing the ABLE. He chooses the WILLING and ENABLES them). So here goes, I hope it blesses you as much as it did us that day. I pray that you can just get a touch, a feel of how powerfully the presence of God was in a room full of women genuinely committing to obey HIM!

………We have all come here today to pray to a most loving Father who we trust and that is wonderful! And in Jesus name, He will hear our prayers tonight. But you know what? Prayer should not just be something we DO. It should be WHO WE ARE. A Pray-er. Prayers should be our way of life. Yes, as a Christian woman of God, prayers should be our lifeblood. God will help us all in Jesus Name. Amen!

But as important as prayer is, that's not really what I want to share on today. We are going to pray. That's for sure but FIRST of all, we are going to do some serious SURRENDERING. In the times we are living in, if we are going to survive with our sanity, we need to totally lose ourselves to God…

I would like to thank you and congratulate you for coming to this meeting. I personally believe that God is going to do some awesome things in our lives. There will be testimonies in Jesus Name. Lives, Homes, Marriages will be transformed. Shackles will be removed. Bodies will be healed. And because I believe this we must not be unaware of the devices of the enemy. So we are gong to put in place a firewall of protection around ourselves and we are going to make sure there is nothing that will give him access to our midst...

First of all, let's use the words of Psalm 51 to ask God for forgiveness of all that would block our prayers here today and give room to the enemy. Let's pray to Him to cleanse of anything that would hinder His work in our lives, bitterness, unforgiveness, gossip, sins of omission, malice, etc. You know these things! Lets remove them, lets ask for grace! (Pray)

In addition, Women of God, let us claim the protective power that is in the blood of Jesus Christ now. Over our minds, bodies and souls. Our homes and family members. Our church. Over this room we are in. All that we will do here today to the Glory of God will be sealed and permanent because of the blood of the Lamb over us. (Pray).

We have all come here today to seek God's face. I just want us to spend sometime thanking God in advance for what He is about to do in our lives individually and collectively.

- Thank Him for all that He had done in your life and is about to do
- Praise Him for all His incredible acts as recorded in the Bible
- Worship God for all His creation
- Magnify His name for all that He has given us in Christ – salvation, redemption, peace, joy,

Living a Surrendered Life (Mark 14: 32 – 35)

Now, the environment has been set. God is here. Praise God. And He is more than enough for us. Amen! But can you do me one small favour right now? You know, all the needs you have come here with today? All you hearts desires? Could you just SURRENDER them along with you LIFE to Jesus Christ tonight? No, this is not some wicked 419. Trust me, we are going somewhere!

Can someone please read Mark: 32 – 36 (New Living)

32 They went to the olive grove called Gethsemane, and Jesus said, "Sit here while I go and pray." 33 He took Peter, James, and John with him, and he became deeply troubled and distressed. 34 He told them, "My soul is crushed with grief to the point of death. Stay here and keep watch with me." 35 He went on a little farther and fell to the ground. He prayed that, if it were possible, the awful hour awaiting him might pass him by. 36 "Abba, Father,"[h] he cried out, "everything is possible for you. Please take this cup of suffering away from me. Yet I want your will to be done, not mine."

Like you and I, Jesus had a desire. That the cup be taken away from him. Like us he was groaning under the strain and stress of this need. Like us, he cried out. He wept. He prayed. But in the end, he submitted to the will of God. He surrendered to God, His Father. He decided that his number one priority was to obey God and to let God's will be done in his life. And his complete obedience paid off. He got a name far above any other name. He got power to overcome death. He ruined principalities and power. You see, my sisters, the key to our requests, the road to abundance in life is SURRENDER and OBEDIENCE.

Are you willing to turn a new leaf today and commit to 150% Obedience with God? Are you ready to say 'I don't care EVEN if my dreams do not come, true, IT IS YOU GOD and nothing else!? May God Help us all in Jesus name. Amen!

Now, IT IS TIME TO PRAY!!
Prayers
1. Help me to surrender my will to you Lord just like Jesus Christ did in Gethsemane
2. Let pleasing you, O Lord, be my number one priority.
3. Help me to trust you more and walk in reverential fear so that I will be blest and lack no good. (Psalm 34:8-10)

(You can sing any Spirit inspired song as led here)

Living a Righteous Life

Yes, ladies, we need to let God have His way in our lives FOR REAL. He needs to be the boss. Ask yourself now. Is God REALLY the Lord over your life? Or is He just your Saviour? Now more than ever we need to ask for a refill of the Holy Spirit so He can help us to walk in the Spirit. Live righteously. To live holy.

Prayers
4. Fill me a new with your enabling Holy Spirit so that I can obey you COMPLETELY
5. Refiner's Fire, Burn away all that is flesh in me today. Help me walk by your Spirit o Lord!
6. Dear Heavenly Father, help me to live righteous so that when I decree a thing, You will back me up.
7. Let this revival in my life bring about ABUNDANCE in all areas of my life.

(You can sing any Spirit inspired song as led here)

Abiding in Jesus Christ (John 15: 7 – 9)

8. Lord, give me the grace to abide in you so that I can bear fruit.
9. Father, Let your words abide richly in me so that when I ask for my heart's desires, you will grant them to me!
10. My Father and My Lord, let me life glorify you and you only!

(You can sing any Spirit inspired song as led here)

Remember, at the onset, I asked you to surrender all your needs to Jesus Christ? Guess what? Now that you and I have committed to make God our number one priority. Now that we are in a right standing with Him. Do you know what? As we stand holy in God today and as we begin to live lives that resemble Jesus Christ, we actually begin to take on the very nature of God. We become his mouth! When God speaks, who can annul it? No one! So as you walk with God, He will place in you the power to decree LIFE into all areas of your life. And that is exactly what we are going to do right now. We are going to decree! And God will back us up in Jesus name! Amen!

1. First of all we are going to speak to all the requests before us today. Pray as the Spirit leads you (best to have your requests written down. Lay your hands on the sheet of paper and pray in the Spirit.)
2. Troubled Marriages –When we live a surrendered life to God, He will fight for us. God should contend with anyone or thing contending with the peace of our homes
3. Fruit of The Womb – As we walk in obedience, now that we are speaking as the mouths of God, let us prophesy over our sisters that though the vision may seem to tarry, at the appointed time which we are decreeing to be 9 months from now, life shall spring forth from them in the form of healthy baby boys and girls. In Jesus name. Amen!
4. Our Children in the Mercyplace
5. Mercyplace – Zechariah 2:3 – 5

6. Nigeria – II Chronicles 7:14

(You can sing any Spirit inspired song as led here)

Walking in the Peace of God henceforth.

11. Heavenly Father, help me to be still and know that you are God over my life. Let my mind be stayed on you ALONE as I leave this place now. It is well with my soul!

1. Psalm 16:8
I have set the LORD always before me; Because He is at my right hand I shall not be moved.
****
Recognizing Your Ministry (Homework)

12. Lord, reveal my own personal programme/ministry/calling and place me in it just like you did in the life of Jesus Christ.
13. Heavenly Father, give me the grace to be useful here on earth even as I remain constantly focused on heaven

Sunday, 25 October
Yet, There is A Place

No matter what happens to us in our lives, I believe there is a place we can go to hide. Maybe it's just me. I find that in my down times, I have a place I can run to that allows me to retain the joy that God has placed in my heart. They joy of knowing that He loved me. That He loves me still. That He will always love me. No matter what. Yes, that thought gives me peace. In troubled times, His love brings me peace.

And Lord knows I need peace right now…loads of it.

Monday, 26 October
Just An Ordinary Boy

The other day, it was bedtime and my son woke me up to pray. Yes, our house is odd like that, I go to bed and then he comes to wake me up when its bed time. Cos we must pray you see. My dear, I have given up on standard bedtimes. If he does not sleep on time, he will pay the price. Yes, I am an odd mom. They like it like that. Lol! So far, our crazy rule works. Anyway, as I was saying, my son woke me up. It was time to pray. As I always do, I tell him to pray cos 'you are so good at it and you know God listens to children's prayers waaaay faster than adults'. For now, this is a story that my son buys. I am happy. Very.

So he huffs and puffs pretending not to like the idea that God thinks he is special and he begins ' In Jesus name...' And he prays like only a 5 almost 6 year old can. He asks God to make sure the 'bad guys' don't break into our house. . He covers his daddy, mommy, sista and miss Rosa and miss Lovette with the blood of Jesus so that the bad guys cannot catch them. And of course he prays against bad dreams from watching too many cartoons! Please, at least he knows he needs cover. And finally, he reminds God that 'this is the house of heaven so nothing bad must happen' I was almost sure he would add a 'you hear me God?' But alas he is growing after all. It is not a joke to be almost 6!

Indeed my almost 6 year old prayed a simple 6 year old prayer and guess what. Like I always do. I felt so secure. I knew that God had heard his son. Priceless. When my son was done and my hubby and I had echoed our 'Amens'. My hubby hailed him' Pastor Aniekan!' And I added, 'that was an awesome prayer. Well done love!' And then he said it.

This dear almost 6 year old son made a loud disapproving sound like *ah-ah,* you people should know better now! Then he raised himself from his knees and replied us simply. 'Awwwwgh am not a

Pastor. I am just an ordinary boy who knows how to pray awesome prayers'…

I know, you are smiling foolishly like me right now, aren't you?

Only God could make a boy so adorably cute and wise.

Shalom!

Tuesday, 27 October
Honestly?

Honestly? I have nothing to blog about. Honestly? I have thought about three different things that happened today that I could blog about. Honestly? I just let them all slide. Why? Cos to be honest, I am beyond **ti-red**. I woke up at 4.30am this morning. And was at work at 6.19am! All in a bid to beat the dreaded traffic from my end to the end of Lagos where I work. So right now, even as I type this, my head is spinning. But in a tired, happy, giving-God-the-glory kind of way.

Yes. Cos honestly? I am happy at how God is moving in my life and the lives of some people real close to me. The enemy is bragging but God, who has the only real bragging rights is showing him who is BOSS. So I just logged on this evening to say to you. Yes, you who may be reading this.

Don't worry. The enemy can roar, *na im get im mouth. E fit take am do anytin wey im like.*

God, our God, will have the final say. And when God speaks, tell me, who can annul it? No one! That's right!

So honestly? I think on that note, I should just mosey on off to bed. *Kachifo!* Goodnite. Sweet dreams....

Shalom!

NOVEMBER

Sunday, 01 November
Talk Less. Act More.

Happy New Month! Yes, God has been faithful and He has seen us through ten months and here we are in November. My uncle is not here. My cousin in not here. My uncle in love is not here. But you are and so am I. So trust me, we have a lot to be thankful for. We are alive! Glory to God! For His faithfulness and especially for His mercies over us all.

It has been said that Nigeria is one of the most religious countries in the world. Our Christianity is however zillions of miles long but not even an inch deep! There are so many born again Christians; so many people professing to be Christ followers. I mean you only have to attend any of the Holy Ghost crusades at the RCCG camp to validate this. Let's not even talk about the other crusades organised by other churches. So, it's certain, there are many of us. So someone tell me, how come, as many as we are, we are having NO impact on our country? Nigeria seems to be moving farther and farther away from righteousness!

Simple. We talk, speak, sing, roll on the ground more than we actually ACT like the God we say we are serving. What's the point of all the:

'God is in control'
' It is well'
'That's not my portion'
'God Bless you'
'I am blessed and highly favoured'
'How far? Far above principalities and powers!'

And all the other christianese we speak if our lives don't reflect God? If you did not open your mouth all day long, would I be able to tell you are a Christian by your deeds? If you watched me all day. At the end of the day, would you conclude that there was something different about me. Then when someone tells you I am Christian. You would be like " A ha! I knew there was some thing different about you! Of course, you are child of God!'

I don't know about you but this month starting from tomorrow, I am 'talking' less and 'acting' more God. Why don't you join me? It only takes one person to start change. Me and you? That makes two. We are ahead already.

Dear Lord, help me to be the Jesus Christ the world sees. Let my life shine for you. In Jesus name I pray. Amen!

Monday, 02 November
At The End Of The Day

I asked a group of women a really hard question recently. I asked 'if you knew without a shadow of a doubt, that your hearts desire would not be fulfilled on this side of eternity, would you still serve God? Would you still come to church? Basically, I was asking them what they were REALLY in church for?

It's November and I know we all have many things we had hoped 2009 would bring our way. And God is an awesome provider who is not bound by time. So 59 days is still plenty for Him to move in. BUT what if He does not. Are you done? I ask you the same question now. If you were told today that you would never get married. That, that your arms would never hold your own baby or that God's plan for you did not include your living in France or Canada.... would you still be sold out for Jesus Christ? I am asking you 'At the end of the day, what are you in this race for?' God's hands or His face? Are you in it for the 'stuff' God is more than able to give you OR for the wonderful relationship He paid such a huge price to enable you have with Him?

You see, the truth is that most of us use God as one of the following:

1. Fireman God - Jehovah, come and save me, I don enter trouble o! Fire is burning o!
2. Banker God - Jehovah, come and bless me financially o!
3. Cupid God - Jehovah, bring my husband o! Let him find me ooooo! Where is my Ruth?
4. Doctor God - Jehovah, touch me and make me whole o!
5. Gyny God - Jehovah, bless me with children o! Make me fruitful in my body o!!!!!
6. CEO God - Jehovah, I need to work o!!!!!!
7. Dr. Phil God - Jehovah, save my marriage o!
8. Baba-*alawo** God - Jehovah, come and destroy my enemies o! *Patapata kia mosa!*

And I could go on and on. I know it may make you chuckle but am I lying? We treat God like He is some kind of ATM machine and our prayers are our' debit cards'. The moment we slot in the prayers and punch in the right 'fast-prayer pin number', we want God to whirl out crisp mint 'notes' of divine provision. I wonder how God feels. Used? Taken for granted? Manipulated?

Hmmmm...God is not man so He is unable to respond like we would to all the above shenanigans but I know God has a heart. A heart of pure love and that all He wants is for His children to want Him for Him. So in addition to talking less God and acting more like God, I am going to stop all my requests to God to come and MOVE in these last 2 months of 2009 and 'action' all my outstanding requests *kia kia*. I have decided to shift gears into neutral and just use these remaining days of 2009 to see how much closer I can get to God in 59 days. Remember, the Bible does say 'Seek ye first the kingdom of God...

Yes, at the end of the day, that is really what matters.

Shalom!

Thursday, 05 November
Simply Trust In His Love

You know sometimes as Christians you have a burden to pray for someone and it becomes so unbearable you just have to lock yourself away and pray the burden through. Do you know the feeling? Well that is how I feel about this blog. I felt like it HAD to be written. I am not feeling too good and have been off work for a bit. Plus the Internet at home is down and I really just want to be in bed cos right now, I can actually see 2 PCs, 2 keyboards and 4 hands typing. (weak smile) BUT this thing, this burden would not let me go. So here I am at the business centre in the estate, heeding the prompting of the Holy Spirit cos I believe someone, not just me needs to hear this.

But first, here is a question I must ask. 'Do you believe that God loves you?' Did you say 'Yes'? I hope so. If you said 'No' then I must refer you to John 3:16. You see when God said 'He so loved the world that He gave His only begotten son....', that little word 'world', yes that one, it included 'you'. God loves you. He killed His son for you. But that's another blog. So do me favour, give God the benefit of the doubt! He loves you. Period (and yes, it has nothing to do with your worthiness! sheesh, none of us was or is worthy!)

Now as I was saying. God spoke to me yesterday, albeit through the lips of a truly lovely sista-divine, Daniella. He said he knew I could not understand all the health issues I was going through. Indeed, He could empathise with all the mental agony I must be dealing with wondering what on earth is up with my body! What kind of testimony is this? Am I not meant to be walking in abundant health? Do you feel me? Perhaps you too are unable to understand why that man has not found you yet. Or perhaps, you just cannot figure out why its your loved one that had to die or how come you are so broke. Are you not a tither? Do you not give your offering cheerfully? And your mother? Why is she so hell bent on destroying your peace? In spite of all your efforts, she is just impossible! Or maybe you just cannot understand how for the life of you are hooked on the drug that was meant to help you deal with pain!!!! Another year is coming to an end and no job! Dear Lord, how come I am going through this. And why! Oh! Why are you not listening to me? Where is my own change? Why is my own child sick? Why? For how long? What?

Yes, we may not comprehend our current situations but let's all comprehend this. **GOD LOVES US** with an undying love. And through Daniella, He reminded me...He is reminding us to 'Trust in His Love for us'. I don't know about you but in that minute I felt my heart relax once again in the warm trusting knowledge that God indeed loves me. Period.

Its all part of getting deeper and closer into God I guess. So 56 days to go and Lesson Number 1 has been established:

'No matter how tough things are, Simply TRUST in God's Love For You. Therein lies your PEACE. Remember, True Christian Peace is not the absence of trouble but the presence of Divine Power'

Be at Peace! THIS too shall pass....

P. S. And yes, the burden has lifted.... am going back home to crawl into my bed and snuggle in the warmth of God's love. Now, I don't mind seeing double of my guardian angels...Two Angel Gabs, Two Angel Mikes, and Two...

Saturday, 07 November
NEPA – And Then There Was Light – Part 1

First of all, I give thanks and praise to my God and Father whose touch has made me whole. I cannot tell you how much we take good health for granted. We really should not. Every morning I wake up with no pain, I will thank Him for the simple blessing of being whole again, in body and mind.

Now on the subject of NEPA. I hope you did not think that I was going to blog about the Nigerian parastatal or institution that is meant to supply its citizens with electricity? It does not need to be blogged about. What it needs is prayer. Nuff said. No, my thoughts are swirling more around a person not an organisation. In this my period of malaise, lets just say I had a lot of 'thinking time' on my hands. Mostly I thought about my life and family and things I would love to do if God would just make me feel better again.

And of course, my thoughts found their way to my mighty good man. He is the subject of this blog. He is the one my university girlfriends nicknamed 'NEPA' on account of how fair he was (and still is). I know, not a really nice moniker but sadly it stuck back then although I stopped calling him that once we started 'going out' but I think one of my friends still calls him 'NEPA!' tills this day! Lol!

Now, I know my mgm and I know there is no way in the world he will read anything longer than a page so this blog will be in instalments! For his reading pleasure so I don't lose his attention you see. Lol!

When you are not feeling good you begin to reflect on the valuables you have. The important things. For me, apart from my salvation and my relationship with God, it boiled down to my husband, my children and then my family. These are the things that keep me going. My 'Reasons for Be-ing'

Love, I know am reaching your thresh hold so this is my last paragraph in this instalment. I hope to take us both down memory lane. I hope you will enjoy the walk or ride. In this effort to capture some of our history, I hope you get it? Get what? That I have always and will always love only you. That, even when you drive me absolutely mad, you are still the light of my world!

Saturday, 07 November
NEPA – And Then There Was Light – Part 2

So, are you comfy? Fasten your seat belt and off we go....

(But before I step on the accelerator, may I say to you, the reader that though this is to and about my mgm, there is something in it for you too. I will call them 'morals' and the moral of Part 1 is this - You too have history. Your story. Think on it. Travel it. Tell it. Most of all cherish it.

So back in the day, there was five us. Five girls. Five friends. We used to do most things together, go everywhere together especially in our year one cos most of our classes were general subjects then. Rita, Edo, Nke, Jackie and myself. Remember? As time went by, the friend-combination changed but we still remained tight friends throughout school. The first time I saw you, we were together *of course*. We were all in line at the University's medical centre trying to close out yet another 'clearance' process.

I think we heard you before we even saw you. This deep voice speaking 'Lagos Yoruba', you know, that crazy English Yoruba combo that tripped us girls back then. Don't ask me why? We thought it was just cool. All these funky Lagos boys coming all the way to Uyo! Anyway, we turned back in unison to see what heavenly creation owned the voice and the lingo.

And Bam! I don't think Rita even missed a beat before she whispered loudly to us 'NEPA!' Indeed you were very fair. And very very tall. And according to them all, very very good looking! Yep! as for me, my Ekiti-ness could not handle all the 'yellow-ness'. I could not see past it to the boyish handsome-ness. Lol! So while they were all busy swooning, I was busy wondering what all the hoopla was all about! Lol! I did like that your Afro centric dashiki though. Remember it? The cream one, opened at the sides with an abstract painting of a cow's head or something. It looked so nice over your black jeans. Funny what a girl would remember EVEN though she thought the boy ' no fine jo!'

That day, you were with your friend Kingsley and am not sure either of you even noticed we were breathing. You swaggered on by without casting us so much as a look. That did not stop my posse. As far as they were concerned, you had just improved the weather on campus. No more dark dreary days. NEPA had come and now there was Light!

As for me, the chubby (OK, the fat) Yoruba girl. As far as I was concerned, EVEN if I thought you were fine, I knew in my 16 year old heart, that I was not your kind of girl either. You were James Bond. In our group and in my head, I was well, Mary. I just did not have a lamb! Lol!

Moral: All the single ladies? Your knight in shining armour may not look anything like the picture you have in your head right now! Lol!

Sunday, 08 November
If It Was My Place (A Poem dedicated to Kuba and Shola)

If it was my place
I would make you both promise me one thing
I would make you both swear me an oath
I would make you both look me in the eyes
And make a vow to love each other
Deeply, Forever
But I cannot.
It's not my place.

If it was my place
I would take you aside Kuba
And tell you how to love my Shola
I would make you tell me over and over
How you plan to protect her, support her, care for her
Deeply, Forever
But I cannot
Its not my place

If it was my place
You, Sola, I would also take aside
And tell you how to love your Kuba.
How to 'speak' love to him and
How to 'show' love to him
Deeply, Forever
But I cannot
One, because am still learning myself and two,
Its not my place

The truth of the matter is this
No matter how much I love you my Sister
And you too, my newest Brother
No matter how much I want you to love yourselves
Deeply, Forever

It is just not my place to make you.

But there is one thing that I can do
One thing no one can take away from me
I can pray. Yes, prayer is my place.
And in that place, I will ask God to give
Kuba, Christ's heart
Sola, Christ's humility
Both of you, Divine grace
and of course, quantum amounts of Agape Love
So that yours would be a DEEP, FOREVER relationship
Yes, THIS is what I shall do
THIS is my promise to you as you swap 'I Dos'
For, this, right there, *IS* my place.

Sunday, 08 November
NEPA – And Then There Was Light – Part *Trois*

That first sighting was in my year one. Over the course of that year, there were many more sightings and with each one, one of the girls or all of them would swoon or make some other totally chic-like comment about how fine you were or something similar and we would debate the whole fairness factor that seemed to be my problem alone. Yep! I still did not get it. Until one day and that all changed.

For some strange reason, I was alone that day walking back to the hostel area from the main campus. I think because by then we were in year 2 and our schedules were no longer the same or perhaps I was just too tired to hang around in the 'Pavilion', which was sort of like the social epicentre of the school. People hung around there in between lectures to commit '*lookery*' and generally fool around. Anyway, I was not up for that on this day. It was a hot day and I was tired and just wanted to get back to the hostel, have a shower and sleep!

It was for sure not the kind of day you want to walk into 'the light'. But you know how these things happen now. There I was hot, sweaty and sticky with my long jerry curled hair in a mess when who do I see approaching me on that dusty road? You and your friend, Kingsley! I tell you, if there was a side road to dodge into, I would have dodged into it! But, alas, there was no way of escape so I took a deep breathe and wished to God I did not look as I bad as I knew I did. Now that I think of it, I wondered why I cared. *Shebi*, I was not interested in you, *abi*? Lol!

Anywho, I slid to the other side of the road as you both got nearer hoping to go past you un-noticed as usual cos you never spoke to any of us before. But alas! To my shock and amazement, you spoke to me! You actually said 'hello' and waved! I promise, even though I knew there was no one behind me, I had to look back to be sure. NEPA spoke to *me?* I am not even sure I responded, I just stared as you both smiled at me and moved on.

You know, I still remember what you were wearing that day. Do you remember that black shirt you had? Sort of shiny? You had that on, with the sleeves rolled up to your elbows on your black jeans. I loved you in black cos it sort of set off your complexion. Yes, eventually, that too grew on me...

Anyway, you later on told me how that was the very same day you and Kingsley made a bet. Aha! A bet! A bet? Yes oh, as they walked merrily away after reducing me to blubber, they made some form of bet and of course yours truly was the object or subject of their wager...see poor little me in the hands of these Lagos boys oh!

Do you remember? Huh? Huh?

But hey, that's the subject of another instalment.

Monday, 09 November
NEPA – And It Was Good! – Part 4

You know its so funny, I can still remember the conversation between Rita and myself that day in the bathroom of our hostel (yes, you would not believe the kind of gisting sessions that were held with bowl and sponge in hand in those days! Lol!) when I confirmed that you had asked me out and I was considering saying yes. She more or less exploded. It was so funny. As far as she was concerned, I had always said you were not my cup of tea so what on earth was going on! I still smile as I remember it cos the thing is its not as if she wanted to go out with you. I think she was just vexed in her own inimitable way, that I was getting what I did not 'work' for. lol! But I knew she was happy for me deep inside. For some bizarre reason, she treated me like her baby.

Anyway, so how did it happen? I really cannot remember well and strange enough, I don't know how you found out my room number and I don't remember how we even got talking per se but I DO remember how you would come to my room window and knock for me to come out. It was always late in the evenings after classes and you would 'rap' and 'rap' and I was just in a daze cos I was not sure WHY you wanted to date me. Do you remember? And in the end, I was right; it was all just a bet. You had bet Kingsley that you could get me to get out with you easy! Ha! Not! I was not that easy o jare and guess what it backfired on you! Lol! Cos you ended up liking me for real, na na na na na (imagine me sticking out my tongue right now at you. Lol!)

The truth is that it was not shakara that made me hold off my answer for all those months. I think it was mainly fear. I had heard you had attended FSAS and even way back when I was in secondary school, we used to hear about all the 'atrocities' that happened in the FSAS in Lagos. As far as I was concerned, all FSASes were the same. Lol! And then I just did not see 'us' together'. I felt people would see us and wonder 'ah ah could he not do better?'. Yes oh, so many insecurities...

But you know, gradually gradually, and small by small, you began to win me over but true to God and not because my daughter is reading these blogs, you can confirm that I did not let you make any FSAS moves on me! Ha! My mama taught me better than that! Abi? Eh hen! Yes o! I was a gooood girl! lol!

So, long story short, after close to 2 to 3 months of toasting, I finally agreed to go out with you. I still laugh out loud when you tell me that, that VERY Same day, you had a 'back up' plan waiting. You had told yourself that if I did not give in that evening. Then game up! Miss G was to be your consolation prize!!!!! Anytime I saw the girl after that, I would smile at her very nicely. If only she knew! Lol! Anyway, so there I was, officially dating NEPA and needless to say, it was a BIG deal and I was given a bronze wrist cuff to mark the occasion. Actually, I believe I began to take over plenty of your mother's jewellery as the days progressed into months and our relationship became one of the official 'campus relationships'. You know the ones, when they begin to call you by the name of your partner e.g. Shade Paul or Umoh Linda! Lol!

Yes, all the jewellery...I remember that bronze wrist cuff. I really liked it cos it was different looking. Then there were the rings. I loved rings back then. I actually wore one on every finger except for my thumb! *Na wa*! Your poor mother, I am sure she must have just given up on wondering what you were doing with all her stuff. Until she met me, that is and then she began to send me things herself. But that was much later though. And you can trust that I never wore them at home. Ha! What would I tell my mother? Yes, we were inseparable. Only apart when we had classes. We would go to lunch together at what became our joint, our 'personal' FIR (Food is Ready) where we became such fixtures that sometimes, we would eat on credit when times were hard. Our purse was a joint one even at that time and what was yours was mine and vice versa.

I remember how we would study together in the Pavilion and how you would get so mad cos I really never studied! I was smart like that. I had what you used to call a 'photographic memory' so while you swotted away I would enjoy myself committing lookery' and gisting with my friends and feeling cool with myself cos I was sitting next to NEPA. Of course by this time, I had stopped calling you that! I only read closer to exam times and I had a simple system I would read my notes. Close the book and steadily begin to download the notes almost verbatim into another fresh notebook. Voila! Study done! It always amazed you and even though I wish I could help you do same with your *orisisiri* agric terms, no such joy! You had to study the harder way. But hey, I was studying a language I loved so it was never like work to me! Sadly, the skill has gone cos it would have been good to have to use for my memory verses!

When you were not trying to remember all those biological terms, we would busy ourselves attending parties. Till this day, you still tell our children that I was a party chic. Not true! I was just a stickler for being on time and so I would prepare early!!!! Like 4pm for a party that will not start till midnight! Lol! Ok, so I liked to dance! But really my excuse then was that where we went to school. there were not taxis and since I had not summoned up enough courage to climb *okada* at that time, we needed to set off early so we could WALK to the venue. Yes, I was young like that! Thank God I had you, cos you really were a bit more mature than I was...as God would have it.

Now, am sure I have lost you cos the blog is too long...but am sure one day, some day, you will sit down to read all this or maybe I am blest and you did manage to get to the end of this one...

Morale: Be careful the kinds of bets you make, you might just ending up marrying the person! Lol! I am sorry, I just could not help that one...these my morals need to get more serious!

Tuesday, 10 November
Indeed, Today is the Tomorrow…

that I was rather anxious about but guess what? ALL is well!

You see, nothing is really ever that much of a big deal if you just let go and let God. Which is what I finally managed to get myself to do as I went to bed last night. I just said to God, you now what? You are the boss! At the end of the day, only YOUR appraisal of me counts. So, forget them! It worked!

So today, I came to work as cool as a cucumber not cos I was *all that* but because my God **IS ALL THAT** and He had my back! Yes, through thick and thin, G.O.D plus D.N.W is equals to 'Winning team!

So, do you have something daunting on your plate? Some assignment you need to submit or a presentation to make or a job or visa interview? Or maybe you are sick in your body and/or mind and just need more courage to face life itself! Do like me. Give yourself a good shake and remind yourself of this one simple truth - God is enough!

I did and here I am all done and all good! Indeed, today is the tomorrow I was anxious about YET now, all is very VERY well!

Shalom!

P. S. Yes, I know its not easy and some days, you just want to crawl under a rock and forget it all! Trust me, been there, done that (many many times!). Do like me, enjoy the wallow. Yes, there is nothing wrong with a little anguish once in while. Even JC must have felt like he was under a rock in the Garden of G. But as you lie there, have this one thought on your mind. *'I will rise again! Don't know when but this is not the end cos its a FIXED FIGHT and in Jesus Christ, I ALWAYS win!'*

At this point, you frustrate the hell out the enemy cos he sees that you may be down but you are **not** OUT!

Wednesday, 11 November
NEPA – And It Got BETTER! – Part V

I am so sure we must have had some huge fights back then but for the life of me, I cannot seem to remember them! I do recall though that the party matter used to always cause small *katakata* cos I would be sitting there in 'Beverly Hills, the Home of the Stars'…Ahhhh yes, that is what you guys used to call that place off campus you all stayed in. I have to stop the above jist for a bit and remind you about what you and I also used to call 'appurtenance situate' on account of that being the fancy legal jargon that the landlord put in his agreement. LWKM! Any lawyer out there? Please tell me, what on earth does that mean!

Anyway, as I was saying, 'Beverly Hills, *the Home of the Stars*' was this block of flats that one landlord decided to STOP building half way and make some cool money renting out the rooms, one by one to desperate students. Yep! I think you guys gave it this name 1. Becos you all thought you were too much like that (and OK, most of the guys that stayed were some of the more 'happening' guys in school). 2. That dump had to be given a snazzy name just to make you feel better. It was just the ugliest building you have ever seen. Till we left school, not sure the landlord ever finished plastering the outside talk less of painting it! 3. Beats me! Only the good Lords knows cos Beverly Hills, it sure was not! Lol!

So you my love stayed in one of the rooms on the top most floor of this building and to be honest, the very first time I visited you there, it was really just a room, a bed, a cement block and nothing else. Cement block? Yes, your cassette player was on it. It was like a…coffee table of sorts. Lol! I am rolling on the floor laughing! This was late into our year two or early year three I think and with time, it gradually became a really cute little room. I still remember it very vividly. I also remember very vividly my many 'near misses' when my dear old Papa would come to pay me a 'surprise visit' and……….let's just say thank God for good friends o! Errrr, in view of the PG rating on this blog, let those who know; let them know where this was going. Lol! Merciful Father, once again I thank you!

As I was saying once again, do you know my favourite memories of this room? Our scrabble games, your fantastic *okro* soup, your even more fantastic beans and then the serious cassettes (yep no CDs back then) of good old oldies. My favourites were MJ's 'I'll be there' and another song I used to call 'Dear Mr. Editor'. I don't know who sang it but I actually remember the words

Dear Mr. Editor, wont you please
Print my story in your magazine
Tell all other lovers
That a cheating heart
Will only end up in misery

Chorus:

I was a lying, cheating fool, treated her so cruel
Broke her heart and made her cry
Broke every rule and that's my true Confession
Please print it in your magazine
This story is my true confession and
I'm sorry that I treated her so cruel
Ohhhh, sorry that I treated her so cruel.

I would call her up and apologise
If I was half the man I should be
But am afraid its too late for that
Cos I bet she wouldn't listen to me
I was a lying, cheating fool ...etc.....

Do you remember? Lo! There were other great songs as well but I don't remember their titles even though I am singing the words of one of them right now as I type.

You are the sun; you are the rain babe (or was it moon now? Lol!)

That makes my life this foolish game.
You need to know, I love you so and
I'll do it all again and again'.

I think this was actually Lionel Ritchie. I loved this one too and I remember the vacation I went with my mom and my sister to visit my uncle in Ireland. Every night as I washed dishes, I would sing this song to the plates and think of you...

Hmmmm, memories...

See now, I got distracted…I will have to stop here and continue my gist about Beverly Hills and oh yes, our fights next time!!!!!!

Thursday, 12 November
NEPA – Its STILL Getting Better – Part 6

OK, so where was I? Yes, Beverly Hills and our fights or the lack thereof. I think I shall conclude my jist on the *Home of the Stars* first cos I know it sounds cute but apart from the upsets over my ever growing need to arrive at parties waaaaayyyyyy before time, I am still trying to remember………ah! OK, just remembered a good one. But first, Beverly Hills.

Please do not get me wrong, I have no grudge against this off campus appurtenance situate (thanks to the reader who actually sent me a definition of this! Thanks to you, am even more confused. Lol!) at all oh! As a matter of fact, you remember that when you went off to another University for a one-year sabbatical of sorts, I became one of the few 'Landladies' of the compound (errr, that does not sound very complimentary at all!) as I took over your 'Suite' in the *Home of the Stars* and I do have loads of fond memories of my time there. WHAT irks me however is this. Considering the amount of money he was siphoning off poor students, could that Landlord not have had the decency to put PROPER bathrooms and toilets in this building?????? I kid you not; you will not believe that in that entire block of 'Flats' (I really am being kind to call it this), there were just TWO shower cubicles. Please calm down; I am not talking about shower as in with ACTUAL showerheads with water coming out over your head. Na ah! I mean two bare rooms we used to carry buckets of water into! Lord of all things bright and beautiful! Now, correct me if I am remembering it all wrong but we ALL had to meander our way round to these bathrooms, at least those of us on the top floor. Just thinking about it again, has me shaking. Nasty! And I am not even going to talk about where the toilets where and WHAT they were! But hey, I guess for all you 'Stars', it beat staying in the male hostel on campus. Hmmm, question for me? If it was so bad, why was I not in my hostel? Lol! Good one, good one!

Anywho, to conclude the matter for now, may I just say that regardless of all of the above, I still smile when I think of the little blue rug in the middle of the room, the huge bed that was almost too soft to be comfortable, the fold away table made out of pine, the cactus plant (or some plant!) and of course the lampshade made out of wicker that hung over the blue and white bulbs and threw light over the study table! Ahhhh. So meagre, yet so, so, well so 'us'. It was ours, yours and mine. So, it was good.

I wonder where all those other 'Stars' are? Anyway, now am sure you have been wondering what that 'good' fight was all about. Well… as this is a 'feel good' blog, am not going to tell you! Ha! This is my trip down memory lane and so therefore I can choose to erase ALL the negatives if I so desire and I desire. Lol! Of course we had issues like any other couple but what's the point in bringing them up now…we have only one life to live o jare and we are living a good life I must say. May not have much, but we have something better than 'much' we have a genuine relationship that has been refined by fire and is getting better with time. I think for me the defining thing is this – Do I love you? Yes or No. Answer is equals to Yes. So therefore NO MATTER what you do OR do not do, this truth will be cast in stone. It's unshakable. I told you abi?

You see, when I woke up to this truth and settled the matter in my heart. *O pari, de talk have finis o,* as my Ibadan peeps will say. So OK, I just might feel like killing you tomorrow when you throw your shirt on the floor right next to the laundry basket but…Ahhhh, that's what makes you YOU. I just might have a fit if you actually put it in the basket. Yes, that would mean aliens had abducted my real hubby. So, at the end of the day I am glad I got stuck with you. And I hope you feel the same way…And if you don't, tough luck, its till the death! Lol!

Oh, and thanks for the 90/10 Principle clip you just sent me. Love it! So true. Ok for all you people reading this and may not know, you can click on the link on the side and watch it for yourself. Bottom line: 10% of life is made up of what happens To YOU. The other 90% is decided by how YOU react to all life throws your way. It's your call. So what's it going to be? Yell cos someone just ticked you off at work OR just move on; maybe HE had a bad night? Anyway, watch the clip!

(Sorry, could not figure how to paste the clip…when I do, I will put it up!)

Oh, btw, my dear Nehneh, you know yourself, I cannot express how I felt listening to my 'Dear Mr. Editor' live last night. Do you know I could not sleep? My head was filled with all sorts of memories like the ones I am trying to share here today but have totally derailed myself again. Lol!

Tomorrow, I will do better. I will talk about how my family reacted to you the first time they say you. And by family, I mean my baby sister – now married woman, Sholly babes! I will remind you about the first time my papa got a whiff that something was amiss. I will remind you about how I used to gaze out of the window of our place in the staff quarters willing you to come out of your uncle's place……….it never worked though! Nope, no ESP jazz happening back then at all

For now, *kachifo*! Good night. Oops, I mean, see y'all later cos its not night here. At least not

Friday, 13 November
NEPA, You are All Right – Part Seven

I knew blood was powerful when the very first time my baby sister saw you; she had the same reaction I had. 'I don't like him. He's too yellow!' Lol! She was 5 years old. So we laughed and thought she was being cute. Naaaah! She was serious. Her 'Ekiti-ness' plus her never-seen –someone- this- white- without-actually- being -white-ness combined together to create a serious high jump for you. But you were sweet and eventually you did win her over. Come to think of it, I think that play date we set up with Essien one time like this was what did the trick!!!!! Yes, you came to pick me and we both went to your uncle's place in Bogobiri where she and your cousin played for hours! She really did not have that many children to play with back then and so this was a treat beyond measure. She still remembers him you know.

And since everywhere I went, Sholly was sure to follow, I also remember how when she would come to visit me in school, she refused to let you carry her when we went out. Sometimes we wanted to take for lunch somewhere a bit further down the road and we would worry that her little legs would get tired. You would offer to carry her and she would shake her head resolutely. So I would have to carry her…until one day, out of the blue, she gave in. We both looked at ourselves and wondered what changed. I guess, she too, like me, had been won over by your irresistible charm! Seriously though, I believe she saw that we were really good friends and it was a matter of 'if you like him, so will I'. Sisterhood! Nothing like it. Abi? Now, she is all grown up and has a man of her own and I am paying her back. Becos she likes Kuba, so will I. And the girl has even gone further than me! Her own *na proper white man*! Lol!

Now to *mi Padre*…. you know I cannot place the very exact date that my Papa got to meet you….If am not wrong, I think he must have figured you might be 'the one' when you were the first guy to appear in my house when my mom died. I will never forget that day. We were actually together when one of my family friends drove into school to see me. He said something that till this day baffles me. It baffles me cos am like 'why could they not have given him a better 'alibi', something that I would have actually believed. Listen to what he says to me. 'Your dad is travelling abroad and he wants you to come and stay in the house with your mom and sister so they wont be alone' or something to that effect...I was like 'huh?'. 1. My dad has been an *Ajala* from time Imo River and not once, not even half of once, have they ever felt that my presence was needed to stand in his gap. 2. Could they not have picked a better time than half way through my final year two exams and 3. Why could he not come and tell me this yarn himself. What did poor Mr...I forget his name now, have to be sent on this errand and with his wife!!!!! I smelt a big fat smelly rat...how did I get on this subject? Pure derailment this is, back to the main jist.... like I said this is a 'feel good' blog so no talk about dead people...even if I love them and miss them to errrr...death? (Sorry, I could not help that)

Yes, my mom died but I don't want to write about that today. This is about when Daddy met you for the first time. After I got home on the day above and had promptly lost my mind.... anyway, you were one of the first friends to land my house from Uyo. You were the first guy. I saw you and just burst into more tears. Oh dear! Can't seem to stop this blog from going tear-shaped.... As I was saying, my Papa must have put 2 and 2 together then. He is a very smart man like that so later on when you became a fixture in my life, I think he remembers how you stood by me in the days and months after, always coming to see me before I went back to school and felt 'This young man is alright'. And indeed, you are all right. You were then and you are now.

Saturday, 14 November
Eleven-Fourteen – A Beautiful Day!

Now, there are two schools of thought out there today. One is that I need to be whipped cos I forgot to wish my dear little one 'happy birthday' on FB! Considering that I have shared every other celebration with wild abandon on the network, I see their point. Lol! The other is that I should not only be whipped but I should ALSO do restitution for my unforgivable act of 'forgetfulness'. How could I forget such an occasion? Now this camp, I have to beg to differ from cos I think I have done the restitution in advance, considering that all the running around I was doing on this said Saturday was to ensure that the dear little one has access to food in his belly! Lol! Actually, there is another third school of thought that just told me to 'chill and forgive myself'. It was actually this sweet encouraging comment that made me stop and think. Hmmmm, this is serious oh! I said to myself.

So like a typical Nigerian politician, let me clear the air oh. Yes oh, before some future mother-in-law to future dota in law would think our family is not 'it' at all and all bets fall off. Lol! Please oh!, I 'only' (allow me to use that word as grave as my offence may be in itself) forgot to wish him happy birthday on Face book oh! Its not that we did not celebrate his b-day at all!!!!!!!

Of course, he woke up to the loud albeit muffled 'shrills' (Shrieks and thrills!) of mgm and I wishing him a happy birthday! He smiled that his toothy smile and jumped off the bed and headed straight for the mirror! I was wondering what was up. 'Hmmm he said, but I don't look different' Lol! Yes, we had a good laugh. Apparently my little bundle of joy, my last-born son fully expected to see some physical evidence of his having attained the grand age of 6. I assured him that even though he could see no difference he was indeed now six years old to which he replied ' OK, I guess you are right. I am six then'. He was just so deliciously adorable as he gave me that his 'if you say so Mama' look. Once this was clear in his head, he looked at me and bolted for the pile of wrapped presents he finally spotted on the settee in the room… and the rest they say is the rapturous story of a six year old ripping impatiently away at gift paper clad toys.... Ben 10 inspired. Of course! What else? I did say, 6-year-old boy. What else? If it's not Ben 10, it's Spiderman!

Anyway, so, while pleading that you forgive a mother for not hailing her baby on FB till 24 hours later, I ask that you trust me on this one. In my heart, there was a quantum (I love using this word!) of gratitude and joy towards my God who saw fit, on that beautiful November day in 2003, my own historical 'eleven-fourteen', to bless me yet again with a child - our little mini-me, our child of promise beyond measure. So while I may be guilty of not letting my FB peeps in on the joy, the quantum was there all the same!

I look at my family, my four 'reasons' as I call them sometimes and the only song that always comes to my mind is the Yoruba songs that goes thus (err forgive the spellings o!, You know I am an Ibibio girl now!)

Emi na a re Olorun. Emi na a re, Olorun,
Mo wa dupe ore amodun modun
Mowadupe ore, amosu mosu
Mowadupe Ore igba gbogbo
Emi na a re Olorun

My paraphrased translation of this song goes like this 'is this really me (imagine a look of total bafflement and disbelief)? Am I really the one basking in all these blessings, Lord I come to thank you for all the years you have been blessing me, for all the months of love and care, I just come to thank you cos you are good to me all the time...Hmmmm, is this really me?

Don't you feel the same way sometimes?

Shalom!

Tuesday, 17 November
This, I HAVE To Share

First of all, 'No' I am not done going down memory lane. I have 2 more instalments on that but I just had to share this. A friend at work sent it to me and my colleague who sits next to me had to beg me to take it easy cos I was laughing so hard. Its just sooooooo funny ESPECIALLY cos I use ALL of these in some form or the other! I am sure my mgm will attest and now, thanks to this, maybe he will finally 'get it' FINALLY!!!!!! Lol!

Enjoy! Lafta is truly the best medicine and this should give you your good long belly laugh for the day!

Women Have a Lingua franca of their own

(1) **Fine**: This is the word women use to end an argument when they are right and you need to shut up.

(2) **Five Minutes**: If she is getting dressed, this means a half an hour. Five minutes is only five minutes if you have just been given five more minutes to watch the game before helping around the house.

(3) **Nothing**: This is the calm before the storm. This means something, and you should be on your toes.
Arguments that begin with nothing usually end in fine.

(4) **Go Ahead**: This is a dare, not permission. Don't Do It!

(5) **Loud Sigh**: This is actually not a word, but it is a non-verbal statement often misunderstood by men. A loud sigh means she thinks you are an idiot and wonders why she is wasting her time standing here and arguing with you about nothing. (Refer back to # 3 for the meaning of nothing.)

(6) **That's Okay**: This is one of the most dangerous statements a women can make to a man. That's okay means she wants to think

long and hard before deciding how and when you will pay for your mistake..

(7) **Thanks**: A woman is thanking you. Do not question, or faint. Just say you're welcome. (I want to add in a clause here - This is true, unless she says 'Thanks a lot' - that is PURE sarcasm and she is not thanking you at all. DO NOT say 'you're welcome'. That will bring on a 'whatever').

(8) **Whatever**: Is a woman's way of saying ***** YOU!

(9) **Don't worry about it, I got it**: Another dangerous statement, meaning this is something that a woman has told a man to do several times, but is now doing it herself. This will later result in a man asking 'What's wrong?' For the woman's response refer to # 3.

* Share this with the men you know, to warn them about arguments they can avoid if they remember the terminology. Share this with the women you know to give them a good laugh, cause they know it's true!!!

Wednesday, 18 November
God Cannot Disappoint Us

I tried and tried to get this out last night but alas! The Internet and I were not chummy at all. My connection at home pushed me to the wall! I was so sure SOMEONE needed to read it but hey! God knows best and for some reason, this was meant to go out on the 18th and not the night of the 17th. I am wise enough to let God be God in my life and that includes when my PC connection agrees to connect!!

OK listen up! Read my lips. Yes, listen very carefully. I shall say this only once.

God NEVER disappoints His children!

We are the ones who most of the time have a different idea of how He should answer our prayers...so when He answers in a different way, the best way for us at that time.... because we already had a preconceived idea of how that situation should end, because, as we prayed we also listed exactly HOW God should answer, we believe He has missed it, disappointed us when He responds in a totally different manner... Never!

God's ways our not our ways and some times we cannot understand why He does what He does, when He does, and to whom He does it. But that should not have any effect on our praise, prayer, thanksgiving or service. I was listening to a CD this evening. As a matter of fact I have been listening to Pastor Shirley Brady (I think I got that right) for the past 2 days on the way to and from work and I agree wholeheartedly with a lot of what she says. I want to share some of the ones that spoke to me the most.

We could use some explanations sometimes

Like her, I really wish God would give me some explanation for the situations I find myself in sometimes. It would make it a whole lot easier for cooperation! Indeed, if we knew what God was up to with our delays, if we understood why the sickness was not going away, if we understood why the husband was not 'finding' us or why our wombs refused to sustain life. Indeed, my brother, my sister, if we knew why the job was just not being offered to us in spite of our qualifications or why that family member was just so intent on ruining the entire family. If only we had some insight into God's divine plans for our lives and why this season we are in or the furnace we have been passing through was so necessary. Yes, then it would make 'holding on in faith' a whole lot easier...

God is God ALL by HIMSELF

Hmmmm but it does not work like that. But like she said, 'God is God ALL BY HIMSELF' (I love that) and if He started it, He will finish it. If He said it, It will come to pass. So my dear one, reading this right now. Know this. You can really go to bed tonight with a smile on your face and peace in your soul cos you are indeed on Child Support (another one I love from this woman of God on fire). You are God's CHILD and He SUPPORTS you with his righteous right hand. Yes, the Creator of the entire universe is YOUR Daddy...and though earthly fathers may fail us, He can never ever disappoint us.

Jesus spent 18 years in obscurity

Or do you know what Jesus was doing between the ages of 12 and 30? But we know that when he arrived on the scene after those 18 years, the world took notice immediately. He became so popular; he had to keep going off to hide from the crowds! So what does that tell you... You may be passing through a time of 'invisibility'. No one seems to reckon with you or even know you but hey, remember Jesus. He went through that to bit because He made up His mind to do ' His Father's will' and put Him first, see what he became in the end. The King of Kings! The God whose name is ABOVE every other name! Praise God!

It was plain old water before Jesus turned it into FINE WINE

So how about you tell the devil to take a hike tonight and go to bed to bed cos now you know that even if you are feel like plain old water today, when God is done with you, when the pouring out is over, you will be the best tasting fine wine there is. Trust me; hold on to God for your BEST IS YET TO COME.

God has said it. He will do it. He never fails. And the only time God disappoints is when He disappoints the devices of the crafty! Amen!

Friday, 20 November
I Take Authority

(Today has been BUSY!!!! but I still thought of you all long enough to KNOW that I needed to share this with you. A good sista-friend sent it to me this morning and I tell you, we need to be declaring this over our lives EVERY MORNING!

I hope to touch base with you over the weekend but if I don't, here is wishing you all a good weekend and remember, no one can love you like God loves you, so make HIM your number one priority. Be at Peace!)

I TAKE AUTHORITY

In the name of Jesus at the mention of which every knee shall bow, be shattered oh ye people and be broken to piece. Gird yourselves but be broken in pieces, take counsel together but it will come to nothing. Speak the word but it will not stand for God is with me.

The Lord of Host has purposed in His heart and His purpose in my life shall stand. His hands are turned towards me and no one can turn it back.

May cruel masters and fierce kings rule over every Egyptian in my life. May unfathomable shame and disgrace be the portion of everybody that is incensed against me. Let all those who strive with me perish.

By the Blood, the power of the Holy Spirit and angelic assistance every signs of the babblers is frustrated and every diviner is driven mad. Their wisdom is turned backwards and their knowledge is turned to foolishness.

Every stronghold is subdued before me and the armour of kings are loosened for my sake. The double doors are open before me and they cannot be shut. Every crooked path ahead of me has been made straight and every bronze gate is broken into pieces. The bars of iron are cut asunder and I receive the treasures of darkness and hidden riches of secret places.

I am free from all captivity and free from every terrible predator. All oppressors in my life will be fed with their own flesh and they will be drunk with their own blood.

I stand on my decree as a watchman, not by my power nor by my might but through Christ in whom all things are possible, in whom I live move and have my being. No force can stand me. I'll leap through walls and run through troops. The hedge of God is round about me so I will not loose anything anymore and no more cutbacks.

This is my season for increase, breakthrough, resurrection, resuscitation and revival. I open my mouth, heart and hands wide and I ask you, lord to satisfy me with goodness so that as I walk, goodness and mercy will follow me and overtake me. I walk in excellent health, wealth, breakthrough, sound mind, prosperity, promotion, multiplication and remembrance. This is my set and appointed time to do and be all that God has called me to do and be.

I am unstoppable, "unintimidate-able" and unshakeable. Nothing and nobody can stop me because God is with me.

Anybody that touches me touches the apple of your eye, Lord so arise and contend with them, fight them to a standstill. Condemn any tongue that rises against me in judgment. Arise Lord and let my enemies be scattered. Let every flesh be silent before you.

Put your spotlight on me, showcase me and make me a billboard. Give me brand new testimonies. Let every mocker come to the brightness of my rising. Let your glory be seen all over my life. Do that which you alone can do. In Jesus name. Amen!

Friday, 20 November
5 O'clock in The Morning

Tell me what can anyone have to say at 5.00am in the morning! Well for one, I can tell you that I have not been able to sleep! Yep and right after I read a mail at work that warned that sleep was very vital to us humans. There was a report about a 42 year old guy who was as fit as a fiddle, did all the right things to keep fit, ate all the right foods but you know what he did not get enough of? Yep! Sleep. And so recently after a nice good workout in the gym as usual, he fell down and died. His heart gave out. He had suffered from some sort of heart failure induced by sleep deprivation! Can you beat that?

So yes, I got off my bed, after rolling round in it for 5 hours just to tell you to please do try and get enough sleep, at least 7 hours worth, the report said. What about me? Fear not, I am going back to bed now...but not after I have a nice pow-wow with God on the matter that is stealing my peace and therefore my sleep. Once am done doing that and My Father and I have our feedback session and agree a way forward, I am going to look the devil in the eye and tell him "Ha! You can only try but you will ALWAYS fail. As we say over here in Nigeria, devil, *Notin for you!*'

Good night.... err I mean Good morning. Lol! You know what, where ever you are, whatever the time, know that there is sleep-deprived- yet-confident-in-God woman in Nigeria that wishes that it be 'Good' for you! And I mean like when God created the world and it was 'Good'. You know that is a whole different level of 'goodness'!

Be at Peace!

Saturday, 21 November
It's A Fixed Fight

I know I really should post the last two instalments of my NEPA series and I shall but not just now. Cos things keep popping up in my head that, to me, seem far more crucial.... perhaps I am wrong but once again, its my blog and I can choose what I want to post!

This time I just need some answers...I am stumped. I have been looking to God, scratching my head and wondering what on earth is going on!!!!! Has the world gone mad! Has the devil really taken over the minds of men? Why am I hearing more tales of husbands going astray? Why do I seem to have more people around me in the throes of marital discord? Or is it that my eyes and ears were closed before? Is it that I was going through life oblivious to reality? WILL SOMEONE PLEASE TELL ME WHY THE ENEMY SEEMS TO BE WINNING IN THIS WAR AGAINST MARRIAGES??????? Sorry for shouting. Forgive me, but I hate to see pain. Especially when it is not deserved.

Over here in this country, we blame it all on 'jazz'. Yes, the women out there have charmed our men. They put something in their drinks or they lace their mascara with some evil potion and voila! One look through their evil-laden fluttering lashes and our men are sunk? But is that not letting you men off easy? So is it really beyond your control? Are you truly always unable to resist the wiles of the enemy disguised as strange women?

Why are so many of you dragging your wives through so much heartache and pain and loneliness? How come, the wife your swore to love till death do you part is now so 'low' in your eyes that you cannot stand to be with her. How come? What changed? Is it true what a male colleague tried to explain to me the other day that men are by their very nature, adulterous? Polygamous? Evil? I cannot believe that. I will not believe that.

I go to bed to night with pain in my heart for the many woman out there waiting for their men to come to their senses Waiting for them to come home. Waiting for God to remove the scales that the god of this age has placed over their eyes, so that they can come back to the wives of their youth. To the children God has blessed them with through the woman God caused them to find. Yes, the woman who now, seems to be nothing in their sight.

I pray no woman reading this can relate. I really pray that no woman reading this recognises herself in anything I have said. I really pray so.... but I know someone who can. And my heart breaks for this beautiful woman of God and I believe what I told her this evening. It's a fixed fight. She has won this battle already. Cos God said so.

Yes, it may seem foolish to the world to keep on loving the man that is treating you so badly. Yes, people may laugh at your decision to see him through the eyes of grace. Indeed, you yourself may cry hot tears as you do your best to welcome him home in the wee hours of the night, offering food. Offering love. Offering you. But in this love and humility lies your power. The world does not preach it. But I honestly believe it. Stooping to conquer! Therein lies our power. Cos only when we stoop low enough can God reach over us and touch these men we love so dearly. In a fixed fight, God wears the boxing gloves and enters the ring. The only thing we are called to do is move out of the way. Stoop.

Be at peace!

Tuesday, 24 November
The Value of Time

As I sit here now waiting for my son to finish his breakfast so we can go to the dentist, one thing is uppermost on my mind. Time. And how I am wasting it. Yes, the clock is ticking and with each passing second, a slice of my life has gone by, wasted. Why? Cos I am upset. Locked in a cold war. Its funny how you do certain things even when you know better. It's funny how it's easier to give good biblical advice to others than to take it. It's funny how you beg others to see people through the eyes of grace yet when it's your turn, you ignore the grace spectacles, stewing, fuming, and wasting time.

I have always done my best to be honest in this place cos there is really no point to the whole thing if I don't So today, in all honesty, I confess to me wasting time…BUT I encourage you all not to. Why? Because really once its gone, you cannot get it back. And then you look back and you cannot even remember what the point was! Let me share some quotes from a mail I got recently:

If you want to know the value of a second
Ask the one who just survived an accident

If you want to know the value of a minute
Ask someone who just missed the bus, the train or the flight

If you want to know the value of nine months
Ask a woman who gives birth to a stillborn

If you want to know the value of a year
Ask someone who has go a re-sit paper to take

if you want to know the value of ……….

Ok, I cannot remember the rest but these quotes above struck me hard cos the true magnitude of how we waste time is never really known until the time has been lost. So why not try NOT to waste your time. Your life. There is really nothing worth THAT.

That's all I have to say today...one thing is sure, the sun will come out tomorrow...Yes, because Jesus lives, I can face today, tomorrow and whatever life brings my way in the times to come...Yes, my life is in His hands...

Be at Peace!

Wednesday, 25 November
NEPA – The Winding Road of Love

Its good to hold on to good memories you know. I have found out that in times when storms gather, if you can travel down the road of yesterday, armed with the wonderful memories you created along the way, you are able to, somehow garner strength to push it through the rain and clouds. So today, even as you read this blog, make some memories, some good ones so that they too can carry you over the storms of life…cos trust me, the storms will surely come.

Anyway, do you remember how I told you my baby sister Sholly was like my little lamb and that wherever I went she was sure to follow? Well, I was the exact same thing to my mgm. Wherever he went, I was sure to make my presence felt eventually. Hmmmm let me count. Ok, so when you went off for your one-year thing in Ife, I found a way to come there to see you. For the life of me I cannot imagine what my plans where when I took off. How did I plan to find you? In that big old school? But you know love gives us wings and we think we can fly most of the time. Lol! I went oh and I did find you and let it not be said outside where I spent that first night cos it was late and I could not locate any of my old girl friends from secondary school (who, by the way, had no clue I was coming!) All I can say is thank God for his manifold mercies on our young stupid lives. So carefree, so crazy. I still have some photos from that trip and I must say, they are quite atrocious to say the least! Do you remember, taking photos by those sculptures near their Fine Arts department?

And then there was my visit to you at Ogudu when they moved your whole campus there. By this time I was serving and staying in Calabar and I remember I actually cooked something to take along. Hmph! Imagine that. Yam pottage I think it was. You know I had to stop typing in a bid to remember 'where on earth did I sleep?' I know the answer is obvious but I am like 'what where we thinking?' I just bless the name of God for my poor father – ignorance was indeed bliss. And I bless His name again for protection over the life of a pretty young thing living *la vida loca* miles away from where she should have been. Lol!

But the best of all my escapades where the ones when I came to Jos to see you. Now, that place I liked. It was almost like going abroad. Lol! The weather was cool; you were serving now and shared a flat with some other corpers. In short without going into plenty details, suffice to say that I have travelled the world…err Ok I have travelled Nigeria for your love! Some of those trips were at night in luxury buses and potentially dangerous. But somehow I did not feel it. I just had one thing on my mind – Seeing you again. And that made the miles go by quick. Now, I shudder at the thought of the magnitude of the risk we took back then. My goodness! But anyway, it was all worth it and so yes, though I was on the road a lot for you, it was good.

It was good because you did the same for me. If I was not coming to you, you were travelling down to meet me. We had indeed become that couple that they call by names. I am sure if back then we had all the 'brangelina and bennifer' name concoctions, we would for sure, have been the 'Mercedes Bhenz' of our era…Get it? Get it? Well, those who know us will get it and you must admit, it does have a certain ring to it……….

And that brings me to the last instalment of my 'NEPA' series, the one that ends in when you put a ring on it! But that comes later so stay tuned!

As we say in France, *a la prochaine*!

P. S. just thought to mention that I am in NO WAY encouraging any young lady out there to go traipsing around your location because of love oh! Hmmmm, me? God was just extra extra gracious to me on account of my naive yet pure love for this guy. My cup and your cup are not the same oh!!!!!!! Plus today, no 18 year old can claim to be as innocent as we were back then. *Una eye done open well well!* lol!

Wednesday, 25 November
Angel Friends

I once read that mothers are angels without wings. I believe it with all my heart. I also believe that God sends some angels down to earth just to be friends to His children. Maybe its just me, but this is what I have come to believe cos I have such angel friends in my life today. And I am grateful.

I have the angel friend who God just sent to call me right at a time when I was so down. His timing was perfect. Her words were on point. My spirit was lifted. Is that not what friends are for? Its funny but the first time we met, it was via a telephone call that lasted hours. We were miles apart but we made an instant connection. Till tomorrow, I admire her strength, her hostess abilities and her sheer determination in all things LIFE. I salute you my London angel friend you. You know who you are.

I have this other angel friend who just wont let me forget what I told her. Lol! As I struggle with certain issues in my life, she encourages me with my very own words. And without even knowing it, she sparks life in me again just by inviting me to think with her. She makes me laugh. She makes me cry cos I also know what she is going through. Yet she makes time to make me laugh. I salute you angel friend. You know who you are.

Now, there is my prayer warrior angel friend. Hmmmm, I admire her even though I have only ever seen her once in my life. She inspires me to do one of the best things I can do. To pray. Her text messages always seem to meet me at the right time. She is my firebrand angel friend. Funny, I know her for just so long yet I know that wherever my name is mentioned, she will back me up. You have some friends for years but this kind of trust is not part of the mix. Yet, for this sista-friend, its like we were meant to be.... you too, I salute. You know who you are.

Then I have my office angel-friend. I doubt if she even knows it. We have a special bond in that we come a longish way back and we both speak a second language and can therefore switch to it when we want to talk about stuff we want no other to understand. Our stuff, we are discussing. But what she does not know is that she too, always seems to ask me questions that push me to a better place. I trust her words. I trust her motives. I am sure you agree that for many 'normal' friends' this is not the case. But for angel-friends, such as this my friend, motives are crystal clear. The motive is love. Agape love. And so I salute you too, *mon ange au bureau*! I really do hope you know who you are.

How can I ever forget my model angel friend? I promise if she would let me I would be her agent. She has the looks like that even battered by life as we know it, she still shines from within and without. Her attachment to God inspires me cos indeed in my opinion, His furnace for her burns too fiercely. She has been through much and still she stands. She loves me with all her heart. I know it. And I love her right back. I know she prays for me even in the midst of her own pain. I know she remembers me. Together, we fought one of the fiercest battles of my life. You must know who you are my *Oge*, I salute you. I salute you! And you know that my special dance is perfect now cos the time is NOW!

You know sometimes in life you wonder what your true purpose is, why you are here. Do you have any value? Yes, regardless of your role as a wife and mother and sister and daughter, you just wonder? How am I making a difference? To you my angel friends, please do not be unmindful of the good you are doing in my life. While I know that God also has grander things for you to do, for me, you are already doing a great thing. You are being more than a friend to me. And I appreciate you. My prayer is that you will count it as a HUGE blessing to be used by God to show His love to another. To a sista. To me. In this, you are relevant. In this, you are fulfilling your destiny. You are an Angel-Friend.

Yes, this is what I believe.

Thursday, 26 November
NEPA – He Put A Ring On It. And It Was Excellent

OK, so here we are at the final instalment and I am already missing this series…I guess I can always come back and read them all over again! But you know, first of all, I just have to give God the glory for His Hand of favour and protection over my mgm and I all those years.

Its amazing the road miles we racked up and through it all, God kept us…our final bus stop however was to be Ibadan. We both did our second degrees there. Me first and then him. His first degree was five years, mine, four (just in case you were wondering how come I did mine first. Lol!). To be honest I hated that one year cos doing a masters was hard work! And you should have seen my face when my academia papa tried to suggest that I continue on to do a doctorate…I think my eyes said it all. He wisely left the matter.

Anyway, so you were still in Ibadan when I started looking for a job in Lagos. And as God would have it, I got one in one of the old French banks as a PA. Life was good. You were even more blest in that your employer came to the campus to look for you! Yep, you already more or less had a job even before you turned in your thesis! I remember praying for you as you attended all the final interviews in Lagos. I remember encouraging you as you went back to campus thinking you had not done your best. I remember calling the HR dept of that bank for you trying to follow up on the offer letter. I remember jumping bus with you at TBS after work on the way home. Do you remember? When I tell our children about our *molue* and *danfo* jumping days. They just give me this incredulous look. Lol! And to think that sometimes I cannot seem to remember how to thank God…. imagine!

Anyway, like I always tell you, I made life too easy for you. Becos we had been dating for so long, we just assumed we would get married. It was never even a subject of controversy. Now, to be honest, I wish it had cos then I would have got to experience all that 'down on bended knee' drama. Lol! So let it be said on record that you, oh my mighty good man, never really proposed to me! We just got up one day and said, OK, this is the date and voila! Plans were on the way! And by plans, I mean, we planned it all. Yep, our parents were all outside of Lagos so we both did it all and everyone just turned up on the day. A nice, no rain day in May, 16 years ago. Good heavens...and we are still both alive. There is a God that's for sure! Lol!

I was happy that day. You were sweating that day. Every time I ask why, the answer is different but always funny. I loved our wedding train. It was made up of family. My cousins. Your sister. My sister. Your brother. And then some of the cutest boys ever who though were not blood, are to this day, still sort of family. You should see them all now, all these young children. All grown up. Some are even themselves now married. The guys wore these awesome *kente* waistcoats while the ladies were in these Princess Di inspired red and white skirts suits which were all the rage then (but am sure Sola and Audrey will kill me if I tried to make them wear them today!) The younger boys wore white and blue sailor inspired outfits while the little girls wore the same sailor inspired (don't ask, I think I just loved the navy look o jare) dresses but in the cutest pink ever. And all these outfits had our initials embroidered on their lapels! Dear Lord, I did fancy myself back then...I designed the whole lot!

As for my dress. It was a dream. And you know what the best part of the dream was? That I was slim enough to fit into it. Lol! I tell you, some of my old friends from University arrived at the church just as I was being taken in by my father and they were so sure they were at the wrong wedding! Cos the last time they saw me, I was three times the size of the bride they were looking at. Lol! I loved it. The surprise on everyone's face when they saw me.... precious!

But you know what my favourite part of the whole event was. Not the church service though till this day I still remember the Sermon. It was titled 'Love' and it was preached by Pastor Joe Olaiya. Back then he was just a nice family friend who had a church somewhere in the North. My aunty, the Mamandant invited him to minister at our wedding and he agreed. So today, I can make *shakara* that one of our country's great Men of God preached at our wedding ceremony. It was not the reception, though I absolutely loved the reckless abandon with which you tried to beat me at dancing. It was not the honeymoon, though I will forever love my papa for getting us those free nights in the Honeymoon Suite at Ikoyi Hotel. That was the best! No, all these were good but my favourite part of the whole thing were our RINGS.

Yes, the rings we exchanged. The rings by which we vowed to commit to the long haul. People have rubbished the significance of the rings now but I just cannot. I know even you don't 'get' my thing about the rings. But you see for me, they are more than just strips of gold. No, they are symbolic of promises made before God and I still value mine. In fact when they mistakenly get stuck in my glove sponge and I don't realise and go out without them! Crickey! I feel naked! I guess that's just the way I am.

The truth is wedding rings should be special to the couple. Ours were specially engraved on the inside. Yours has my name and the word *'Together'* and mine has your name in it and the word *'Forever'*.

Forever Together. Together Forever. That was our hope and prayer then. That's my hope and prayer now. I don't know the future. But I know the God who does. He was there on the day when we exchanged those rings. He blessed our union. He said it was good. So I am counting on Him to give us the grace to hold strong for another sixteen years and more to see our three children grow up, marry and have their own children. Yes, that would be good. Actually, that would be excellent!

Saturday, 28 November
I Have Learnt a Life Lesson Today.

For the second time in my whole entire life, I felt like someone had stuck a knife in my heart. The pain I felt in my heart, in my soul...only God could have kept me breathing. Honest. Only God. But therein lies the life lesson I learnt.

God is TRULY enough.

Do me a favour. Don't bother about what could be the reason for what I am saying. Do not try to fathom who could be the perpetrator of this painful act. The person is after all, only human. What do you expect? What does the bible say about the heart of humans? Yes, desperately wicked. So, let's leave that matter.

Let's focus on a better matter. The matter of a God who is indeed a PILLAR. A BUFFER. And today, I have found out. He is also a one-of-a-kind BULLET PROOF and DAGGER PROOF shield!!!!!!! I learnt today that because, for some reason, as if I had known what was coming my way today, this morning I had sang loud and strong to God reconfirming His position as THE ONLY PILLAR of my life. Because of that reaffirmation, God had wrapped Himself around my heart. My fragile heart in preparation for the onslaught to come. What a wonderful wonderful loving Father we have in this God who sees into the future!

I learnt today that it is true. I can stand all things because Jesus Christ will give me the power to stand. Because He is there behind me holding me up in the face of the windy storm or in this case the storm of words. Mean, below the belt words. To me. Me? But God will judge...but no, I will not go there...I will leave that matter...

But suffice to say that I learnt a life lesson or two today my people. But hey! I am still standing, I am still smiling, and I am still here. Devil, you can try another one cos once again. You have failed this one. I don jump am pass!

I share this with anyone out there who may have been hurt by someone really bad and you think you just want to die. To crawl into a ball and shut the lights out for the next one year! Don't do it! Call on God. Call on Jesus. He will hear you and He will give you the strength to bear up under the weight of the pain and better still. He will take the pain away... like He is doing for me.

Shalom!

DECEMBER

Wednesday, 02 December
Humility – Controlled Strength

I have been thinking about this word for sometime now, maybe cos of events in my recent history. Yes, everyday, we are making history. My story. Your story. It's all our history.

The definition of 'Humility' I love the most is one my dear departed pastor read out to us once - Humility is 'controlled strength'. I loved it then. And I love it now cos people tend to see being humble as some sort of weakness. But Jesus was not weak. Far from it.

He was the excellent personification of humility yet the very embodiment of divine and supreme power. Jesus was meek yet mighty. He was peace loving yet passionate about all things God. Jesus had every right in the world to ask Pontius Pilate ' do you know who I am? Do you know who you are talking to? If I call down fire on you now, you will see! Me? Son of God that I am!' But no, this was not His style. That was just not the way He was. Why is that the way we are? Why is that the way I am? (Yes even if I don't say it out loud?) Who am I really? Who am I that God did not make? What do I have that God did not give me. Where am I that God did not place me? A friend of mine was trying to count her blessings the other day and decided that it would be easier to count the sand at Barbeach! Yes, that's how much we owe God for who we are. So why do we go off on a tangent when someone pokes our puny egos? (Selah, I hear this means 'pause and ponder' so pause and ponder right now before going on. Lol!)

I like something else my dear departed pastor told us. He said apart from Jesus, the only thing that can be compared to him in terms of meekness and humility is the earth we live on. Yes, we dig it, stand on it, build on it, plant on it. Sometimes we even pee and poo on it. Yes, and then we seal the deal by performing all sorts of *orisiri* sacrifices all over it. In short we do anything we like and yet it remains silent. It allows us. It does nothing. It says nothing. It is humble. But at the end of the day, that same earth we have treated as we like will open up its mouth and swallow us all up! Now, tell me who has won the matter in the end?

Can I be like the earth? Will people not think I am a *mumu*? So was Christ a *mumu*? We all know that He was not. And our aim is to be like Him in ALL ways. So check yourself like I am checking myself...Recently I relearnt the power of true humility. I wept from the pain of being obedient to God. I rocked myself to and fro trying to release myself from the agony of 'stooping to conquer'...it was haaaaaaaaarrrrrrrrdddddd but I did it cos through Christ, it is always do-able. Today, I can tell you that the returns are plenty-fold!

Hmmmm, indeed, this race is a process, a marathon. God will help us till the end. In Jesus name. Amen!

Be at Peace...and oh yes, be humble. You really have no boasting rights. Your boast should only be in Christ Jesus. This is something else my dear friend above always says. And she is right.

Friday, 04 December
Flashes of Colour In The Sand

I take the back road to and from work every day. It's the only way to get to work in 1.30mins instead of three and it's the only way to get home in three hours instead of five. Yes, that's my commute time to and from work every day. I spend 4 hours on the road to and fro. It should take me 2 hours tops! On top of that, I get to have all my intestines tumbled around and around in my tummy as a bonus! But hey! I should be thankful (and I am) cos I have the four wheeled drive to enable me take this 'scenic' route.

Indeed, perhaps if I were not so tired after a grinding day at work, I would actually take time to enjoy the scenic view of the ocean as I bump along. Perhaps if my confidence in the massive tyres of my 4 x 4 was 100% then I would take my mind off the possibility of sinking in the sand and actually enjoy the sway of the palm trees that lined the beach road. It's only in our dear country that another man's misfortune is someone else's gain (well apart from when you think about people who make coffins. I wonder how they pray for good business? 'Dear Lord, please increase my business, let plenty of people die today!?). You see, just as you have palm trees lining this scenic beach route, so do you have 'beach boys'. They too line the route. They are not swaying in the wind to delight you. They are waiting, praying for your car to sink in the sand. They help you out. You pay them. Good business and quite lucrative, don't you agree?

Anyway, my blog today is not about sinking cars. Nor is it about beach rollers (am really tempted to call them 'beach bums' or 'beach rogues' but I am holding myself back. Oops, just did! Lol!). Today am just musing about what happened to me today on the way to work. There I was on my bumpy way to work, trying to relax my muscles cos its less painful when your body is relaxed. There I was trying to open my 'Open Heavens' at it bumped up and down on my laps. Yes, there I was mulling over how I would love to be like Elisha and see the heavenly hosts that God had assigned to watch over me...when something caught my eyes outside the window of the car. There it was again, a bright flash of colour in the midst of all that, for me, had always just been whitish brown sand littered with pure water bags and all manner of debris.

I looked again and am not sure what surprised me more, that there were so many of these bright pink flowers on the side of the road or the fact that I have NEVER seen them before! Honest, If you had asked me to describe this beach route my response would have been...sand, bumpy road, sand, bumpy road, trash, waves, more waves, beach huts, beach bum errr...sorry, beach boys, coconut husks, more trash...' and on and on I would have gone but not once would you have heard me say, 'bright pink lovely to behold flowers'!

They were not everywhere and after a while I did not even see any more of them...in fact I noticed just as we hit another milestone on the route (for alas there are 5 major milestones to this route, at least from where I live), I saw one lone pink flash and then the colour became whitish brown again. No more flashes. No more loveliness. But, one word struck me? Possibilities.

If it was possible for those lovely bright pink flowers to somehow spring up and be sustained in the middle of the sandy desert road. Then I as a Christian should also be able to spring up and be sustained even in the midst of a dry and sandy environment. Who says things have to be perfect for me to continue to be bright and lovely to behold. It has not rained for days. I know cos that's why so many more cars are sinking; the sand is so loose now. Yet, those pink flowers look as vibrant as ever. Yet everything else around them looked dry, arid, withering, lifeless – uninviting. That means, somehow, nourishment is getting to those flowers. Somehow, something or someone is feeding them. Somehow, they manage to STAND OUT.

SOMEONE too feeds me. Yes, my God is feeding me. Physically and Spiritually. And I know He is doing much more for me than for those flowers. So why then does my colour not shine as bright as theirs? Why am I not bright enough to catch the attention of the casual person bumping along by me on this sandy bumpy road called Life? If they can survive in the midst of that arid land, then I dare say, so can we. And we too can be bright flashes of colour along the hot, sandy road so that as others pass us by, they too will catch their breathe in silent wonder. What a beautiful sight! How odd, yet how wonderful to see such in the midst of all this evil! Such wholesomeness. Such godliness! Such, such, such Christlikeness!

I get the sense I have rambled abit in this blog. But in my head, its clear what am trying to say…hopefully, you too will get the gist of the matter.

Arise and Shine!

Be the 'Brightness!

Yes, that sums my thoughts up rather nicely.

Be at Peace!

Sunday, 06 December
The Wonder of The Snowflake

I know I had heard it before but today as my Pastor B preached her message and said it again, it took on a whole new meaning for me. She was telling us about the wonder of the snowflake. How every single snowflake that softly falls to the ground is different from the next one. Can you imagine that? When you sit by the window watching the snow fall from the sky, every single one you see, every single one has a different make up. How awesome is that? To the ordinary eye, they all look the same, don't they? Snow is snow is snow! But no, our God is such a genius God that He created each one unique. Special. Beautifully so. Just like He created you. And me.

Yes, we too are so created. On the outside we all have the same features. Like each snowflake is white and powdery-like to our human eyes, so all human beings have one head, two arms, two legs, a mouth, two eyes, a nose, one heart.... you get the picture? On the outside, we all look the same but God has made us all so incredibly different. So wonderfully unique. There can never be another DNW. Never. There might be someone out there that looks a bit like me, even sound like me maybe, perhaps even think like me in some ways but there is NO ONE out there that IS me. There is only one of me on the entire face of the earth. And guess what. Ditto for you. There is no one on the face this planet like you. You are fearfully and wonderfully UNIQUE like one of those awesomely created snowflakes. Wow!

So we have no business comparing ourselves to anyone else. We are what we are by the grace of God and God has a plan just for you. Just for me. It's only a lack of understanding that makes us compare ourselves to other people and want what they have or want to be where they are. The truth is that we never really now the TOTAL picture of that person. If we did, you would be like " Dear Lord, forgive me, I DO NOT want any of that situation!!!!!' So all you might see may be the Gucci bags, or the lovely children or the fact that she drives a different car every time you see her BUT do you know that she cries herself to sleep every night from loneliness. Do you see the brother battling with low self esteem late at night when the doors are closed and his chauffeur driven car drops him at his mansion of a house. None of that stuff can block those choking feelings of being a 'nobody' that he tries to mask with all the 'effects'.

And you know something else? When you stop looking at what God is doing in the life of the other sister or brother. When you begin to focus on your own walk with God and begin to see what God is doing in your OWN life for good, then you will be able to give true THANKS in all things. And as we close 2009, if there is one thing we ought to be right now, it is thankful.

So why not get wise today and appreciate God for your uniqueness. Thank God for making just ONE of you and because God does not make things just for fun. There is talent on the inside of you that you must bring out. If you don't, you are depriving the world of something ONLY you can give to it. Just like each snowflake that falls from the sky brings its own unique crystalline beauty to us, so you my friend have plenty of beauty to give to our world. So bring it on. In your own unique way.

Shalom!

Tuesday, 08 December
Oh! What A Wonderful Feeling

Oh! What a Wonderful Feeling! Oh! What a wonderful day! I have a wonderful feeling; everything's going my way!

This is the song that came to me sometime during the course of today, which was really just going on like any other day until…

First of all I was still floating on cloud nine from seeing my corporate identity come to life in the hands of some genius I will simply call Frank and his team. Yes, I have a little 'something something' going on and my heart is still singing with the remnants of the joy that filled it yesterday as I tried my best to choose my favourite. They were all so good. So showery. So just what I would have done myself had I the skills! May God continue to send down showers of blessings on you Frank. I am grateful. You brought my dream to reality on paper.

And then today. Oh, this was a big one. I got a phone call. Yes, from 'overs' as my people in the eastern part of the country would say. And, even though it is early days yet, I have a wonderful feeling everything's going my way. People have always told me certain things and they still keep telling me even know, even yesterday, someone told me the same thing. ……err, sorry not telling you! Lol! But, I will some day soon or perhaps you will 'see' it as it unfolds God willing.

But I am in an extremely happy place today. Actually, I just had a thought, I have not been happy, I have been joyful. Cos to be honest, there have been some specks of irritation crossing my path BUT alas! They could not burst my bubble. Is that not what the joy of the Lord is all about? Its not about your circumstances (even though mine have been quite wonderful lately), its more about the joy you have from knowing that God has got your back no matter what. It gives you strength to still be bubbly like me even when those irritants fly by… Amazing to think that I was in the mood to kill someone just over the past weekend or so. Lol! You see why we should anchor our emotion to God? Everything else is so fickle. So here today and gone tomorrow!

So I am talking to myself now as I end this, 'DNW you must remember to be joyful and full of the bubbliness that you are now floating on… regardless of what happens on Saturday, regardless of what happens in the end as per that call from 'overs'. Yes and even if that mail that said you had won a freaky amount of money turns out to be a hoax (as you well know it is!! Lol!), you will still go around floating on your God-high, humming under your breath ' everything is going my way!' You hear? Yes, that is what you will do, for therein lies your strength!

In the joy that comes from God!

Shalom!

Tuesday, 08 December
Don't Let the Grinch Steal Your Christmas

I was on that bumpy road to work this morning. Remember the one I told you about the other day. It was not too bad this time cos I had my MGM's hand to hold on to! Lol! Yes, one of the rare days when we got to go to work in the same car. Small gist here and small gist there. A little silence here and there as we got lost in our own thoughts and then he said it.

He made a comment that made me laugh till tears ran down my cheeks. He was talking about the man at the helm of affairs somewhere and how he was just really throwing a spanner in the works for most families. How he was 'the Grinch who had stolen Christmas'. It was funny all by itself and then add to that the way he said it. I could not help laughing out loud. A real belly laugh. If you have seen that movie, you will understand! All I could see in my mind's eyes with this little man in a bow tie carting off the country's Christmas tree! Lol! Oh dear, pardon me, but my sense of humour is not always in line with most of the population! Anyway, it was good to share a comic moment with my main man.

But as the laughter died down and we bumped along, I sobered up. I turned to my main man and said defiantly ' No, we will not let him steal our Christmas!' I refuse to let him or anyone have that much power over me. Over mine. Saying that he had the power to steal my precious Christmas was like giving him the power to stop baby Jesus from being born. Lailai! It was like making him the custodian of all that Christmas really represents - Love, Peace and Joy to the world. Of course, he could not steal that away from me. From mine.

Naira and kobo, presents, and plenty rice, we may not have in reckless quantities, but I will make sure, by the grace of God that my home does not lack quantum amounts of love and joyful merriment this Christmas. These are free! Yes, neither man in a bow tie, nor man in *agbada* nor any other principality or power will rob my home of all that Christ's birth signifies. As my only princess will say in her funny Yoruba accent *'Rara o!'*

Yes, no way, Jose! The Grinch shall not be stealing my Christmas this year or any other year for that matter

Don't' let him steal yours either! And trust me, the 'Grinch' can manifest in many different ways. So be ready, be prepared…and block him! Do all in your power to have yourself and your family a very merry Christmas time!

Feliz Navidad Prospero Ano y Felicidad!

Wednesday, 09 December
Are We Truly Thankful or Are We Just Being Polite

I did my Masters at a university in the South of my country (now that sounded funny. Do you 'do' a Masters degree or 'undergo' it or perhaps like me, you 'suffer through it!' Lol!). Anyway I am sure you get my meaning. And while I was there, every weekend or most weekends actually I would board one of the rickety cabs that this ancient town was famous for and watch the road through the gaps in the cab floor as I headed to my aunty's house. It was always nice to get away from campus once in a while and my auntie treated my like a princess so I loved to go there. But the thing I remember the most was Sundays at her church.

Now my auntie used to go to one of the CAC churches. I am pretty sure she still does and I remember during testimony times watching in utter amazement as people would come up, give their testimonies with so much gusto which always crescendo-ed into this spontaneous rolling on the floor from side to side. They said that what God had done for them was so far beyond their ability to praise Him in words alone that they just had to do something more. And their 'more' was to roll on that hard cement floor from one side of the church to the other!!!!!!! I just could not understand it.

NOW, I do.

Yes, now that I am a bit older (OK, a lot older) and much wiser (hopefully) and have definitely seen more of life and how 'BUT for God, there go I wretched and hopeless too' I NOW fully comprehend the need to give crazy praise to the God I serve. The one who loves me more than I can understand. Whose love for me I sometimes question. Not because I don't believe that He loves me. But because I don't know WHY He loves me like He does.

What am I trying to say here? It's like this. As a child we are taught that it is polite to say 'Thank you' when someone does something nice for you or gives you something. That it is the polite thing to do. Yes?

Good. But I have figured out that most of the time, when we are saying 'thank you' to God, that's all we are being. Polite. Cute, well-mannered, well brought up. Don't get me wrong. There is nothing wrong with being well brought up oh!

But would I be terribly wrong to say that our God deserves much more than our cute courtesies? Will you want to smack me upside the head if I tell you that the God who woke you up this morning. The one who gives light to the eyes you are using to read this blog right now. The Jehovah God that gave you the very breath that you just took just now. Will I be mad to say He deserves much more than just a polite 'thank you'? Our Omnipotent, Loving, Faithful, Patient, Gracious God and Father deserves our crazy heartfelt roll-on-the-floor, jump-on-the-table thanks and praise!

So next time you are in church or even just in your room and you want to thank God, give it to Him with ALL of your heart cos YOU know what God has done for you. If you sat down to THINK, to CONTEMPLATE your life, to CONSIDER all that God has done for you, you know He is worthy of mad praise and thanks....

You know what? Let's switch gears. Try to think about ALL the stuff God has delivered you from that YOU DID NOT EVEN KNOW about. Try that and see if you too will not throw aside all your cute praises and polite 'Thank You's' and give your God some reckless, crazy praise!!!!!!!

Yes, be polite to your fellow man.... but our God? He deserves much more than that! Don't you think?

Shalom!

Friday, 11 December
A Letter To The Enemy

Now hear this.

Yes, I would not even grace a letter to you with any form of greeting. I see you are on edge and cannot stand that fact that my God and Father is about to take me to another level. Shame on you. Oh, I forget, you don't know the meaning of the word. But let me tell you something now and let me tell you short and simple. YOU don't scare me anymore. I know who I am in Christ now and I am confident that greater is my God in me than you can ever dream of being. If you had any sense at all, you would give up this your age-old bid to be like God. He is better than you, bigger than you.... in short, why am I wasting my time trying to compare you with my JEHOVAH? There is NO ONE Like Him.

You know, its almost laughable your attempts to mar my excitement and ruin my joy at this particular time. You must be so frustrated. Well, you know what, you devil you? Get used to it. Cos my God and I are on a journey and you CANNOT stop it cos when my Father in heaven commands a thing. IT STANDS FAST. And He has commanded that I enter into a new season in my life and nothing you do can negate God' spoken word into my life.

So to paraphrase what Jesus Christ told you in the wilderness when you tried to stop Him from entering into His ministry too - 'GET LOST!'

Saturday, 12 December
Father Lord, We DID It!

'Hear this song from a grateful heart; anytime I think of you, my praises start. I love you sooooooooooo much Jesus, I love you sooooooooooo much!'

Yes, this is the song that has been in my heart and on my lips all evening! God, my Father, you are just too much and I love you so much cos today? At my first official bridal shower under our brand, QB's Showers of Blessings, Lord you surpassed my wildest expectations. I thank you from the bottom of my heart.

People of God, God did it! I may say 'we' in the title but I know it was really God doing his business. I was simply the tool. His partner. Read this testimony (I shall be sharing more in the coming days. And in Jesus Christ's name, this good thing He has started in my life, He will continue to perfect. Amen!

To all my sista-divines who supported me in prayers and words of encouragement, I say a big 'Mmmmmwaaaah!'

My day with QBSB

I had an exciting time at this event organised by QBSB today. It wasn't like the regular bridal showers that are usually filled with playing crazy games and all. It was fun and at the same time spiritual.

The whole concept of the organising gave me a new view of bridal showers and I am really glad that I was a part of this.

QBSB, you are doing a great job and God will continually increase you in ways that you have never imagined.

I honestly did not pay this lady to say this. Honest! Lol! It just goes to show that God is a faithful God and I just want to say thanks to

Him with a lifestyle that is worthy of His faithfulness and love towards me!

Join me please. It's the only way to go as we close out 2009 and cross over into 2010.

Shalom!

Sunday, 13 December
Desperate? Yes, Desperate

I promise to continue sharing my bridal shower testimonies right after this blog. Just bear with me for a few hundred lines of blog. Lol!

The year is coming to an end and I feel a need to re-state what I am all about. What this blog is all about. And why on earth I have stuck with my blog title or at least with the use of the word *'desperate'*.

Its funny how such a little word can have so much impact or cause so much…well, discomfort in our minds. At least, in this country, to be a 'desperate woman' is really not the best at all. For the life of me, I cannot understand why our first thoughts are not about how she could be 'desperate for health or desperate for a good life or desperate to find out who she really is or what her purpose is or maybe simply desperate to learn how to drive'!

Why oh why does the word have to immediately connote a woman desperate to find a MAN at all costs??????? I cannot count how many raised eyebrows I have come across in the course of writing this blog.... especially when am trying to sneak in a little something something at work and someone gets a peek at my PC screen, there it is again, that 'ah ah' desperate ke?' I used to always try to explain but now, not really....

But today before 2009 closes out I am going to do so again.

My *desperation* is to be like Jesus Christ. Period. Why? Because that is what I believe I am called to be and that is what gives me joy knowing that in my every day life I am trying to emulate my Father in heaven. My God who is so loving. My God who IS Love personified. Yes, I am **desperate** to be like Him. To be loving and to BE Love.

Yes, I know that it is easier said than done. Trust me I too have some **quantumly** (I just love this word and I try to use it as many times as I can EVEN when some other word would have done a better job!

Lol!) unlovable people on my path of life but that's where God's grace comes in, *n'est pas?* This walk with Christ is not something that comes naturally to me. The race I am running is a grace-assisted race and every moment of every day I try to stay plugged in to the source of that grace. So that I can live a life that is a true reflection of who I am - the daughter of the most High God who is altogether lovely. Altogether worthy. Altogether wonderful. To me.

I am *desperate* for people who may never go to church or read the Bible, to learn about God's love just be watching how I live my Life. Yes, I am *desperate* to be in the words of Kirk Franklin, the 'Jesus' the world sees.

I am *desperate* to bring up my children in the fear of the Lord and to live a life that shows them by example how to serve and love God with all one's heart even in this mad world we live in.

I am *desperate* for my relationship with my mgm to reflect the union between God, His son, Jesus Christ and the Holy Spirit- Three yet indivisibly one. In our case, two, yet indivisibly one, bound by the agape kind of love.

And you can bet I am also *desperate* to make heaven. So I can see my mother, my Pastor and my uncle and most of all so I can hear Jesus say those sweet words ' Well done, oh ye faithful servant'. Hmmmm, this is a major desperation point!

But don't get me wrong, I have absolutely nada against any one out there who prefers to do this God thing, calmly, coolly and collectively. Dance like crazy in the discos and nightclubs and come be 'too cute' to dance for God in church. Wake up at the crack of dawn to be on time for that meeting with that human boss but take your royal time on Sunday and come to church dressed anyhow for the God who gives you breath. I am not judging you. *Who born me?* Please by all means, to each his/her own

As for me, I am a **desperate Nigerian woman** and I know it, I know it and I ain't too proud to say it! I CHOOSE to put God first cos I am desperate like that!

Phew! OK, so now that is clear, I shall be back tomorrow with some more bridal shower testimonies...For now, I wish you all a 'just-as-it-should-be, God-ordained week ahead!

Yours desperately

DNW

Wednesday, 16 December
The Mind Is a Very Powerful Thing

I am at work so this will be a short one. We really need to be careful what we fill our minds with. I know we all know this already but today I just got confirmation of this in a very real way. Let me explain as my dear Supervisor always says.

I have been meaning to go for an eye exam for the past 3 months. Yes, I should be whipped. I agree. By the time you are 'meaning' to do something for 3 months and you still have not done it as we speak, you have become highly irresponsible. And this is especially so if this something is related to your health. Then you know you should be flogged. So if you can find me, I give you permission to come and flog me. Lol! But this is a serious matter cos my eyes have been feeling 'funnier' and funnier' as the days go by and yet I did nothing.

But tomorrow I SHALL. Why?

Because today, I was in a meeting and a colleague said my eyes 'crossed'!!! Or rather, ONE eye crossed!! So I looked like I had a quarter to four squint. Lord of heaven and earth! Do you know that since then, I have all kinds of funny feelings in that particular left eye. My vision through it has been cloudy, hazy, and even non-existent. So you can bet that I do not need to be told to find my square root to the eye doctor!

You see, I am sure my eyes are pretty much as bad as they have always been (I know, don't confess negatively but I am not confessing. I am only stating a fact. I know God will correct my sight via divine touch or via the knowledge He has given to the eye doctor! Lol!) Anyone He chooses to use, as long as Moses and I share the same testimony of being very old yet still have 100-watt eyesight. Yes, I am sure nothing had really changed but the moment the words my colleague spoke penetrated my mind, it began to spiral out of control. In 25 short minutes, I was completely blind. In my mind.

What am I saying? Be careful what you let 'penetrate' your mind. Cos the enemy is always trying to get a share of your mind cos that is where his control begins. So unless the 'inflow' is profitable to your total well being and state of mind, be like the duck and water - hear but don't absorb. Let it slide...

In closing, please ask me on Friday if I have seen the eye doctor and if I say 'no'. Please look for me and flog me!

Shalom!

Thursday, 17 December
Off Duty on Christmas Day.

First of all, I would like to say that you can all put away your whips cos I did go to see the eye doctor today. But I must say that I was quite chuffed with all the mails and calls I got from people telling/reminding me to make sure I did go. Lol! Thank you all. And in about a week or two I shall be duly bespectacled.

Anyway, so that is that. I am on here today just to say that we really need to rest this holiday season. I mean it. I don't know about you but I am tired inside my bones. So I have made up my mind to take it easy this Christmas. I shall do the very barest minimum of cooking and all that. IN FACT I am looking for (and I think I have found actually) someone else's house to go and camp at for Christmas. For a change, I will be the guest and not the hostess. Yes, it's the perfect plan. Let someone else worry about food and drinks for a change. Yes, let someone else worry about children running around making so much Christmas noise you want to just run to Jerusalem and hide in the manger! Lol!

NO, I am not being lazy (OK maybe just a little) but after playing hostess for 15 out of all the 16 Christmas days I have had as wife and mother I believe that a woman is entitled to an off day on Christmas once in a while. And this 2009 Christmas is it for me. Yes, I am off duty on Christmas day. Actually, I did get lucky last year cos we went to spent it in Calabar and I quite enjoyed being waited on for a change. Hence my stance this year. Lol!

But seriously whatever you are doing this Christmas holidays, being a full blown hostess a la Martha Stewart or playing it lazy like me, moving from one hosting home to another (yes now, are they not the ones that declared 'open house' so through the open doors I shall be marching filling myself with all the *orisiri* small chops, jollof rice, *asun*, etc. Whatever is on offer, I shall be involved. Lol!), just remember to rest. OK?

Yes, rest your bodies. Rest your mind. Rest Your Spirits. Spend time charging all these areas of YOU. Spend time with your Maker. It's His Birthday after all. I don't know how we manage to celebrate some one's birthday without inviting the celebrant!

We will not be like that *abi*? Good. Also remember to love, show love, express love, in all the ways possible. And please, remember to thank your God. It is He that has brought you to this season. Many were here last year. They are no more. We are still here. Don't' you think He is worthy of our thanks?

Sunday, 20 December
Motherhood and the Gift of Christmas

In the space of two days and one night, I have welcomed home one son and watched while one daughter and another son played the parts of the angel of the Lord and a wise man respectively.

And I can safely say that there are not many things that can melt a parent's heart like the above. I thought I would be all nice and cool when I finally spotted my older son at the airport. There I was speaking to him on the phone trying to get him to spot me in my ridiculous Santa hat and before I knew it, as I watched him look for me, smiling that his wry smile that teenagers seem to perfect for situations when parents are behaving badly or embarrassingly, I broke into a run. Yes, I began to run cos I was excited. All coolness flew out of the window. My son, my baby, my first child was home. Safe. Sound. I could not help it. I had to run. And as I reached him, I wrapped my arms around him and his big Afro saying 'my son, my son, you are home. Praise God!' Yes, and for a split second, he forgot his own coolness too and hugged me back. And then the moment was gone and AK, the cool dude was back. Lol! But I could see he was glad to see me, even if I did have a silly red hat on my head. At least I did not cry ... I tried jo! All the way home, I had a nice warm feeling in my heart. I was grateful to God. He had kept my son safe.

And then today, at church, the warm feeling was made even warmer as I watched my only princess float across the stage delivering the 'Fear not' speech of the Angel of the Lord to the Shepherds watching their flock by night. I have nicknamed her Love Angel on account of her name meaning 'the love of God'. So now that she is an angel...it's only natural that she should become my personal Love Angel. Abi? Lol!

And as for my little husband, my mgm's mini-me. He was a wise man. A wise man who completely forgot himself on stage and became so engrossed in the band that he had to be dragged off the stage as he stood there all alone after everyone else had marched off singing. Lol! That's my son o jare. At least he was the only one that took a bow after giving Mary and baby Jesus his gift. Not sure where that part is in the bible but in his mind, it was the right thing to do! Lol!

Yes, in these 2 days, I have been proud. Proud to me the mom of these three children. But even prouder (or is it 'more proud?') to belong to a God that decided that I was worthy of such a privilege. The privilege of motherhood.

To all the moms out there welcoming children home from school or just having the house full of all their 'Christmas is coming noise' I throway salute to you all! As we sneak around with their fathers or grandparents buying all the gifts and all, let's be sure we sneak in some of the good stuff too. Lets be sure to tell them about the greatest gift of all - Jesus Christ, the gift that keeps on giving. Our children must 'get' the real message of Christmas. We, their moms, we must find a way to get that message across to them, whatever their ages.

Can I count on you to join me in doing this? It's important. It's our responsibility as Christian moms.

God will help us all in Jesus Christ's name.

Amen!

Tuesday, 22 December
God Does Not Give Us Rocks

I know its Christmas and this is why I am determined. Yes, determined to be of good cheer. I tell you, I am so happy right now. And so sad too. Yes, I have laughed many belly laughs in the past 2 dozen days (in fact, I thought I would collapse in fits of laughter yesterday during our office end of year party! But that is another blog for later…on second thoughts, maybe not!) But then again, I have also shed many a tear too for myself and for my friends. My sista-friends.

Its like there is the angel from heaven fluttering about the skies with a bowl of happy Christmas cheer dust, sprinkling it down on us, God's children. And then along comes along this evil red midget-minion of the devil doing its best to scatter ashes into the mix. Lailai! I shall not let him. Neither shall you

You see ehn? Today, you and I are going to determine to STAND our ground. To HOLD on. We will NOT look at what we are still lacking in our lives. We will not cry over any 'down' aspect of our situations. No, today, you and I will focus on the good. Not the bad. The beautiful. Not the ugly. On the half-full cup. Not on the half empty one. You will look at the one shiny star on your Christmas tree and not dwell too much on the fact that there are fewer presents under its branches.

Yes, you and I will determine to believe that if God cannot give you rocks, then whatever you have right now must, in some way, be His bread for you (I know, he could have at least tried to add some sugar to his bread mix, but hey! Are you gonna question your God Almighty? Thot not). Its no fun losing your job just as Christmas peeked its red shiny nose round the corner. That's tough. But at least you are alive, and life is still a privilege and as you are still exhaling and inhaling and reading this blog, God obviously believes you are still worthy of living. That's still something, isn't it?

So, be a good man. Be a good woman. Join me today in building up our faith to stand against the wiles of the dastardly one. Listen; if you were not valuable to God in some way, the enemy would not have your time. Like I shared with a lovely lovely sista of mine yesterday as she wiped her tears and blew her nose, 'You are going somewhere in 2010 and it scares the hell out of the devil (not sure that's possible, but you know what I mean) so he is trying to knock you out now with this latest blow. But you WILL NOT let him. You must rock this Christmas like you know what's up!

People of God? So must WE. As we do this, we will rock the devil's boat cos if there is anything that frustrates the enemy, it's our joyful praises to a God who will always be better than him. A God who does not give his children rocks.

Tuesday, 22 December
There Comes A Time When

I don't care. I am still happy. But I want to share this with you all. Cos I feel we all need this right now. We need to know when to be still 'verbally' and let God be Lord. Sometimes we women need to know when to quit talking and let God be God over our lives.

Trust me, God can do more than any 'nagging' can accomplish. And I have not seen one man who told God to back off cos He was just being a nag. No, when God speaks to the heart of man, man listens. Simple. Our prayer should be that God speak to our men. That God wake them up in the middle of the night and talk to them in a terrifying manner. So that they will KNOW that God is God.

So women of God, wives of God's men. Quit talking. Quit nagging. It does not work. Instead be that woman God has called you to be. If you must talk. Channel your talk via prayers. God is always ready to listen. He will work on your behalf. As you release yourself to Him. As you obey His words and seek to Obey Him. He will move on your behalf. But I must tell you. It is HARD. Cos the flesh is not naturally a forgiving-let-God-Have-His-Way kind of flesh. It wants its own way too. So be ready for the conflict. And make up your mind to let God be the LORD of your life. Be prepared to defer to HIM no matter how bad it feels. Cos trust me. Been there. Done that. There is no sweeter victory than the one God gives you because you obeyed Him even when it hurt.

So let this be the time when you let go and let God. Believe me; He will give you the final victory. Just hold one. Just stand firm. OK?

Thursday, 24 December
Because I Am a Christian

Because I am a Christian, even in this, I will give praise to my God.
Because I am a Christian, I know that ALL things will work out for me, for mine, for good.
Because I am a Christian, I must take my mind off what I am seeing, hearing, feeling
I must focus my mind, stay my mind, and set my face like a flint
On my God.

Yes, because I am a Christian, I know, without a shadow of doubt, that
At the end of the day ONLY the counsel of the Lord shall stand
For me. For my mgm. For my family. At this time.

Because I am a Christian
I know that no one has power over me. Over mine. Save that which God gives them
In their darkness, they consider themselves powerful
No, they are just mere tools

Because I am a Christian, I will stand resting on my Pillar
I tell you one thing. I am so grateful to God for this simple truth
Yes, it sounds so simple, so childish, and so easy. This my Christ-identity
Actually, it's not any of these
Its just TRUTH
One that I hold. One that holds me. Keeps me. Thankful. Praise-full. Hopeful.
Even when faced with stuff so dreadful.

Yes, I am a Christian.
Lord, Thank you!
Yes! I am Christian.
So I praise you! Now. Always.

Thursday, 24 December
Do Me a Favour, Please.

I am on a quest. Yes, am determined to totally, fairly and squarely, 100% frustrate the enemy.
You know something? I am actually enjoying this cos regardless of what is going on, somehow, somehow, my expectations of what God is about to do has not been tainted in any way. I am still so excited about my future. Our future. So excited.

So this is the favour I ask of you. Tomorrow is the day we celebrate the birth of our Lord and Saviour Jesus Christ. Yes? Yes. Good. I want you to please please pretty please join me in celebrating this one like you have never done before.

Celebrate it in a way that makes a point
Celebrate it in a way that makes people look at you and wonder.
Celebrate it in a way that shows the devil that he is no match for your God
Celebrate it in a way that proves to God that He is your number one
Celebrate it in a way that shows you know the reason for this season.
Celebrate it in a way that casts down fears and imaginations
Just celebrate my people, rejoice for a child has been born to us
And HE has overcome the world for us.
Becos of Him, we are not afraid. Not of arrows by day, nor moon smites by night.
No, we are not afraid. Our heart is fixed. Our peace is sure.
Praise His Name!
Praise His Name!
Praise His Holy, Awesome Name!

Just do me a favour, praise God tomorrow. Praise him as you eat. Praise him as you gist and visit with family and friends. Just do me this one favour. Praise our God so that He knows that some people on earth know what time it is.

Thank you in advance.

Friday, 25 December
How Shall This Be? (The Million-Dollar Question in 2010)

First of all, I would like to take a moment to hail Pastors Seye Kosoko, John Hagee and Rod Parsley. These three men of God have, today, jointly delivered to me a very special Christmas morning. Thank you and may God refresh all of your anointing this day and may all of your dreams and aspirations for 2010 come through.

Now, to my question. 'How Shall This Be?' This is what Mary asked the Angel that brought her that one of kind message more than 2000 years ago. I mean if I was 14 years old too, still a virgin, never been married and never been with a man and someone came up to me and told me I was going to have a baby, I think that would be a fair question for me to ask. Don't you think?. Yes o!, 'How Shall This Be?'.

How shall it be that I will be able to pay my rent/children's fees in January when I just lost my job?
How shall it be that I will be pain free after living with sickness for most of 2009?
How shall it be that I will finally have a child with all these negative reports?
How shall it be that I will be married before the close of 2010?
How shall it be that this my business will prosper when the economy looks so bleak?
How shall it be that I will get a job in 2010 when 2009 brought nothing?
How shall it be that I will do exploits for God when my life is such a mess spiritually right now?

And I could go on and on and on...Indeed, ALL of us have something we are trusting God for but the truth is that, lurking in our hearts is this unasked question ' 'Lord, How Shall It Be?' It's not that we don't want to believe, its just that the reality looks so...so ...well so contrary. But, still there is an answer to this million-dollar question.

Yes, the answer is in our Bible and I give it you today as my special Christmas present to you (OK, it might be a second hand gift cos God gave it to you already in His Word but how for do, Take it like that. Lol!). The answer is this:

"WITH GOD, NOTHING IS IMPOSSIBLE'

I don't know about you. As I wrap up 2009 and cross over into 2010, I am beyond expectant. So excited. I am holding on to this answer with all my might. Like I am 2 years old. I will not even second guess it or try to figure it out. I know ALL that God has spoken concerning me, my mgm, my family and my friends. And if God said it. I know He means it. It's not my business HOW He does it. The only thing I need to do is make sure that, in 2010, I walk in complete TRUST and OBEDIENCE just like Mary and Joseph did.

Then I, too, will SEE and EXPERIENCE How This CAN BE. Yes, in 2010, the same divine power that brought forth a virgin birth will be at work in my life.

And yours too as you join me.

Shalom and *Meri Keresimesi* once again!

Monday, 28 December
Stop! Detoxification In Process

2010 is going to be a one of a kind year. I can feel it in my bones. We need to be ready. Yes, ready in the Lord!

So I have made up my mind to set out EARLY. I am going to get ready 'physically' and more importantly 'spiritually'. None of my angels must pass me by. No way! None of the blessings God intends to shower on me must be held back. *Lai lai*! So what am I doing? I am taking spiritual stock of myself and my walk with God. Painful but necessary. Let me give you an example.

I tend to be quite short- tempered. And to my great astonishment, I recently discovered that being easily irritated or quick to 'lose it' actually points to.... wait for it...Pride! I would have 'beaten my chest' anywhere to attest to the fact that I am most definitely not a proud person (hmmmm, is that in itself not already an indication that I am indeed quite 'pride-full'? Lol...human nature!)

I might be laughing but this is really no laughing matter. There is so much God wants to do for us in the coming year. But are we ready? I woke up the day after Christmas still feeling ridiculously 'stuffed' from my over indulgence of the previous day and as I stared down at the folds of my tummy, I forced myself to give my life some heavy-duty thoughts. The truth of the matters is I could be better.

Yes, I thank God for where I am today. It's all by His Grace. But, still I know I could be fitter in body and in spirit. And I aim to begin the process now now. I am not waiting for 31st of December to begin declaring New Year resolutions. I actually intensely dislike those 3 words. I actually believe that the moment you declare your intentions under that caption, you automatically jinx yourself. New Year's Resolutions are by their very nature, un-doable! Un-keep-able! At least, in my opinion.

So me? I have kicked off what I am calling a detoxification process of my own. Its sort of the 1st steps towards laying down some '2010 Commitments'. Yes, first I am ridding myself of all the toxins in my system - physically and spiritually. Pride must go. Bitterness and resentment must go. Negative attitudes and 'had I known' thoughts have got to go. Unforgiveness and Malice? Got to go too! And on top of all of that, excess belly fat and all other unwanted kilos must go to return NO MORE!!!! Lol!

I am serious oh and I have a good feeling about kicking this off now. No need to wait. Yes, this is the time to sit with my Coach/Dietician a.k.a The Holy Spirit and agree on how we will enter into the first quarter of 2010, physically and spiritually. And that's another thing. 12 months is too long to make realistic commitments. I shall be taking it 3 months at a time.... In April, we shall re-evaluate, re-group and re-commit.

There is much to be done. Much to be won! But we must not be faint hearted! No, we must not be unmindful of the plans of the dark one. One thing is sure; he will try anything to keep us from what God wants to do in our lives in 2010. We must thwart him.

Aluta Continua in the strength of my God!

Tuesday, 29 December
Now, I KNOW I Am On To Something Good.

Yes, I am sure beyond a shadow of a doubt. Do you want to know why? Cos I fell so badly last night it is almost unbelievable considering how confident I was about my stance.

I know I scared the devil cos he came at me with a vengeance.... and somehow, though I am ashamed at how quickly I fell, in some strange way, I am pleased.

Yes, I am pleased cos NOW I am sure I am doing the right thing. Starting now to get my act together. I have confused the camp of the enemy. Praise God! So here I am dusting myself off and getting back up again...thanking God for the gift of another day....

Lord, thank you. For giving me another day. Forgive me for dragging you through that again...Thank you for cleaning me up again and assuring me of your love. I know you hate the sin I get into. Yes, you cannot stand it when I walk in the flesh but oh! How much you love me. So boundlessly. And I just want to show you how much I love you too by living a life that makes you smile.

So people out there, as long as God has given us TODAY, we are still in the race. If you too have missed it. If you too have fallen. If you too have caused God sadness by living below His plans for you, it's OK. Join me. Get up. God loves us enough. He is still rooting for us. Can't you hear Him?

The failure is not in our fall. Its in our not getting back up. So, we have NOT yet failed cos, YES! We are getting back up RIGHT NOW!!!!!!

Like I said, Aluta Continua...One step at a time...holding on to God's hand.

Shalom!

Tuesday, 29 December
True Love Is Not Mushy At All

I have a friend. Her name is Saratu. She is one of the funniest people I know. She it was that taught me one of my favourite love quotes. Never mind that we were both still in our twenties and probably knew very little about what real love was. We were discussing about errant boyfriends and she said "If you truly love someone you have to be prepared to let him fly away, out of the cage. If he flies away and never comes back, he was never meant to be. But if you open the cage door and he flies away and then comes back to you, then you know it was meant to be'. It was 1989. I was twenty-one and thought it was the most profound statement I had ever heard about love. Especially coming from someone who usually only managed to crack me up with her quirky, totally mad behaviour. I miss Saratu.

Anyway, this is not about Saratu really. But it is about love. True Love. Real Love. People usually think its some sort of bubbly, mushy, butterflies in your tummy feeling, cant eat, cant sleep sort of feeling. And while I can consider that it could make you feel all of the above, I have come to learn over time, that the real deal love is not soft. Nor is it mushy at all. No, the love worth finding and having is tough. It has to be, cos it will be called on to make some pretty tough choices. Choices that soft and mushy cannot make.

I love watching telly and once in a while, I actually get to sit and watch something other than the Disney channel or National Geographic. I get to watch and cry over such telly delights as Extreme Makeover - Home Edition (yes, I cry over every single edition. My friend, Funmi, thinks I am a total sap! Lol!). I also get to watch tear jerker movies like the one I watched this evening - Mom at Sixteen. This is what reminded me about when love has got to be tough. About when love is called on to make hard decisions.

I watched a mom showing tough love to her daughters because she wanted the best for them. I actually began to dislike the woman cos I did not get her at first. But I did in the end. I also watched her young teenage daughter make one of the hardest decisions of her life. She gave up her baby for adoption because she truly really loved him. Her love drove her to give him up to a couple she knew would love him and give him the life she so wanted for him BUT could not give him herself at that point in her life. For her, it was about 'what was best for her baby'. She might have been sixteen but she had learnt the meaning of true love.

Two days to go and 2009 will be history and as part of my detoxification process, I have decided to take a close look at how I have been 'loving' people. Is it about them or about me? Is it about getting or giving? Does my love suffer long or just make people suffer? Does my love cover a multitude of sin or does it keep a black book of remembrance? In short, is my love mushy or is it the real deal? No one sets the standard for true love like our God. He not only loves, He **IS** Love.

Yes, come 2010, I believe one of my commitments will be to walk in love better. To demonstrate true, self-less, sacrificial love more.

Like the love God has for me. For you.

Wednesday, 30 December
DNW's 2009 Hall of Fame Awards

While I am loving my less than 40 minute, traffic-less ride to work these days, there is a down side. I can no longer enjoy those long (albeit bumpy) early morning reveries along the beach road. Yes oh! The roads are beautifully empty on account of more than half of the inhabitants who live along my axis being away on holiday somewhere. In fact, yesterday I sent out a plea on FB asking them to all stay in their various villages and not come back. Lol!

Nevertheless my mind still managed to do some travelling. It took my on a journey over my time on this earth and the various people that God has placed on my path. To help me. Bless me. Challenge me. Encourage me. Motivate me. Pray with me. Pray for me. In short, God has, over the years, built a wall of support around me for each season of my life. A People wall. A Love wall. Today, the last but one day of 2009, I say to you ALL - **THANK YOU from the bottom of my heart**! You should know who you are but just in case, I will name a few names in a randomish, hall of fame-ish kinda way!

DNW's 2009 Favourite People (apart from family of course!)
My Out of Office Sistas-Divine (Ms. B, Shola L, Ekene, Nkechi, NGSam and Yemosh)
My Office Sistas-Divine (Banwo, Rita, NK, Uche N, Funmi, Nyada & IQ)
Femi F, Jide A, Jibs A.

DNW's 2009 People I Am Most Proud Of (apart from my mgm, my sister and my children!)
Oroms and her hubby
Uchechi, Bola M, Lanre E
Olubunmi O., Gloria A

DNW's 2009 Favourite Place To be (apart from my bedroom! Lol!)
Mercyplace Parish on Thursdays during Power, Praise and Pentecost

DNW's 2009 People I Am So Blessed To Know
Pastor B!, Yinka J, Uju Oge
Nneamaka O, Pastor Seye, Rosemarie O
Ohunene, Bimbo I, Oye O

DNW's Happiest Moments in 2009
Every time my baby son said ' I love you mommy, very much too much!'
Every time, I heard my only princess play the piano
The night after my first official bridal shower on 12/12/2009
The day I had enough grace to 'truly' be still and let God.
The moment I spotted my oldest son at the airport the day he came home for Christmas!
The day I saw JJ back on Facebook after her surgery!

DNW's 2009 Lifetime Achievement Award for 'making me feel supported regardless of how many times I see you or not'
Sola DB, Ekaette!, Angela OD, Ifeanyi T, Yemisi TA
Lizzie A, Femi O, Yewande TS, Foluke M, Habiba, Mrs. P!

DNW's 2009 Most Missed Person
Tokunbo, Uncle Abiye

DNW's 2009 Most Helpful Person in a Day to Day Way
Oga Oye

DNW's 2009 Favourite New Person
Bukola A. Fash
Ana Renee
Ade O

OK, there is really no way I can do it all but if you see your name up there somewhere, then you are one of the people, who in some way or another, helped me during this 2009 leg of my life's journey. I hail you. I am grateful. So very grateful. And outside of my mgm, my children and my family, y'all are my 'Personal People'. Much love!

Like I always say, I can only thank you but God will reward you for every seed of love you have sown into my life. Wait and see.... Just wait and see.

For now, listen, can you hear it, its a standing ovation for you! Take a bow! Go on take a bow! As far as I am concerned, you have more than earned it!

Mwaah! Mwaah! Mwaah!

Thursday, 31 December
Good-bye Two Thousand and 9. Hello Twenty-Ten!

It was quite foggy today as I stepped out of my house and into my car. For once, it felt like harmattan was upon us. I liked the feeling. All through my commute to work, I talked, on and off to God. I thanked Him. I praised Him. I sang along to my 'High Praise' CD, giving Him more praise but most of all, I questioned Him. I asked Him to tell me about 2010. What will it be like? How will it be different? How should I be different? HOW shall all that You have promised me and mine BE? God was patient with me as usual and allowed me to assail Him with all these questions. God is good like that

You know some days, I think that Pastor Adeboye somehow wrote some of the 'Open Heavens' entries just for me, for that day of my life. You know those days when the entire word for the day would just hit the nail on the head of the situation I was going through or provide clarification for the thoughts running riot in my head. Today was one of those days.

Today, God answered my '2010 How Shall This Be' questions through the word in 'Open Heavens'. His answer was short and simple - Win me some souls. Yes, in 2010, if I am too enter into all that God has for me and mine. I have to aggressively commit to giving God the one thing He is hungry for. Souls. Right now, as I type, not sure what I am going to do to up the ante on this but one thing is sure. It will be one of my key 2010 commitments. The Lord who is asking will show me how and at the end of the day, its really all about sharing. Its the Holy Spirit that brings in the harvest.

My dear NK also provided an answer to my question in a different way, which actually ties in to the detoxification process I am currently undergoing. I tell you, you will not believe the quantum amounts of toxins we leave to pollute our bodies, minds and spirits just because we fail to take time to look deep into ourselves. Its not easy and you need to let the Holy Spirit have his way and accept ALL that He brings to your attention. Anyway, we were gisting, this sista and I and we came to the conclusion that many of us will wake up one morning to discover that we have missed the rapture. Why? Cos we were in an 'unrapturable' condition on account of some negative situation in our lives which will become TOTALLY IRRELEVANT the moment you realise you have missed heaven! Morale of the gist? Get over it. Let it go. Say you are sorry. Forgive. Break the ice of the yearlong malice. Love the unlovable. In short. Be the LIGHT in this mean, dark world! Because, at the end of the day, these people, these situations? None of them will matter. None of them is worth you missing eternity with Jesus Christ.

So are you asking 'How shall it be in 2010 O Lord?. Permit me to give you an answer using my personal paraphrase of the response the Angel gave to Mary when she asked the same question:

'It shall be, because with God nothing shall be impossible to those who **aggressively win souls in 2010 cos that is your Heavenly Father's favourite meal**. Yes, feed God and let **your lifestyle glorify Him always**. Then you shall see **HOW** He will make **ALL** that He has promised you **BEcome reality in your life.**'

I love it! And I think its just the best *last word* that I, your DNW could leave you with as we close out 2009. So on that note, from me and mine, I wish you and yours a stupendously awesome Twenty-Ten!!!!!!!!

Happy New Year!!!!!!!!!!!!!!!!!!!!

At The End of The Day

At the end of the day, where will I be? Where will you be? I may have written all the blogs you have just managed to read till the end but no matter how godly and saintly I may sound, at the end of the day, it is God that sees my heart. And yours. So what does He see?

I am no pastor but I have made a promise to my Maker to make my life count for something. This book you have just finished reading (I hope!) is not just a book. It's a cry for help. Yes, a cry for help to you all out there.

Why am I crying for help? What do I want from you? Not a whole lot really. I just want you to take a look at your life, a real close look at it and tell me you don't need the Cross.

The Cross brings us salvation, cleansing, provision, protection, healing, peace and joy. Now don't you believe that the world needs more of these blessings?

If you do, then this book is a cry for help to you to *help* me bring one more life to the feet of this Cross. I am desperate to lead just one more life to a place where he/she can enter into these blessings via a relationship with Jesus Christ. Yes, just one more life—**Your life. Yes, YOU.**

At the end of the day, that is all that really matters. Saving lives for Jesus Christ. Come to Him today. Now. He is waiting. It is not hard at all. Just pray this prayer from your heart:

"Heavenly Father, have mercy on me, a sinner. I believe in you and that your word is true. I believe that Jesus Christ is the Son of the living God and

that he died on the cross so that I may now have forgiveness for my sins and eternal life. I know that without you in my heart my life is meaningless.
I believe in my heart that you, Lord God, raised Him from the dead. Please Jesus forgive me, for every sin I have ever committed or done in my heart, please Lord Jesus forgive me and come into my heart as my personal Lord and Savior today. I need you to be my Father and my friend.
I give you my life and ask you to take full control from this moment on; I pray this in the name of Jesus Christ."
Amen.

You did it!!!!! Praise God! I promise, there is a whole lot of rejoicing going on in heaven right now just for YOU. If you don't already have one, look for a true bible believing and spirit led church and begin attending. Go dust off your bible or buy a new one. Continue the conversation you just started with God above and step into the best days of the rest of your life! God Bless you!

In His Love and Mine
DNW
(desperatenaijawoman@ymail.com)

Lightning Source UK Ltd.
Milton Keynes UK
19 June 2010

155846UK00001B/5/P